Developing Teaching Skills in Physical Education

SECOND EDITION

Daryl Siedentop

OHIO STATE UNIVERSITY

 MAYFIELD PUBLISHING COMPANY

For Bobbie . . .

Copyright © 1983 by Mayfield Publishing Company
Second edition 1983

Library of Congress Catalog Card Number: 82-60884
International Standard Book Number: 0-87484-550-5

Manufactured in the United States of America
Mayfield Publishing Company
285 Hamilton Avenue
Palo Alto, California 94301

Sponsoring editor: C. Lansing Hays
Managing editor: Pat Herbst
Manuscript editor: Linda Purrington
Designer: Al Burkhardt
Compositor: G & S Typesetters, Inc.
Production manager: Cathy Willkie
Printer and binder: George Banta Company
Cover designer: Al Burkhardt

Contents

Chapter 3

Chapter 4

Chapter 5

Chapter 6

Chapter 7

Chapter **11**

Chapter **12**

Preface

During the past fifteen years, more has been achieved in understanding the nature of effective teaching in schools than was achieved during the previous 100 years. Only a decade ago, Herbert Kliebard (1973) reviewed the history of research on teaching effectiveness and concluded that, despite the good intentions and honest efforts of early researchers, the search to discover the secrets of successful teaching had been mostly misdirected. Kliebard was critical of the past and pessimistic about the future. While he was correct in his appraisal of pre-1965 research, he most certainly was wrong about the future.

We have learned a great deal about the way teachers operate in those classrooms where students achieve and have positive attitudes about themselves and their school experiences. This is not to suggest that we know everything about effective teaching. We no doubt have just scratched the surface—but the results have been reasonably consistent and point to practices that can be passed on to those preparing for a teaching career.

In essence, that is what this book is about—providing effective teaching methods for those who will soon begin teaching and for those who are already teaching but whose preparation was less than complete.

Virtually all of the teaching practices suggested in this text have been identified through research; they do not represent just one person's view of how teachers should teach, nor do they represent an idealized set of skills that can be developed and used only by supermen and superwomen. Indeed, many of them simply represent what Nate Gage (1972, p. 195) has referred to as "tools of the trade":

> Other professions and crafts give their practitioners whole arrays of techniques, instruments, tools, devices, formulas, strategies, tactics, algorithms, and tricks of the trade. . . . But, in teaching we find relatively few of these ways of making complex tasks more manageable. Teachers are expected to rediscover for themselves the formulas that experienced and ingenious teachers have acquired over the years. Each generation of teachers benefits too little from the inventions of its predecessors. Too little of the wisdom of the profession gets saved and passed along for the benefit of the novice. What teaching needs—if it is to be improved in the hands of ordinary persons, who are not geniuses or inspired artists, and if it is to be improved with resources at a level not inconceivably high—is a much more abundant and helpful supply of "tools of the trade."

Although certain aspects of teaching effectiveness can be attributed to consistent and appropriate use of basic "tools," other aspects of teaching are more complex, requiring the teacher to attend carefully to the dynamics of a teaching lesson and to respond to emerging situations with the appropriate action at the right moment, in the right amount, and of the right quality. But even this kind of skilled artistry can be analyzed, studied, practiced, and improved in various kinds of preparation experiences. As Denemark and Espinoza (1974, p. 193) have observed:

> Basic to the effectiveness of both field operation and classroom simulation is the capacity of the teacher educator or teacher education team to analyze the processes of teaching and learning in a manner that permits the identification of critical elements of different contributing operations and the subdivision of the whole complex of teaching into distinguishable and manageable parts.

Many kinds of teaching practices will be advocated in this text, but I have not attempted to formulate or defend a particular theory of teaching or even a style of teaching that I believe is superior to others. My basic contention has always been that the critical characteristics of effective teaching can be found in many different styles—but the adoption of a style without these characteristics results in form without substance.

There are many ways to practice teaching skills, and most of them are explained in this text. The development of skill will progress most rapidly if those who practice have clear goals and ample opportunity to practice and regularly receive feedback about how they are doing. Although that may sound quite basic and simple, the central problem of teacher education still remains how to arrange simulated and real teaching experiences so that trainees have a chance to practice critical skills and receive frequent, accurate feedback about their use of those skills. Clearly, a teacher-to-be will develop few professional skills sitting at a desk in a university classroom and listening to a lecture about teaching. Receiving information in that fashion is no doubt necessary, but it is the actual practice of teaching skills under appropriate conditions that results in improvement.

Education and educators are under ongoing critical attack in our society. Students are less literate. Discipline problems abound. Taxpayers revolt. Teachers burn out. Many laypersons and professionals question whether teacher education is relevant, useful, or even necessary. Given these circumstances, one would expect teacher educators to welcome promising research on the practices of effective teachers and to implement the results as quickly as possible so the next generation of teachers might be better prepared to acquit themselves skillfully and professionally early in their careers. But, for many reasons, such is not the case. Dissemination of research is slow. Translation of technical research into readable, usable prescriptions is seldom done. Many teacher educators simply ignore professional outlets where they might encounter information on teacher effectiveness research. The process of change is slow; yet within physical education there is a ready and growing audience of teacher educators interested in teaching research and willing and anxious to use it in their own programs. And there is a growing number of teaching researchers in physical education who have responsibilities in teacher education programs. Thus, the future is not bleak. There is reason to expect that future physical educators will move into their first jobs better prepared and more highly skilled than many of their predecessors. To push that entire process along more quickly and efficiently has been a major purpose of this text.

Research on teaching is seldom done in isolation—and it almost always requires many helpers to complete even one project, let alone to staff a research program over the years. To my physical education colleagues who participate with me in the ongoing research process, I give my thanks—much of your effort is in this text. The usefulness of our future efforts will be determined by the degree to which we can maintain the fruitful relationships we have established.

In my own research program at The Ohio State University, I have had the opportunity to work with faculty colleagues, graduate students, undergraduate majors, and local physical educators in a series of studies designed to extend our understanding of the complexities of teaching/coaching and ways to improve skills in those areas. To all of these people, particularly to the physical educators who allowed us to be guests in their gymnasiums, I offer my sincerest appreciation.

My own Ph.D. students continue to be my major source of professional satisfaction—and their contributions to the development of the ideas and methods in this text are considerable. Through their work at Ohio State, and later at their own institutions, they continue to extend the frontiers of our efforts and improve the quality of our research products.

I must again, as I have done in other places, express my gratitude to Charles Mand, Director of the School of Health, Physical Education, and Recreation at Ohio State. He not only is an able and facilitative administrator, but he continues to be a knowledgeable, honest, and caring critic of my work. I also want to thank colleagues who reviewed preliminary drafts of the manuscript: John Cheffers, Boston University; George Graham, University of Georgia, Athens; David C. Griffey, University of Texas, Austin; and Thomas J. Martinek, University of North Carolina, Greensboro.

My wife Bobbie is the elementary physical education specialist at the Maryland Avenue School in Bexley, Ohio. When I came to Ohio State in 1970, I got to know her because she was widely reputed to be the best elementary specialist in the Columbus area. Those who gave me that information were right! She is the most effective teacher I know—and I gratefully continue to learn from her on a regular basis. In a fundamental sense, she and I have the same goals. I do not pursue teaching research as an end in itself. She does not try continually to improve her own performance and her program as ends in themselves. We are both interested in helping students in the schools in our society to have a better physical education experience—one that is more positive, one that is more successful, one that equips them with more skills and the desire to utilize those skills. Indeed, that is a set of goals to which we all might rededicate ourselves.

D. S.

Developing Teaching Skills in Physical Education

CHAPTER 1

Systematic Improvement of Teaching Skills

Teacher education, both at the preservice and the inservice level, should adopt as primary goals the development of the competencies needed to create and maintain the learning environment, to engage pupils in learning-related activities, and to implement the kind of instruction that research indicates is provided by effective teachers. There is an abundance of practical knowledge available about how to do these things; what has been missing in the past is a clear conviction on the part of teacher educators that these things are what teachers ought to be doing.

Donald Medley, *The Effectiveness of Teachers* (1979)

CHAPTER OBJECTIVES

To distinguish between the art and science of teaching

To explain the ingredients of a systematic approach to the development of teaching skills

To define teaching

To explain the role of feedback in skill development

To distinguish among and explain the stages of skill development

To explain the ways in which teaching skills can be practiced

My three goals in writing this text are to help you to better understand the dimensions of effective teaching in physical activity settings, to help you to improve your teaching skills, and to make you want to teach better, both now and in the future. Of those three goals, wanting to teach better—the motivational component—is probably the foundation on which all else is built. The saddest of all professional conditions exists when a teacher has good teaching skills but lacks the motivation to use them regularly. It isn't bad teaching that plagues physical education so much as it is *non*teaching (Locke, 1975).

If you are properly motivated, the acquisition of teaching skills is not enormously difficult. The combination of skills and motivation to use the skills results in effective teaching, which, in turn, usually results in student achievement. As you acquire teaching skills, so too you acquire understanding of them. And as you fully acquire basic skills and achieve higher-level skills, your level of understanding increases until you, the experienced teacher, can anticipate situations before they actually occur and adjust your teaching to take advantage of them. At this point, a level of real artistry is achieved: The skilled teacher orchestrates a repertoire of finely tuned skills to meet the ever-changing demands of the learning situation. Few things are more enjoyable to watch than a motivated, skilled teacher totally in control of a learning setting in which students are not only learning but also obviously enjoying the learning.

Unfortunately, instructors in too many physical education methods courses teach for understanding and expect skill and motivation to develop naturally. The result, over the past several decades, has been a generation of physical education teachers who understand something about teaching but have not had the chance to improve their skills, and whose level of motivation remains largely unchanged throughout their undergraduate programs. This text challenges you to be a better teacher. The skills necessary to be an effective teacher are described in the chapters that follow. As you practice them, you will come to a better understanding of what constitutes effective teaching and what you must do to become more effective than you are now. But first *you must want to do it!*

Systematic feedback is necessary for skill development. For a long time we have known that to be true for motor skill development. It appears to be true as well for the development of teaching skills. A major feature of this text is that it provides a systematic approach to the development of teaching skills. The skills themselves and the situations in which they can be used are explained clearly. Methods for evaluating your use of the skills and ways of charting your improvement are presented. The chapters that follow define teaching skills, describe data collection systems for observing the skills as they are practiced, and examine methods for using the collected data to provide feedback for further improvement.

The major purpose of Chapter 1 is to alert you to the basic assumptions that underlie the systematic approach, especially its data collection features, and to provide a rationale for their use.

Basic Assumptions Underlying a Systematic Approach

Every approach to teaching is based on some underlying assumptions. Stating the assumptions explicitly can provoke discussion, provide some understanding, and suggest the kind of accountability that becomes possible when an approach to teaching is examined carefully for consistency with its own underlying assumptions. A so-called scientific approach to teaching in which no data are regularly collected is obviously mislabeled. An "experiential" approach to teaching that doesn't provide for a substantial amount of actual teaching experience is likewise inconsistent.

You may not agree with all the assumptions stated in this chapter. There is room for much disagreement in teacher preparation even when the major ob-

The Reality and the Hope!

Do things *always* get better naturally? Or do we need to *act* to improve things?

> The generally accepted goal of improving our schools may be chimeric. This is not to say that school improvement is impossible. But it is to suggest that, given the circumstances surrounding schooling today and what is needed to effect improvement, we—that is, our society—may not be up to it. Indeed, given certain of these circumstances and conditions, our schools may deteriorate, and dissatisfaction and disaffection may increase. [Dr. John Goodlad, Dean of the Graduate School of Education, University of California at Los Angeles, January 1979]

Fact: More than one-half of 585 public school teachers in a large city recently took standardized tests and failed them, even though they needed only 31 correct answers to the 60 math and language questions.

Fact: In 1976, one of every three applicants for teaching jobs in a southern state failed an eighth-grade general knowledge test.

Fact: The illiteracy rate of the United States is three times higher than that of the Soviet Union.

Fact: When teachers are asked about the concerns they would like to see addressed for inservice workshops, they increasingly ask for guidance related to "stress management."

Fact: In 1969, 75 percent of parents asked in a national poll indicated that they would like to see their children become teachers. By 1972, that percentage had dropped to 67. By 1980, only 48 percent of parents polled wanted their children to become teachers.

Fact: Teacher unions in certain states are beginning to bargain for what they call "assault leave"—time off from their teaching duties because of physical and psychological trauma resulting from assault by students.

What is the best, quickest way to improve the picture in schools?

> The effect of schooling on the individual pupil depends to a considerable extent on who his teacher is. Personnel costs themselves represent so large a share of the day-to-day cost of education that the best hope for improvement in cost-effectiveness lies in improving the effectiveness of the teacher. [Professor Donald Medley, Professor of Education, University of Virginia, 1979]

jectives are agreed on. Consensus can be achieved only when the issues have been debated thoroughly. I hope that the following sections provoke discussion among you, your fellow students, and your instructors. One of the best ways to focus our views on teaching is to be made to explain and defend our assumptions about physical education teaching skills and how they can be developed.

Science and the Art of Teaching

The development of teaching skills is approached in this text as if it were a science—that is, amenable to systematic evaluation and capable of being broken down into a series of tasks that can be mastered. This does not suggest that teaching can or should be viewed as a mechanistic enterprise. Nor does it suggest that there is no room in effective teaching for personal style, inventiveness, or intuition. It is probably most accurate to define **effective teaching** as the artistic orchestration of a set of highly developed skills to meet the specific demands of a learning setting.

Some people, however, view teaching solely as an art. They believe that teaching skills cannot be taught—that good teachers are born, not made. This view implies that we can discover nothing about teaching and cannot pass on what we *do* know to other people. Because the public schools employ so many teachers, we can sincerely hope that chance of birth is not the sole or even major contributor to a teacher's effectiveness. Clearly, if teachers are born, not made, then enormous sums of money are being wasted each year on so-called teacher education.

People who seriously argue that art and science constitute a dichotomy are raising a pseudo-issue. Anybody who has ever attempted to learn an artistic skill will attest to the fact that much of what is learned can be examined from a systematic, scientific point of view and can be improved as a result. Art—in the forms of music, painting, sculpture, and dance—most often requires training based on systematic, scientific principles. Thus, we can understand the dancer's use of leverage, the painter's command of color, and the conductor's mastery of sound and balance. Viewing an artistic performance from this perspective does not render it less artistic, nor does it dehumanize the performer. The scientific approach does not claim to account for the entire artistic performance. The dancing of Rudolf Nureyev equals more than the sum of all the principles of mechanics. The paintings of Picasso equal more than all the principles of color, perspective, balance, and theme in art. Yet neither Nureyev nor Picasso could be truly creative in their artistic performances unless they had mastered fundamental skills. The same is true for teaching. Before you can become a master teacher, you must develop the basic skills that provide a foundation for skilled performance in real educational settings.

In recent years we have learned much from a systematic study of teachers teaching, and we can learn much more from a continuation, extension, and refinement of this systematic research effort. Everyone understands and supports the notion that anyone eager to become a highly skilled basketball player has to master fundamental skills. As playing experience is gained, these skills gradually become more finely tuned. A basketball player must learn to respond to hundreds of small situations that arise during a typical game. Certainly, a player goes into the game with a game plan, a well-practiced offensive pattern, and a set of defenses. But once the game begins, the player's ability to orchestrate all these plans and adjust to the demands of the game spells the difference between victory and defeat. Even at the highest levels of skill, players and coaches agree on the need to continuously practice fundamental skills. The systematic study of basketball and other sports enables coaches and players to perfect individual skills and team efforts. Many statistics are kept, both for practices and for games. Although this may seem obvious for basketball, it is much less well accepted for teaching.

In this text I am not attempting to account for all the individual styles that contribute to good teaching. I do not (to use the basketball metaphor once again) attempt to explain all the effectiveness of a "Dr. J" (Julius Erving). I *do* explain basic fundamentals of teaching (such as dribbling, passing, screening, and rebounding in basketball) and basic teaching strategies (such as zone and individual defenses, fast break, and other offenses). No attempt will be made to fit all teachers into a single mold or to deny individual styles except when such styles are clearly detrimental to students' achievement and growth. The fact that there is some personal artistry in teaching (as there is in basketball) does not mean, however, that all aspects of good teaching should be left unexamined or cannot be passed on to a new generation of prospective teachers.

The aim of the materials presented in this text is not to fit you into some preconceived mold of how all teachers ought to operate. Rather, the text aims to help you to want to improve your teaching, to understand what improved teaching means, and to develop the skills and strategies of better teaching through practice under appropriate conditions. With more, and more highly refined, skills and strategies, you in your own way will have a unique impact on the students you teach and coach.

A Definition of Teaching

The basic task of teaching is to find ways to help students learn and grow; to design educational experiences through which students will grow in skill, understanding, and attitude; and to do so in a manner that enables students to enjoy both the learning experience and the activity or subject being studied. The most meaningful way to define teaching is by reference to what happens to the students being taught. It is increasingly difficult to assert that a teacher taught but the students did not learn. We must begin to evaluate teaching in terms of its impact on students. Without such reference, the activities of teaching become abstract and meaningless.

If teaching is defined primarily in terms of its impact on students, then it is necessary to observe what is happening to students in order to describe and evaluate what kind of teaching is being done. Thus a consistent strategy in this text is to link teaching activities to their impact on students. One useful way of evaluating your own teaching is by consistently monitoring what your students are doing. In other words, if you are ever asked to evaluate a teacher and are allowed to look at only one aspect of the educational setting, my advice is to look at what the students are doing rather than at what the teacher is doing. The *appearance* of good teaching is one thing. The real evidence of good teaching is to be found by watching the students. For example, an elegant demonstration and explanation of the volleyball bump pass may seem to demonstrate good teaching—but not if it is followed immediately by students' trying to take each others' heads off in an impromptu, unauthorized game of bombardment.

Improving Teaching Skills Through Practice

The best way to improve your teaching skills is to teach. That doesn't sound like a revolutionary statement. But if you examine your undergraduate preparation, you will probably find that you have spent very little time teaching, either in a real situation or in some simulation of the real situation. This is true today despite a trend in professional preparation toward more teaching experience. One now finds early field experience, miniteaching, microteaching, peer teaching, and extended periods of student teaching in many physical education programs. Unfortunately, the sum of all these teaching experiences may not equal the time you spent in a freshman biology lab or in lectures for an anatomy course.

You may have learned a great deal about teaching. But learning about teaching is no more fruitful than learning about tennis. You can learn about tennis by reading books, watching instructional films, watching people play on local courts, or watching top players on television and hearing commentators discuss their styles and approaches to the game. Much of this can be enlightening and a great deal of fun. You might even be considered an expert on tennis, having read so much and seen so much that you know more about it than most other people. If I pursued the analogy much further, I might suggest that if you really learned a great deal about tennis, a college or university might hire you to lecture to other people, perhaps on Mondays, Wednesdays, and Fridays at 10 A.M., on what you know about tennis. As you know, none of this will help you hit your backhand better to get more spin on your second serve.

The only way to improve your tennis skills is to play tennis. Not only do you have to play, but you will also probably have to play against someone who is better than you or receive instruction from someone who can help you improve your skill as you play. Books, films, and all the rest are important, but they should be seen in proper perspective—as support sources for skill development, not as substitutes for direct experience in the skill itself.

Similarly, no one would dream of conducting a tennis class or camp without having the students play tennis a large part of the time. The skills involved in tennis are difficult to master, and a great deal of practice is necessary.

Teaching skills may not be defined quite as easily as those in tennis, but this does not mean that they should remain undefined and unpracticed. What kind of practice have you had in developing teaching skills? You probably know a great deal *about* teaching. This does not mean that you are a competent teacher. You may be a competent teacher, but one can only guess at how much your knowledge about teaching has contributed to your abilities as a teacher. How often have you had the opportunity to practice your teaching skills under conditions that allowed you to improve those skills?

Simple practice, of course, is no guarantee of learning. And if learning does occur, simple practice does not guarantee that the learning will be an improvement—you may learn bad teaching habits. When you send someone out to learn tennis, he or she may learn bad habits just in order to stay in a game with the opponent. When you are sent out to teach, you may learn bad habits just to maintain order, or to get the students to like you, or for many other reasons. In order for you to improve your teaching skills, you need clear goals and feedback that provides information about your performance relative to those goals.

Goals and Feedback

Feedback is usually defined as information generated about a response that is used to modify the next response. Feedback is a necessary condition for learning. In order for you to learn how to draw a line 17 inches long, you would have to receive feedback after an attempt to draw the line: Someone would have to tell you the length of the line you drew or how far short of or beyond the 17-inch goal you went. If you receive this kind of feedback, you will learn to draw the line quickly and with great accuracy. You could also learn this task if someone simply told you "too short" or "too long" after each attempt, but it would take you longer than if the feedback were more precise. The precision of feedback is determined by the information content of the feedback and how it relates to the learning task.

Obviously, feedback cannot be very precise if the learning task has not been well defined. Suppose that someone asks you to draw a "medium-length line." After your first attempt to draw a medium-length line, you are told that the line you drew was 23 inches long. This feedback, even though quite precise, is absolutely meaningless because the learning task was not sufficiently defined for you to use the feedback. If either the task or the feedback is not precisely established, you are put in a situation where learning will be difficult and frustrating. You may know how long a line to draw, but you may not be able to get anybody to tell you how well you are doing in your attempts to draw it. Or you may not really understand what it is you are supposed to be doing. So it is too often with learning how to teach.

The goals of teaching cannot be stated as simply, specifically, and in such neatly quantifiable units as those of line drawing. But teaching need not be so vague and imprecise that you have no idea about what skills you are supposed to develop as you practice teaching. It is possible to formulate some precise goals for teaching and to provide sources for feedback to a teacher on his or her progress toward those goals. The total of all the precise goals will not necessarily equal good teaching, but it will improve teaching. There is much about good teaching that we do not yet know, and many teaching skills cannot be stated in terms of precise goals and feedback. This should in no way deter us from doing what we can to improve teaching. This text does not claim to include all skills that constitute good teaching. What it does is take those important aspects of teaching that can be stated precisely and provide clear goals and feedback channels for developing those skills.

Too often the preservice or inservice physical educator is told, "Be firmer with students," "Be more emphatic," "Relate to them more on their level," or "Give your directions more clearly." These not-so-clear goals are followed by equally imprecise feedback such as "Much better," "Okay," or "That's not quite it yet." The method usually employed to monitor teacher and student performance in such cases is "eyeballing." The supervisor sits and watches the class for a session and then provides unilluminating feedback. This kind of supervision is no longer adequate.

Data-Based Approach to Developing Teaching Skills

Most of the suggestions for improving teaching skills that are presented in this text require collection of some data in order to work toward the skill development goal. This is a fairly new way of working for many people. Physical educators are not accustomed to using a data-based approach in practice teaching or simulated teaching situations. Usually someone watches the teaching intern perform and then provides some verbal or written comments on the performance. This type of datum lacks specific information related to specific goals. And far too often the report of the peer, supervisor, or master teacher is so insignificant that nothing of any substance is gained from the experience.

This text suggests the collection of various kinds of data on your performance as a teacher and the performance of your students. Counting behaviors, using watches to record time, and other data collection methods will be unfamiliar to many of those with whom you will share this experience. But the techniques are fairly easy to master, and getting regular feedback about progress toward your goals will be valuable for you and for those with whom you work.

The fact that this text is based primarily on a data collection format does not mean that you cannot or should not take every opportunity to learn through informal conversations with peers, supervisors, and cooperating teachers. The data collection format provides a base for developing teaching skills. It is not a substitute for the many subtleties and nuances of skill that can be passed on to you by an experienced teacher. Every opportunity to discuss teaching openly and frankly with peers, supervisors, and cooperating teachers should be vigorously pursued. The right piece of information about a student's home life, the right tip about voice articulation, or a good bit of advice about organizing for a particular activity can help you tremendously. This text makes no claim to cover all the factors that contribute to good teaching. It does provide a format through which a solid foundation of good teaching skills can be built. The degree to which this foundation provides the base for further professional development rests largely with the professionals and peers with whom you are working.

Chapters 2 and 14 provide more material on data collection and assessment techniques.

Ways of Practicing Teaching

Teaching can be viewed partially as a set of skills and strategies that can be practiced. These skills and strategies can be defined, goals can be set, and feedback can be provided for teachers so that they can improve their performance. But how does one practice a teaching skill? How does a preservice or inservice teacher improve, short of actually trying out the skill or strategy in a regular class? Fortunately, there are many ways of practicing teaching skills, outlined briefly in this section.

First, it is important to understand that actual teaching with a full group of students in a real setting is not the only way to practice, or even the best way in many respects. True, *eventually* you need to try it all out in the real setting, but first it helps to have a great deal of other kinds of practice. In learning a sport, you clearly can't perform well under game conditions until you have had a chance to work on the fundamentals and to practice under more controlled conditions. Coaches use drills to isolate crucial components of the performance so they can be practiced thoroughly without the complicating distractions of the full game setting. Players often practice skills alone, or in small groups. Eventually the coach moves to a controlled practice setting, which we usually refer to as a **scrimmage**. The scrimmage is closer to reality, but it is still not exactly like the game itself. Throughout their careers, players participate in drills and scrimmages. Even when they become highly skilled game players, they still need to practice the fundamentals, and there is always something new to learn that will help improve their overall performance. Most of what is true for sports practice is true for teaching practice, too!

Teaching skills can and should be practiced in ways analogous to practice in sport settings. You cannot expect to read about a teaching skill or strategy and then go out and do it in a real setting without having first practiced it in more controlled settings. If coaches tried to do this, they would probably lose their jobs quickly—their teams certainly wouldn't perform very well. Unfortunately, teacher educators have been doing this for far too long. Recently, however, there has been an increased recognition of the importance of teaching experience in teacher preparation. Teaching skills and strategies can be practiced in several ways.

Practicing Alone

It is often useful to practice certain skills alone, especially when you are first trying to learn them. For example, praising students seems like an easy skill, but it is not. First, you have to learn to say the right words, and you have to learn to use nonverbal communication (see Chapter 7 for suggestions on this skill). You have to build up a variety of ways to praise. You can do this by yourself. For example, watch your nonverbal behavior in a mirror. An audiotape recorder is useful to record your own attempts so that you can listen to them later. A videotape system is even more useful so that you can "teach to the camera" and can later watch and evaluate your efforts. You will feel a little uncomfortable doing this at the outset, but this kind of practice is potentially as useful as shooting baskets alone is to a basketball player.

Peer Teaching

It is often useful to practice skills by simulating situations with a small group of peers. Short teaching episodes can be arranged so that they focus on a limited number of skills (such as providing learner feedback as they practice or giving quick, clear instructions about a game). If these sessions can be videotaped, it is useful to watch them later for evaluation and feedback purposes.

Microteaching

The microteaching strategy is like peer teaching in that it has a limited scope, a specific focus, and a small number of students. But, unlike peer teaching, microteaching uses real students, either in a school or brought to the college or university where you are studying. Microteaching sessions usually have a limited time focus. Again, videotaping these sessions is very useful.

Reflective Teaching

Reflective teaching is a technique pioneered by Cruikshank (Cruikshank and Applegate 1981). It is like peer teaching, but with added features. In reflective teaching, a group of college students (your methods class, for example) is divided into smaller groups, usually six to eight in a group. One teacher is selected from each group. The selected teachers are given a descrip-

---

Practicing Teaching Skills Informally

Do you need a specific assignment to practice important teaching skills? Do you need a microteaching setting or a trip to a local school? No! Teaching skills can be practiced in many places—indeed, in almost any place where you interact with other people.

For example, becoming a more effective praiser can be practiced with brothers, sisters, or roommates. Asking clearer, better questions can be practiced in other classes, in an informal discussion with classmates, as a church school teacher, or as a volunteer at a youth agency. Providing direct, informative feedback can be practiced at a summer camp, as a YMCA volunteer, or simply helping a neighbor child jump rope in the backyard on a weekend afternoon.

The point is that many important teaching skills can be practiced on a daily basis in the settings you now frequent as part of your daily routine. You simply need to pick out one skill at a time, consciously try to improve your use of that skill, and be sensitive to how you are doing. Some of the techniques for self-assessment presented later in the text may also be very helpful in such informal practice.

If you want to improve, try practicing on your own.

---

tion of what is to be taught. The teaching task should be a skill in which the other learners have had little prior experience. The instructions include a specific objective of what is to be learned and a way of evaluating the students after the learning experience. This teaching task should be handed out at least one day in advance of when the teachers will be expected to teach the short lesson.

The next time the class members meet, they divide into their groups, and each teacher teaches the lesson as he or she sees fit. After the designated time, (usually 10 to 15 minutes maximum), the learners are evaluated on how well they learned the task. The learners also fill out a questionnaire that allows them to react to the method by which their teacher taught the task. The entire class then reassembles to discuss how well the various groups learned the task and to share their reactions to the methods by which they were taught. The learning data and the reactions of the learners provide the basis for "reflecting" on the lesson in the discussion. From these "reflective" discussions, insights and understandings about teaching grow. Reflective teaching is a promising, cost-effective technique for practicing teaching skills.

Small Group Teaching in a Real Setting

Eventually, the time comes when the teaching skills must be tried out in a real setting. It is very helpful to be given the chance to try them out with real students but in a setting that is slightly less demanding than one would encounter in real teaching. The best way to accomplish this is to reduce the number of students to a manageable number: usually from five to ten. You might then teach a 10- to 20-minute lesson or series of lessons to such a group. This technique is especially useful for practicing instructional teaching skills (it is far less useful for practicing managerial skills).

Large-Group/Short-Time Teaching in a Real Setting

Managerial and organizational skills and strategies are usually best practiced with a full class of students, but with a limited time focus—often no more than 5 to 10 minutes. The purpose is to practice those aspects of teaching that deal with getting classes started, getting equipment out and/or away, helping students to make transitions efficiently, and other managerial and organizational tasks.

Real Teaching

Full-class, real-student teaching is the final kind of practice before a preservice teacher actually gets into the "game." The game, to carry the analogy, is the student teaching experience, when the preservice teacher will have full responsibility for many classes over an extended period of time. If other practice techniques have been used wisely, the student teaching experience should be comfortable and enjoyable. The student teacher should be able first to survive the early part of the experience and then to grow in the later parts of the experience.

In each practice setting, the data-based, systematic approach to teaching skill development can be used. Without specific goals and good feedback, it is difficult to determine, in any practice setting, how much you are improving.

Stages of Skill Development in Teaching

One research program has experimented with ways of helping preservice and inservice teachers to improve their teaching skills (Siedentop, 1981). This research program, which has been underway for more than a decade, has used many different kinds of teaching skills, teachers, and settings. Throughout, the program shows that people go through similar stages of development as they acquire teaching skills. These developmental stages may not be absolutely necessary for every teacher, but most teachers seem to go through them. It is important that you understand that there are stages of development, that people do go through them, and that they may be necessary stages if you want to improve your teaching. These stages are particularly evident for people who are attempting to acquire and refine interactional instructional skills such as giving feedback, praising, stopping misbehavior, questioning, and other similar skills.

Stage 1: The Initial Discomfort Stage

It may be hard for you to learn to interact in new ways. You may have a limited repertoire of words to use to convey your messages. You may even feel embarrassed in saying phrases in ways that are new. This is particularly true for learning how to praise students effectively—and this is an important skill. For some reason, people have very limited practice in being nice to one another. Teaching alone or small group peer teaching is especially useful to help you to get beyond this stage. Please do not feel that you are unusual if you feel awkward, discomforted, or even embarrassed at learning to behave differently as a teacher. It seems to be a first stage, and most students grow through it quite quickly.

Stage 2: Learning a Variety of Techniques

When you first learn to praise or to give specific feedback or to be more enthusiastic, you will have a limited repertoire of ways to do so. And you will tend to repeat the same phrases and do the same things over and over again. In giving positive feedback and praise, you will be giving what one research team once labeled as the "global good"; that is, you will interact more frequently with your students (you will have increased your rate of interacting), but you will have a limited number of ways of interacting (for example, saying, "Good job" over and over). This, too, appears to be a stage most people experience. Don't worry! If you persist, and if you get help through systematic feedback, you will learn a greater variety of ways to give feedback, to be enthusiastic, to praise students, to use your nonverbal behavior.

Stage 3: Learning How to Do More Than One Thing at a Time

The next stage seems to be learning to focus on improving one skill or strategy while still being able to do other things at the same time. This is an important stage, because it indicates that you have progressed far enough so that the skill is becoming more habitual. This lets you focus on other important aspects of teaching. Now, for example, you can continue to improve your feedback skills while also focusing on the improvement of some managerial techniques. When you have reached this stage, you are on your way to becoming a skilled teacher!

Stage 4: Learning How to Use Your Skills More Appropriately

It is one thing to learn how to give feedback, to say the words, to increase the variety of things you say. It is another thing to give the right feedback at the right time. The early stages of development of this kind of skill are like hitting a baseball off a batting tee. Batting tees are a nice way to learn a smooth swing, the transfer of weight, and a good follow-through. But eventually you must hit a pitched ball! You can also learn many good techniques for praising students, both verbal and nonverbal. Now you must learn to praise the right student at the right time for the right behavior. In other words, you must learn to *apply* your skills appropriately and accurately. Here, too, it helps immensely to have specific goals and regular feedback as you try to master this stage of development.

Stage 5: Confidence and Anticipation

The final stage is where you have practiced the skill, used it, and can see the benefits of it in the reactions of your students. Skills eventually become habits—good habits, in this case. Teachers with large skill repertoires, and confidence in their ability to use them, gradually acquire the ability to anticipate the demands of the settings within which they work. They acquire what teaching researcher Jacob Kounin calls "with-it-ness" (see Chapter 5 for more about with-it-ness)—they seem to have eyes in the backs of their heads! This is the stage you are working toward—but most of us need to work through the other stages first.

Sources of Help

It is worth repeating that experience alone does not guarantee improvement in teaching. This is true for real experience, and it is also true for simulated experiences. Each teaching experience you have will no doubt change you a bit. But it would be foolish to assume that every change is a change for the better. Bad habits are learned, just as good habits are. A systematic approach to the development of teaching skills helps maximize the chances that you will learn good habits and helps minimize the chances of your acquiring bad habits. You can no doubt learn a lot on your own, just as you might learn how to be a decent tennis player without any instruction or coaching. But it is also true that you can be even better if you get the right instruction and coaching along the way. Now, who or what can help you?

First, a systematic approach can help you. You may not always like to have specific goals for a teaching episode. You may not always like to have your teaching observed. You may not always like to have to deal with feedback about what you did. Very few of us like to be held accountable for achieving goals. But these constraints help you improve. Having a goal gives an experience the necessary specificity to make it useful. Learn to ask for clear, specific goals. Similarly, observation is the only way to develop good feedback. The observation process is a main aid in helping you to improve. You should want to know how well you did. Just as a player likes to know his or her statistics, teachers should want to know how well they did relative to the important skills of their "game." In other words, the systematic approach is your friend, not your enemy.

Second, you can help yourself. Mirrors, audiotape recordings, and videotapes can all be used in order to help yourself improve. Third, your instructor can help you improve. Your instructor is not just your evaluator but should also be your helper. If you have specific goals to achieve, then your instructor can provide practice and feedback to help you improve. You are partners in teacher education. You are on the same team. That doesn't mean that you will always get along in every situation. It simply means that you ought to keep in mind that you both have the same goals—becoming a better teacher.

Your peers can also help you improve. This can be done specifically through techniques such as peer teaching and reflective teaching. It can also be done by having the peers observe you as you teach and provide feedback to you afterward. Most importantly, improvement can be enhanced through the development of a professional attitude within your peer group—an attitude that takes teaching seriously and motivates discussion, questioning, and a desire to improve. If you and your undergraduate peers do not care much about learning how to teach now, there is no reason to expect that you will care much about improving once you get on the job.

Finally, practicing physical education teachers in schools can help you to improve. They can do so in the first instance simply by allowing you to watch them—*if you watch specifically with a goal in mind.* Learning through observation is more than sightseeing. Teachers in schools can also help you by discussing specifically what they do in certain situations or how they organize or manage. A skilled teacher makes certain tasks look effortless. Don't be fooled. When you talk seriously to such teachers, you find out very quickly that they have worked very, very hard to achieve that "effortless" look.

Developing Teaching Skills in the Age of Accountability

Professional educators are increasingly called to account for what happens under their tutelage. There are probably three primary reasons for the widespread acceptance of education accountability. First, economic resources have become scarce as education competes with other societal needs and as the costs of education soar. This creates a public mood that tends to welcome some kind of accountability for the expenditure of those resources. Second, as teachers become more organized and militant, it is inevitable that the public at times takes an adversary position. Because the public controls the purse, it is not surprising that it seeks to hold teachers more directly accountable (especially by making salary increases based partially on the productivity of students). Third, there is growing evidence that in many schools students are not performing well in such basic skills as reading. Education is one of our biggest national industries, and the public does not take kindly to evidence showing that many students reach high school without being able to read the materials necessary for success in high school.

Most teachers concede that accountability will more likely strengthen education than harm it. If teachers want a higher status and the remuneration and professional privileges that go with it, then more specific measures of accountability should be used in making decisions about their professional advancement. Teachers pay taxes, too! Education is a function of government in our system. Most of us would be very happy to have the government be more accountable for the way it spends our tax dollars. And certainly, wherever students are so ill served by the educational system that they reach high school without being able to read, the system needs to be corrected.

This text provides you with a measure of accountability for developing teaching skills, especially those developed in reality-based field experiences (see Chapter 13). When you come to the end of this experience, you should be able to point to specific teaching skills that you have developed or improved. You will have some direct measures of your performance and of your students' performance that will help you improve now and in the future. They can also be used to make judgments about what further experience you may need in order to become certified as a teacher.

This text can also help your instructors to serve you better and thus be more directly accountable for their performance as educational specialists. To what extent these materials will be used as accountability measures will be decided by the university and school personnel who work with you in your program.

CHAPTER **2**

Assessing Teaching and Its Outcomes

Teaching makes only the difference it can make; it is not magic. Teaching is vital because it is the only factor we really can do much about in the short run. It is impossible to change a student's heredity, and socioeconomic conditions change only slowly over generations. The quality of teaching, on the other hand, can make an immediate difference. . . . A small but substantial portion of what any student achieves in the gymnasium is a consequence of what we do as teachers. It is now possible to find out which behaviors are effective and how they work. It is possible to learn from teaching.

> Larry Locke, *Learning from Teaching* (1979)

CHAPTER OBJECTIVES

To distinguish among teacher process, student process, and student outcome variables for assessment of teaching

To explain relationships between how teaching proceeds and how a student learns to like or dislike a subject

To distinguish among discrete teaching behaviors, analytic teaching units, and criterion process variables

To define a unit of ALT-PE

To distinguish among emotional climate, management of student behavior, and management of learning tasks as separate elements of educational settings

To explain the difference between management through established structure and management through current interaction

To respond to common arguments against the measurement of teaching and learning

To explain the importance of behaviorally defining teaching and learning variables

To explain the importance of specificity in goal setting

To explain how baseline data are used to improve teaching

To distinguish between goal achievement and goal maintenance

Chapter 1 emphasized the distinction between knowing about effective physical education teaching and knowing how to teach effectively. Another distinction was added—that of wanting to teach well, of being motivated to continuously try to improve your teaching.

Obviously, knowing about effective teaching is important. College and university programs are usually quite good at helping you to learn *about* such things as effective teaching. Frequent quizzes, study objectives, study guides, lectures, discussions, term papers, and exams all help you to learn about effective teaching. But these same programs are less adept at helping you to learn *how to teach well*. Here, of course, the lectures, discussions, quizzes, and exams are less important. You may learn about teaching by listening to a good lecture or by reading a good book, but neither will help you to teach well unless you have an opportunity to practice the teaching skills. Likewise, a written assessment in the form of a quiz or exam doesn't provide any information about how well you can teach.

17

In order to assess your physical education teaching skills, you first of all must be put in a situation where you actually teach. Only then can teaching skills be assessed and eventually evaluated. The purpose of this chapter is to alert you to various ways of assessing physical education teaching and its outcomes. The specific techniques for conducting the assessments of teaching and its outcomes are covered thoroughly in Chapter 14, although some mention of assessment techniques is made in this chapter.

This text strongly advocates the regular assessment of teaching; however, it should be made equally clear that no single assessment of teaching gives a complete picture. Similarly, no individual statistic from a basketball game allows evaluation of the play of any single participant. Several indicators are needed before a complete picture begins to emerge. Similarly, teaching is an extraordinarily complex process that can be viewed from a number of different perspectives. The vignette on page 19 indicates clearly the complexity of the teaching act and shows that no single view of that act is sufficient, in and of itself, to understand that act fully, let alone assess and evaluate it.

But this is no reason not to assess specific skills when and where you can. The more good information you have about your teaching, the more you will understand it. The more specific the information is, the more you will be able to act in order to improve. Thus, the complexity of teaching should not deter us from measuring what we can and using that information. A major goal of this chapter is to identify assessment techniques that provide specific information on the development of isolated teaching skills and other techniques that provide a more global tool for evaluating teaching. Both types of techniques are necessary for the full development of teaching skills and strategies.

An Assessment Model

Three assessment categories are suggested here. The first category consists of **teacher process variables**. These include teaching skills such as giving instructions, questioning, providing feedback, stopping misbehaviors, and praising appropriate behavior. Teacher process variables also include strategies for organizing the class, managing behavior, helping students make transitions, and dealing with intrusions into the flow of an activity. Teacher process variables relate directly to the teacher's performance and are measured by direct observation of the teacher while he or she is teaching.

A second assessment category consists of **student process variables**. These variables begin to shift attention away from the teacher and toward the learner. Student process variables relate to those actions performed by students that potentially contribute to or detract from learning. Examples of such variables include the amount of time it takes for students to move from one place to another, the level of misbehavior in a class period, the amount of appropriate learning time an individual student gets in a 40-minute period, the number of skill attempts a squad gets during a volleyball lesson, the per-

The Teacher as Ringmaster

The instructional act itself has one pervasive quality—complexity. In full swing, a class of 35 fourth-graders doing a gymnastics lesson is a seething mass of human interactions. Events happen at high speed, with high frequency, in multiple and simultaneous patterns, and take subtle forms. In one recent clip from two minutes of that reality, the following was observed:

> Teacher is working one-on-one with a student who has an obvious neurological deficit. She wants him to sit on a beam and lift his feet from the floor. Her verbal behaviors fall into categories of reinforcement, instruction, feedback and encouragement. She gives hands-on manual assistance. Nearby two boys perched on the uneven bars are keeping a group of girls off. Teacher visually monitors the situation but continues work on the beam. At the far end of the gym a large mat, propped up so that students can roll down it from a table top, is slowly slipping nearer to the edge. Teacher visually monitors this but continues work on the beam. Teacher answers three individual inquiries addressed by passing students but continues as before. She glances at a group now playing follow-the-leader over the horse (this is off-task behavior) but as she does a student enters and indicates he left his milk money the previous period. Teacher nods him to the nearby office to retrieve the money and leaves the beam to stand near the uneven bars. The boys climb down at once. Teacher calls to a student to secure the slipping mat. Notes that the intruder, milk money now in hand, has paused to interact with two girls in the class and, monitoring him, moves quickly to the horse to begin a series of provocative questions designed to reestablish task focus.

That was only 120 seconds out of the 17,000 the teacher spent that day in active instruction. No description fits this picture of complexity so well as Smith's concept of the teacher as ringmaster [Smith & Geoffrey 1969]. Surrounded by a flow of activity, the ringmaster monitors, controls, and orchestrates, accelerating some acts, terminating others, altering and adjusting progress through the program, always with an eye for the total result.

Source: Locke, L. The ecology of the gymnasium: What the tourists never see. *Proceedings of SAPECW*, Spring 1975. (ERIC Document Reproduction Service No. ED 104 823)

centage of time a class is on task during a lesson, and the amount of time students spend receiving information. These variables are linked directly to learning. Student process variables are measured through direct observation of students while they are in class.

A third assessment category consists of **student outcome variables**, or student **product** variables. Such variables indicate student achievement, changes in learners that are considered to be evidence of learning and growth. Generally speaking, these variables are typically more familiar to physical educators than the preceding two categories because they consist of increased skill, better game-playing ability, higher levels of fitness, increased knowledge about the subject matter, and improved attitudes toward physical education. Such variables are most often assessed by tests or other evaluation instruments, usually at the end of a teaching unit. But there are also other forms of outcome or product evaluation, such as the achievement of objectives, the completion of designated tasks, the reaching of criterion levels of performance, and direct observation of performance on a regular basis.

It is useful to consider the differences between short-term outcome measures and long-term outcome measures. Long-term outcome measures are much more difficult to assess, but they may provide valuable information relative to the overall goals of a physical education program. Physical education has always been concerned with "carry-over" values such as fitness, participation in leisure activities, and proper sportsmanship habits. Many of these cannot be evaluated fairly in the short term simply because their long-term strength gives evidence of the degree to which a program has achieved its goals.

The basic assessment model proposed, then, suggests that teacher process variables influence student process variables, which in turn influence student outcome variables, both in the short term and in the long term. Schematically, the model in its most basic form is shown in Figure 2-1.

This basic assessment model needs two additions to make it even more useful for the systematic development of effective teaching skills. The first addition is a set of feedback loops that represents the *use* of assessment information to change teaching strategies. One feedback loop uses information on student process variables to change teaching strategies. For example, an assessment that showed low rates of on-task time for a gymnastics class might lead to a different instructional format designed to increase on-task time. A second important feedback loop uses information on student outcomes to change teaching strategies. Here, for example, evidence from fitness scores of poor upper body strength might lead to devoting more practice time to activities that contribute to upper body development. The addition of these feedback loops implies that information generated about student processes and student outcomes must be *used* if it is to improve teaching.

One other alteration to the basic model is needed to have it better repre-

Figure 2-1. *The Basic Assessment Model*

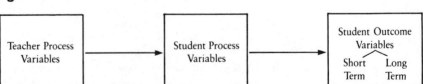

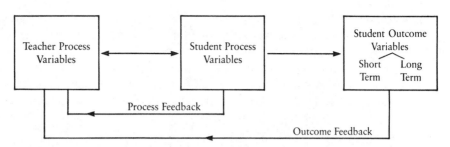

Figure 2-2. *The Complete Assessment Model*

sent the realities of physical education teaching. The line between the teacher process variables and the student process variables should show arrows in both directions. Far too often we assume that teachers exert influence over students in a unidirectional manner. The fact is that teachers are influenced very directly by students! Sometimes it is difficult to tell who is more in control of a lesson, the teacher or the students. Unless this dual-directional influence is understood, many mistakes in interpretation can be made. For example, when it is suggested that enthusiasm is related to achievement, we should not automatically assume that enthusiasm *causes* achievement. Such an assumption represents a unidirectional view of the influence between teachers and students. Teacher enthusiasm does influence achievement. But teachers who are in classrooms where learners are achieving also tend to be more enthusiastic as a result of their association with such learners. Drawing arrows in both directions underscores the complexity of the teaching setting, so that interpretations can be made more carefully. The complete model then appears as in Figure 2-2.

Information on techniques and instrumentation for measuring variables in the teacher process and student process categories are explained in Chapter 14. Techniques for monitoring student achievement are discussed in Chapter 11.

A Universal Objective for Education

Assessment produces information. Information then is used for making evaluations. However, evaluations must always be made with some frame of reference in mind. Usually, the frame of reference for evaluating teaching is the goals of the educator and the school. Goals may be developed relative to skill development, movement capabilities, games skills, fitness, sportsmanship, self-concept development, and other similar characteristics. There are many, many different ways in which physical education goals could legitimately be conceptualized. Each of us no doubt would differ somewhat in our selection of goals. I would like to propose an underlying, universal goal for education both in the gymnasium and in the classroom, for math teachers,

English teachers, and physical education teachers. That goal is to teach in such a way as to develop in the students a growing commitment to the subject matter.

In education, product and process are unalterably intertwined. You cannot separate the results of an educational experience from the nature of the experience itself. The atmosphere of the learning environment will teach your students something just as lasting and important as the actual skills learned within the gymnasium, playground, or athletic field.

Three levels of learning should be recognized. For example, if you are teaching volleyball, students will learn the skills and strategies of volleyball. This is the most obvious level of learning. But at another level, students will learn to like or dislike volleyball, and at still another level they will learn to like or dislike the very process of learning. Robert Mager (1973) has said that the objective of all education should be to help students like what they are learning and like the process of learning. Mager believes that students learn to like or hate a subject while they are learning it, and that these cumulative experiences eventually determine whether people come to like or hate the very process of learning.

> The object of this paper is to discuss the importance of designing learning experiences in such a way that they do not teach students to hate the very things about which they are learning. It is the object of this paper to suggest that each and every instructional sequence or event, each and every lecture, each and every program, should have as its number one objective the intent to send the student away from the learning experience with approach tendencies toward the subject matter equal to or greater than those with which he arrived. [p. 3]

Students who experience a consistently negative and coercive environment or who experience consistent failure will learn to hate the subject taught and eventually to hate learning. A consistent feature of this text is emphasis on the positive aspects of a learning environment or, as Mager would put it, teaching for approach tendencies toward the subject and toward the learning process. An approach tendency is simply any behavior of students that would allow one to conclude that they find the subject and the learning experience satisfying, enjoyable, valuable, interesting, challenging, or some combination of these.

It is difficult to predict how students of today will spend their leisure time 30 years from now. If past evidence is at all reliable, we know that they will have to continue to develop skills and learn new skills in order to have a productive leisure life. Indeed, to obtain any of the benefits of regular physical activity and play, they will have to participate regularly. If students' physical education experiences are to promote such growth tendencies, then physical education teachers must teach in a manner that strengthens the students' approach tendencies toward physical activity and toward learning physical activities. Mager contends that this is what distinguishes the true professional educator from the hack teacher.

It has been said that better than 50 percent of all the students now in our elementary schools will ultimately be employed in jobs that do not now exist. If this is true, and if we are to achieve the goal of educating for the future, we must not create students with aversion to learning. We must accept the responsibility for organizing our instructional efforts in ways that will maximize approach strengths toward what we are now teaching and toward the act of learning. We should accept as a universal objective the intent to send the student away from each instructional experience with approach tendencies equal to or greater than those with which he arrived. Not to do so is to run the risk of educational malpractice. After all, any hack teacher can teach hate. But to send a student away as eager to learn as he was on the first day of school is a challenge for a professional. The issue seems clear: shall we be hacks or professionals? [Mager 1973, p. 6]

The teaching skills emphasized in this text are those that will contribute to this universal objective, specifically tailored to the needs of the physical education teacher.

On-Site Assessment of Teaching

The assessment of teaching can be viewed from three levels or three different perspectives. These levels provide a useful framework for examining teaching regardless of whether it is in a microteaching lesson on campus, small group teaching in a local school, or student teaching. These levels of assessment can be used to generate information that is useful immediately both to help teachers improve and to evaluate their teaching. Information in each level is generated through direct observation of teachers and students:

Level 1: Discrete teaching behaviors
Level 2: Analytic teaching units
Level 3: Criterion process variables

Each of these levels provides different information, useful for different purposes. Each should be used appropriately relative to the specific goals of any practice teaching episode.

Level 1: Assessing Discrete Teaching Behaviors

It is often useful to define important teaching behaviors carefully and then to measure the degree to which they occur during a teaching experience. This level of assessment is particularly useful for the early stages of teaching skill development where teachers practice skills in fairly controlled settings, teaching to camera, microteaching, and other simulations of real settings. Discrete teaching behaviors can be defined as specifically as need be to meet the goals of the practice session. Feedback for skill attempts is an example. If desirable, feedback can be subdivided into negative, corrective, and positive feedback. It can be still further subdivided into feedback statements that are general in nature, as opposed to those that have specific information content. Categories such as feedback, reinforcement, questioning, and prompting are often included in observational formats for the assessment and evaluation of full-scale teaching efforts, too. The focus at this level of assessment is on a teaching act that has a definable beginning and end (and is therefore discrete) and can be postulated as important in the teaching and learning process.

Sometimes it is useful to assess discrete teaching behaviors in terms of their frequency of occurrence, simply by counting the occurrences and showing them as a function of the lesson length or as rate per unit of time. Thus, rate of specific feedback per lesson, rate of praise statements per 30 minutes, or rate per minute are useful in comparing performances or in setting goals for a teaching episode. Another technique is to watch a teacher for a set interval (usually from 5 to 20 seconds in length) and record the behavior of the teacher that best characterized the interval. Information thus generated can be expressed in terms of percentage of total intervals in which a behavior occurred during the teaching episode. For example, a physical education teacher might initially deliver positive feedback to students at the rate of 12 percent of the intervals in a 30-minute lesson and then, after practicing, improve to the rate of 40 percent of the intervals in a lesson.

Discrete teaching behaviors can also be assessed by their accuracy rather than by their frequency alone. Thus, the appropriateness of a feedback statement could be the target for the observation. The resulting information could be expressed as a ratio of appropriate feedback statements to the total number of feedback statements made.

Level 2: Assessing Analytic Teaching Units

Single, discrete behaviors often do not give information that is sufficiently rich and complex to provide useful assessment information for the improvement of teaching. For example, knowing how many managerial behaviors you emitted during a 30-minute teaching episode would provide only limited information about your overall managerial skills. In such cases, it is necessary to develop new ways of looking at the teacher-learner process in order to generate information that is most relevant to a particular kind of teacher function such as management, organization, or instruction. Units that consist of more than one discrete behavior or the combination of teacher process variables with student process variables are referred to as **analytic units** (Dunkin and Biddle 1974).

A very useful analytic unit is the **managerial episode**. A managerial episode is defined as a sequence of time that is initiated by a teacher managerial behavior and culminates when the next instructional or practice activity begins. For example, consider a situation where a teacher has four squads involved in two volleyball games. The time has come for the two sets of teams to exchange opponents. The teacher initiates this transition by blowing a whistle to stop the action. The teacher then explains that Squad A will now play Squad D on Court 2 and Squad C will play Squad B on Court 1. The teacher then signals for the teams to change. The teams change. Eventually,

---

Observing Teaching: Supervision Is More Than Sightseeing

Traditionally, the observation of teaching has been little more than an infrequent visit to a school, a short time watching the teaching intern, perhaps some nonspecific summary comments afterward, and a brief and too often meaningless period of chit-chat to conclude the visit. This supervision method—if you can call it a method—is what I refer to as **eyeballing**. This method is inadequate even for those who have enormous experience and a very heightened capacity for intuitive judgments about teaching. Good observation requires some data collection—our intuitive sense of what is going on in the gymnasium is not often sufficiently specific or precise to provide useful feedback for the teacher. The teacher is trying hard—the observer should try hard, too.

Anecdotal records in the form of detailed note taking, rating scales, and checklists can be helpful. The rating scales and checklists are easy to do, but the information they provide is less than precise and not often sufficiently specific for teachers to improve from session to session.

Observations are best done with a system developed for the specific purpose of the teaching episode. These involve counting time, behaviors, and instances of analytic units. Chapter 14 describes many kinds of observation systems. Observation can be done by peers, by an instructor, or by a cooperating teacher (or by you, if the session is videotaped). Wouldn't you like to know what you are doing—specifically? Without such information, you are much less likely to improve.

---

the new games begin. The managerial episode began when the first whistle was blown. The managerial episode ended when the games actually began again. The total length of time recorded (perhaps 2 minutes) would be the time for that managerial episode. The lengths of all of the managerial episodes in a lesson add up to the total amount of managerial time. The managerial episode is judged partially by what the teacher does and partially by what the students do. It is an analytic unit.

Another useful analytic unit for assessing teaching skills in physical education is the teacher prompt → student response → teacher feedback cycle that occurs so often during an instructional session. This cycle can be observed and evaluated from several points of view. This analytic unit is a combination of discrete behaviors. The teacher gives a brief prompt about what to do ("Keep shoulders level when swinging"). The student makes a response. The teacher evaluates the response and then provides some feedback about the response ("Much better, they were nearly level"). The teacher then provides yet another prompt ("Watch me and copy what I do"), and the cycle is repeated. Assessing these behaviors as a unit provides a much more meaningful view than would viewing the separate components only as discrete behaviors.

Level 3: Assessing Criterion Process Variables

Often we need on-site assessment of teaching in an overall sense. We need to provide for a teaching intern some information that represents the degree to which he or she is "doing the job." Because student achievement data usually are collected at the end of a unit or term, we need evidence that is strongly linked to achievement but that can be observed at any time in a teaching unit. What is needed is a measure that provides, on a day-to-day basis, direct evidence of the degree to which students are learning. This can be accomplished by assessing **criterion process variables**, ways of conceptualizing process-oriented variables that provide direct evidence of student learning. It can also be argued that certain kinds of ongoing process evaluation provide a better measure of student learning because they are less contaminated than are typical achievement measures. (Achievement measures are influenced by many factors over which the teacher has little or no control—mainly, the skills and aptitudes with which the student entered the learning experience.)

I would like to suggest two criterion process variables for which there is strong evidence of a direct link to student achievement. They can be thought of either as "proxy" measures for achievement or as even more direct measures of student learning. Actually, there is strong evidence to suggest that the two variables are simply different ways to measure the same phenomenon, the degree to which students have the opportunity to engage in appropriate learning tasks.

One criterion process variable to measure appropriate student engagement in learning tasks is **academic learning time** (ALT). In physical education (PE), one might think of ALT-PE as a strong criterion measure for student learning. A student would be judged to be in ALT-PE when he or she is engaged in a physical education learning task in such a way that the chances of success are quite high. ALT-PE is measured in time units. The method most often used to measure it is referred to as **interval recording** (see Chapter 14). During repeated, periodic intervals, students are observed to see what they are doing. For example, they might be actively engaged in a learning task in such a way that they can be successful. If so, that produces an interval of ALT-PE. The ALT-PE intervals can then be summed and expressed as a percentage of total intervals. A time estimate can also be generated simply by multiplying the number of intervals by the length of the observation interval. In this way it has been shown (see Chapter 4) that individual students often have as little as 2 to 5 minutes of appropriate activity engagement per lesson. Five minutes of appropriate engagement per lesson isn't much time to learn skills such as the volleyball serve or hurdling techniques in a track unit.

> ### Academic Learning Time-Physical Education (ALT-PE)
>
> Academic learning time-physical education (ALT-PE) is a unit of time in which a student is engaged in relevant physical education content in such a way that he or she has an appropriate chance to be successful. Appropriate success rate is usually about 80 percent probability of doing the task correctly as it is defined in the lesson. ALT-PE is thought to be a powerful way of evaluating the degree to which teachers perform effectively. In a recent study of teaching physical education, in which over 100 lessons were evaluated, Professor John McLeish (1981, p. 31) concluded that
>
> > It was one of the major impressions received in the use of the ALT-PE system that this supplies the missing element, or indeed, the major component, for evaluating effective teaching in physical education. Time on-task, academic learning time, opportunities to learn—call it what you will, and measure it if you can—this is the vital component of effective teaching in general.
>
> What percentage of total time will your students be engaged in activities in which they have a good chance to be successful?

A second way to provide a criterion process assessment is to count the number of trials a student gets at any particular learning task where he or she has a good chance for success (there is no sense counting attempts to high-jump 4'6" when a student cannot yet do 3'6"). The number of learning trials (for example, four trials per 30-minute lesson) is also a good measure of student learning—classes in which students get more opportunities to try out skills are those classes where they will learn more.

The concept of opportunity to respond, measured through ALT-PE or by frequency of appropriate trials, represents the best criterion process variables to use in assessing teaching skill. These measures also allow for useful diagnosis and assessment of other discrete teaching behaviors and analytic units. For example, it might be logically and empirically determined that fewer and shorter managerial episodes are related to increases in ALT-PE. These criterion process variables also represent a legitimate way to operationally define improved teaching; that is, the teachers who organize and instruct in such a way so as to create more opportunity to respond are doing a better job of teaching. This is thoroughly consistent with the definition of teaching presented in Chapter 1: Good teaching exists where students learn. ALT-PE and rate of appropriate trials are good on-site measures of student learning. Thus, teachers who produce more of these variables are producing more student learning, and are therefore, by definition, doing a better job of teaching. Let's not dodge the issue. What I am suggesting is that your overall teaching skills be assessed by reference to what your students are doing rather than by how well you give initial instructions, how often you give feedback, or how enthusiastic you are. These last three criteria may be related to increased student opportunity to respond. Then again, some of them may not! The point is that improved teaching skills should show up in more and better opportunities for students to learn. The teaching skills themselves have little inherent meaning. They derive their meaning from their influence on student learning and therefore should be evaluated in terms of criterion variables that are valid measures of student learning. Criterion process variables such as ALT-PE and rate of appropriate learning trials have been shown to be valid measures of student achievement (indeed, many would argue that they are better measures of student learning than are achievement measures derived from end-of-unit tests).

Understanding the Learning Environment

It is important to have a clear and accurate set of concepts with which to analyze and evaluate the teaching-learning process. Educators and the public have traditionally viewed the learning environment with concepts that do not hold up when compared with research results. The following set of statements is typical of common misconceptions:

"Permissive teachers are warm and supportive."
"Negative settings are tightly controlled."
"Highly directive teachers produce negative climates."
"Firm control of pupil behavior results in high time on-task."

The problem with these statements is that each confuses two or more aspects of the teaching-learning process. There are at least three distinct dimensions of the teaching-learning environment that need to be separated in order to be understood, analyzed, and evaluated (Soar and Soar 1979). These three are (1) the emotional climate of the setting, (2) the manner in which student behavior is managed, and (3) the manner in which learning tasks are selected and carried out. These three major dimensions are schematically represented in Figure 2-3.

Research has shown these dimensions of the teaching-learning process to be distinct and separable. But educators too often tend to confuse one dimension with another—for example, assuming that a permissive teacher (mobile

Figure 2-3. *Dimensions of the Teaching-Learning Environment*

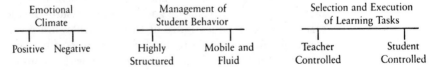

Table 2-1 / *Dimensions of the Teaching-Learning Environment, Related to Teacher Types*

Teacher Type	Emotional Climate	Management of Student Behavior	Selection and Execution of Learning
1	Positive	Structured	Teacher controlled
2	Positive	Fluid	Teacher controlled
3	Positive	Structured	Student controlled
4	Positive	Fluid	Student controlled
5	Negative	Structured	Teacher controlled
6	Negative	Fluid	Teacher controlled
7	Negative	Structured	Student controlled
8	Negative	Fluid	Student controlled

and fluid management of student behavior) is automatically warm and supportive (produces a positive emotional climate). Another common misconception is that negative educational climates are necessarily associated with teachers who structure student behavior highly and tightly control the management of learning tasks. Although some teachers certainly do represent those particular combinations, other teachers represent other combinations. In fact, there are eight possible combinations of the three important dimensions. They are listed in Table 2-1.

Which type of physical education teacher would you most like to be? Which type do you think has most often been associated with physical education settings where students achieve more? Which, if any, do you think might be associated with settings where students tend to achieve less or have better or poorer attitudes? The answers to these questions should become considerably more clear to you as you read Chapters 3 and 4.

The major point to be made here is that the assessment of physical education teaching and its outcomes must be done within a framework that allows for useful distinctions and analysis, ones that reflect the realities and complexities of real-world teaching. In some highly structured settings both learning and behavior are tightly controlled by the teacher, yet the emotional climate is strongly positive. And some teachers allow for much more fluid and mobile student behavior yet still control and direct the learning tasks themselves. In some settings student behavior is highly structured and controlled by the teacher, yet the learning tasks are more under the control of the students. It is important that you do not look at just one dimension of the teaching-learning process and then *assume* that you also know what the other dimensions must be. This is especially true for the distinction between emotional climate and the management of student behavior. The only way to understand both of these dimensions of classroom life is to examine them both!

Obviously, you will seldom see teachers who represent the extreme positions the model indicates. To be realistic, the model must be viewed as a continuum. Teachers fall somewhere between the positive and negative poles of the emotional climate continuum. They fall somewhere between the structured and fluid poles of the management of behavior continuum. And, likewise, class settings fall somewhere between total teacher control of learning tasks and total student control. Although this makes the model, and the concepts, a bit more complex, it also makes them considerably more realistic.

One further addition is necessary to use the model as a framework through which to analyze and evaluate information gathered about physical education teaching. As teaching is observed, one tends to focus on the interactions that occur, especially on interactions between the teacher and his or her students. The observation and analysis of current interaction patterns are no doubt important to understand the setting. But current interactions should also be viewed in terms of the **established structure** of the setting (Soar and Soar 1979). In fact, it is useful to gauge the degree to which a setting operates on current interaction as opposed to established structure. Established structure means the patterns of behavior and routines of the setting that have been established in the past to such a degree that students have internalized them and now operate in a routine way without constant teacher direction and supervision. Current interactions are visible and often quite noticeable. A teacher is constantly prompting students, giving directions, and organizing. A teacher is constantly providing reprimands and corrective feedback in order to keep students moving along in the lesson. Established structure is less visible and often goes unnoticed unless you look for it carefully. When structure has been established, students know what to do and do it without prompting and without attention from the teacher.

In physical education class, if students move from place to place and task to task quickly and without constant prompting or correcting from their teacher, you can be assured that the teacher, at some time in the past, established structures that now operate without his or her constant attention. The students have learned the important class routines and now operate on this structure rather than on the basis of interactions from the teacher. This is an important distinction. As you will see in Chapter 3, an effective teacher tends to establish a structure early in the school year and then depends on that structure for many of the moment-to-moment operations in class. Teachers who manage by high rates of current interaction tend to be associated with class settings where achievement and attitude gains are less powerful.

General Plan for Improving Teaching Skills

You will learn more *about* effective teaching in physical education as you read this text. If you have a chance to actually try the skills described in the various chapters, you may also be able to improve your teaching skills. But in order to improve skills, there must be planning, defining, specific goal development, and criteria set. There must be observations of your teaching, with data collected, and those data must be used to provide feedback to you. This is all necessary no matter whether the teaching is to be done alone, in a micro-teaching setting, with a small group of students in a school, or in student teaching. What follows explains the essentials necessary for the systematic improvement of your teaching skills: the need for measurement, behavioral definitions, specific goals, and the use of baseline data to guide achievement and maintenance of goals.

Measuring Teaching as It Occurs

Many professional educators object to a strong emphasis on measurement because they feel that the things that are most easily measured may be the least important aspects of teacher and student performance. This is a legitimate criticism, but when examined closely, it is not really so much a criticism of the use of measurement techniques as it is of the lack of imagination in defining performance categories that are educationally important. Performance categories that are easy to measure are almost always easy to define. The number of push-ups completed or the number of laps run are easy to define and easy to measure. Good form in hurdling or successful solutions to movement problems are less easily defined and consequently are more difficult to measure reliably. Some social characteristics such as cooperation and sportsmanship are even more difficult to define and therefore even still harder to measure reliably. But it should be recognized that the problem of measurement is secondary to the problem of definition. If cooperation could be defined adequately, it could be measured easily by counting the frequency with which it is observed (event recording is discussed in Chapter 14).

Another objection to an emphasis on measurement is the more radical view that many of the most important educational outcomes cannot be measured. Not too long ago, while discussing the need for greater accountability in teaching, a colleague told me that most of the important things that occurred in her classes could not be measured. This is not an uncommon stance. There are two obvious counterarguments. First, rating some occurrences during a class as important implies some judgment about the relative importance of the many outcomes in the class. Such a judgment can be made only if the relative outcomes have been measured in some way, no matter how crudely. For example, a teacher who adopts this stance toward measurement can usually rate his or her various classes on the degree to which each demonstrates a feeling of unity. If a feeling of unity is considered more important than improvement in basic skills, then some judgment has been made about this feeling of unity, and it must be based on a measurement system of some kind.

Second, and perhaps even more basically, the simple recognition that something has occurred implies a measurement. When a teacher says, "We had fun today!" he or she is making a measurement. The measurement may not be precise, and the teacher may not even understand clearly on what basis the judgment was made, but the fact that the statement is made implies that a quality or element was measured in some way. So the question of measurement again appears to be secondary to the question of definition. When someone suggests that a quality or element of teacher or student performance can't be measured, what is implied is that it can't be defined. Once an element or quality is defined, it can be measured. The relative crudeness or sophistication of measurement systems depends primarily on how well a quality or element has been defined. Undefined qualities are judged by crude and often unreliable methods of measurement. Undefined qualities usually are highly susceptible to the personal bias of the observer. Undefined qualities cannot be made public and cannot become realistic goals for any educational venture. If such qualities are considered important, then every effort should be made to analyze them and to generate definitions that can be observed and made more amenable to more reliable measurement systems.

Recasting Definitions in Behavioral Terms

For important characteristics, qualities, or elements of teacher or student performance to be useful as educational goals, they need to be recast in behavioral terms. The term *behavioral* refers to things people do that can be observed. Feelings cannot be observed and are therefore not behavioral, but verbal reports about feelings can be observed. Many important constructs in physical education have existed for years without anybody having any clear idea of what they mean in behavioral terms. Physical educators deal with such constructs as positive self-image, body image, ego strength, competitiveness, leadership, and sportsmanship without specifying what each of these means. It does no good to encourage a student to show leadership if one cannot describe to the student what showing leadership means in terms of what he or she should do in a class or on a team. Likewise it is counterproductive to berate a player for lack of competitiveness if one cannot describe to the player how he or she should behave in order to improve in this quality.

One value of attempting to recast definitions in behavioral terms is that it forces each of us to examine his or her own beliefs. It is fine to talk glowingly about sportsmanship, but it is another question to have to list what would be acceptable evidence of good or bad sportsmanship. It is easy to tell a teaching intern that he or she should care about his or her students, but it is an entirely different matter to describe clearly what evidence would be accepted as a demonstration of the degree to which the intern cares.

Nobody can systematically improve in any quality unless he or she understands what the quality is and how it is demonstrated. If as a teaching intern you are told to demonstrate maturity, initiative, and enthusiasm, you have every right to expect someone to tell you what it means to behave maturely in a teaching situation, what kinds of things are counted as proof of initiative, and what is meant by enthusiasm in teaching.

Contrary to some opinion, the recasting of definitions in behavioral terms is not a totally recent phenomenon. In the 1920s, W. W. Charters and Douglas Waples were conducting widespread investigations concerning the goals of teacher education and desirable characteristics for effective teachers (Kleibard 1973). They polled "experts" to find the 25 most desirable traits for teachers, and then they attempted to give them meaning by citing behavioral referents for the traits. For example, the trait of adaptability was then considered important, as indeed it might be so considered today. But in the 1920s an adaptable teacher was defined as one who "does not dance nor play cards if the community objects" (Charters and Waples 1929, pp. 223–244). You may wonder what adaptability means in a more modern context. The point is that unless there are fairly clear behavioral specifications, a term such as *adaptability* is largely meaningless. Each of us might infer something entirely different from that term, and the confusion and misunderstanding that might occur if it is used without behavioral specifications could be a source of potential conflict in the internship experience.

Achieving Specificity in Goal Setting

The goals developed for a teaching experience may be few or many, depending on the nature of the experience (microteaching goals should be few, while student teaching goals will be many). But regardless of the number of goals set, each must be *specific*. Specificity is achieved in two ways. First, the precise definition and meaning of the teaching skill must be agreed to and understood by the teacher who is supposed to show it in his or her teaching. It is not enough to suggest, "Let's focus on improving management skills." Instead, it is better to agree to try to "reduce total management time," "reduce the average length of managerial episodes," "reduce the number of transitional episodes," "initiate the beginning activity more quickly," or "have equipment exchanges go more quickly" (always with a specific time criterion stated). Each of these must be defined sufficiently well so that they can be measured reliably. To measure reliably means that two observers using the same definitions and watching you at the same time would agree on what they recorded.

The second aspect of specificity is setting a criterion goal. This could be done in terms of a time criterion or a percentage criterion or in several other ways. What is important is that the goal be established realistically yet still be a challenge to you to improve your skills. If the goal is set too low, you won't be challenged to improve. If the goal is set too high, you will be set up for failure. An example of a criterion goal is "The student teacher will spend no more than 10 percent of class time in managerial activity."

Both goals and criteria must be adjusted to make them relevant and fair for the situation in which you will teach. Giving feedback at a high rate per minute in a peer teaching situation in your own gymnasium on campus is one thing, but achieving the same rate per minute in a real setting with a difficult class is something else. These situational factors should be kept in mind during the goal-setting discussion.

Using Baseline Data for Diagnosis and Prescription

Once goals for teaching experiences have been defined specifically, how does one know how high or low to set the initial criteria for achievement?

With management time per class, for example, is 20 percent the right goal, or 15 percent, or 10 percent? There are three ways to set initial goals. First, results of research in physical education could be used to establish some goals—the materials in Chapter 4 will be helpful for this. Second, the experience of the student or instructor could be used (that is, goals established on what previous teachers and interns have been able to do in previous micro-teaching or student teaching experiences). Third, and perhaps most importantly of all, the initial goals could be set on the basis of your initial efforts, on the basis of data collected on your own teaching, what is called **baseline data**. No doubt some combination of the three ways would be useful. By keeping in mind what descriptive research in physical education has found, modifying it by what is known about the local situation in which you will teach, and putting that together with baseline data from your own teaching, a realistic set of criteria could be developed.

Baseline data are descriptive results of your own teaching efforts used to set further goals and to make comparisons. If possible, it is good to have more than one teaching session contribute to the establishment of your baseline levels of performance. If two or even three such sessions can be used, then the teacher behavior and student process data from these sessions can be used in two very important ways. First, baseline data reveal your strengths and weaknesses (we all have them). You may be very good at giving feedback, but may not be quite so skilled at providing appropriate behavioral interactions (you may nag the students a lot). You may have a low level of management time for beginning and ending sequences, but a too-high level of transition time. You may provide very good demonstrations and instructions, but the ALT-PE of your students may be too low. Baseline data reveal the priorities for your own skill development.

Second, the baseline data also provide evidence useful for setting criteria for improvement and, later, the basis for comparing subsequent performances to baseline for evaluative purposes. If your management time during baseline is 37 percent of total class time, then setting an initial criterion of 25 percent is realistic. Eventually, you might be able to manage well enough to achieve 10 to 15 percent, but that is unlikely in the beginning. If your baseline reveals no capacity to deliver positive behavioral interactions (verbal reinforcement of appropriate social behavior among students), then clearly the initial goal must be to help you to do a few each class period. Only after you get through the initial stages of skill development should a criterion of 1.5 per minute be established (1.5 praise behaviors per minute is 45 positive reactions in a 30-minute period, and that is a lot for someone whose baseline was 0.0).

Achieving and Maintaining Goals

Experience in helping physical education teachers to improve their teaching skills shows that they can accomplish much in short periods of time. You, too, will improve if you have the chance to practice, if you try to improve specific skills, and if you regularly get some feedback about how you are doing. As you improve, criteria can be changed to take into account your growing skills. The chapters in this text contain information about what to do in order to improve—how to manage more efficiently, how to prevent and remedy discipline problems, how to interact more humanely and effectively, how to give more and better academic feedback, how to implement your instruction better, and how to improve the interpersonal relationships between you and your students. Chapter 14 contains detailed information about building observation systems through which these skills can be regularly coded so as to produce good feedback. Goals can be achieved—you simply need to want to do so and you need opportunity to try the skills out.

Although goal achievement has been fairly easy for most trainees I have worked with, goal maintenance takes a little more care. Goal maintenance means that once you achieve a goal, you must then move on to other goals, but at the same time try to maintain your new skills from the previous goals. For example, once you achieve some goal in the feedback area, you might then move on to work on behavioral interactions. What happens to the feedback? Hopefully it stays up somewhere near the level it was when it was the main goal. To help to achieve better maintenance of developed skills, it is helpful to use **maintenance goals**. A maintenance goal is a target criterion for a skill you have previously worked on, but are not working on directly at the moment. A maintenance goal should be set at a realistic level, high enough so that it is evident in your day-to-day teaching. Then, when an observer does code your teaching session (or you code yourself from a videotape), several skills can be observed and the resulting data can be used to give you feedback not only on the target for that teaching session but also on how well you are maintaining previously developed skills. In this way, you gradually build a repertoire of teaching skills, and they eventually become habit. When high levels of skill are displayed as permanent features of your teaching style, then you will have developed into a truly effective professional teacher.

Maintaining One's Own Performance

The final phase, time permitting, will be to shift control of your teaching performance away from your supervisory team and onto your shoulders. When you teach full time, you will not have the support of the supervisory team. This does not mean that you should abandon the method used to develop your skills. For example, suppose you use a cassette recorder to tape one class session per week. You can later code this tape yourself to check on certain aspects of your verbal behavior such as feedback and positive interactions. A section of this text is devoted to methods for maintaining teaching skills in the absence of supervisory team help (see Chapter 13). This is the epitome of good teaching. A teacher takes pains to develop and maintain skills and then periodically checks him- or herself to make sure that the performance endures. There is no guesswork and no eyeballing. There is hard evidence. This means that the teacher has taken the responsibility for holding him- or herself accountable for what goes on in his or her gymnasium.

CHAPTER 3

What We Know About Effective Teaching

The effect of schooling on the individual pupil depends to a considerable extent on who his teacher is. . . . Personnel costs themselves represent so large a share of the day-to-day cost of education that the best hope for improvement in cost-effectiveness lies in improving the effectiveness of the teacher.

Donald Medley, *The Effectiveness of Teachers* (1979)

CHAPTER OBJECTIVES

To describe the major reasons why pre-1960 research efforts so often resulted in failure

To describe and explain why the development of systematic observation systems were important in improving the research picture

To describe the major research model through which teacher effectiveness has recently been investigated

To describe major limitations of the present research effort

To describe the major features of effective teaching

To explain and provide examples of teacher strategies that contribute to teaching effectiveness

To explain and provide examples of teacher strategies that have correlated negatively with effectiveness criteria

To explain the general relationship between academic achievement and attitude gain

To explain and provide examples of the relationships between classroom management and teaching effectiveness

To explain the concepts of with-it-ness, overlapping, smoothness, momentum, group alerting, and accountability

To describe the manner in which the developmental status of the learner, the socioeconomic status of the learner, the aptitude of the learner, and the subject matter being studied tend to modify the general pattern of teaching effectiveness

Each of us has no doubt experienced what it means to be in contact over a period of time with a truly outstanding teacher. What teachers do is extraordinarily important. A skilled, motivated elementary classroom teacher can, in one year's time, afford a young boy or girl untold chances for personal and academic growth. A high school teacher can open up the riches of a subject matter during a particular term. At the same time, a poor or uncaring teacher can make an elementary year seem like an eternity and can be responsible for what John Dewey called "miseducation"—the stunting of personal and academic growth. A poorly skilled junior high school teacher can "turn off" the minds or bodies of an entire class. In these cases students wrongly assume that the subject matter is not interesting or useful, when in fact it was the teacher who was dull and uninspiring.

Education is our largest industry. We spend more on education than we do on national defense, and that is no doubt wise

36

because in the long run a well-educated citizenry is probably our best source of ongoing security. There are over 2 million full-time teachers in our nation's schools. They account for the largest part of the expenses of education. The importance of having effective teachers is, therefore, quite clear. Both from a personal, experiential point of view and from a purely economic or societal point of view, more effective teaching in schools should be a national priority. Moreover, as problems in schools mount, teaching becomes more and more difficult. As society expects more and more from its schools, the issue of what constitutes effective teaching becomes more and more crucial. When students come to you full of eagerness, highly motivated to learn the subject matter for which you are responsible, well disciplined from previous experiences, persistent in their efforts to learn, accustomed to long stretches of on-task behavior, able to delay gratification, and equipped with whatever basic skills are necessary to launch fully into your subject matter, then effective teaching is quite easy to achieve. You simply point them in the proper directions, put them into contact with the right materials, see that they get some feedback, and generally stay out of their way as they explode with enthusiasm into the learning process. But don't expect to encounter such a group very often in your career! Most groups of students might have a few such learners, some who exhibit a few of those characteristics, and some who exhibit characteristics opposite to those described. That's the real world, and to be effective in the real world requires more than good intentions and the ability to point students in the right directions. That is what this chapter is about.

What makes a teacher successful in the real worlds of classroom and gymnasium? This question has been asked, in one way or another, quite consistently for most of this century. The question has been asked philosophically and scientifically, but until recently the answers have been less than satisfactory.

False Starts and Inappropriate Techniques

Research on teaching doesn't have a very good reputation. It has suffered through a long history of inconclusive results, inappropriately asked questions, and less than useful techniques. Most of what transpired in teaching research between 1900 and 1960 is gathering dust on the back shelves of university libraries, and deservedly so. Many of the early researchers attempted to sort out the personality profiles of successful teachers. There were two major problems with this approach. First, success was too often judged by the ratings of supervisors, principals, and peer teachers, some of whom may never have seen the teacher teach. These rating and judgment systems were invalid and unreliable. They most certainly were not good indicators of success in teaching. A second problem was to have hypothesized in the first place that "personality" had something to do with effective teaching. Personality is most often judged by responses to questions on paper-and-pencil tests, and

The Educational Romantics of the 1960s and 1970s

Ever since A. S. Neill's *Summerhill* appeared in 1960, there has been a continuous series of educational manifestos vilifying the public schools and describing organizational and methodological reforms that would supposedly lead us all into a bright new era of schooling. The names of those who led this reformist movement are now familiar—John Holt, Jonathan Kozol, Ivan Illitch, Charles Silberman, and others. Their words have been powerful and persuasive. They have had a major influence on educators, those teaching in schools, those administering schools, and those helping to prepare teachers. We have been told to individualize, personalize, and humanize. We have been told to teach less directly, and instead to exert subtle indirect influences. We have been assured that when we do these things creativity, self-growth, positive attitudes, and better academic achievement will follow shortly.

Most of the romantic reformists of the 1960s and 1970s were more concerned with the question "What are schools for?" than with the question "What is the most effective way to teach?" As they sought answers, they tended to confuse the two issues. Nonetheless, we have all been influenced by their visions and their persuasive writings. Unfortunately, little of what they said was based on a comprehensive and reliable analysis of teachers teaching and children learning.

Teaching research, by necessity, responds first to a scientific peer community. Reports of its outcomes are hardly ever written as well or circulated through the same channels as any of the popular educational manifestos. But, as a Stanford University education professor, Nate Gage, has said, "in the long run, the improvement of teaching—which is tantamount to the improvement of our children's lives—will come in large part from the continued search for a scientific basis for the art of teaching" (1978).

there is little reason to suspect that responses to these kinds of tests told anyone much about what kind of teacher a person might be. The results of these efforts were uniformly inadequate. They revealed little other than that teachers had different personalities and this related little to their success as teachers.

Another research strategy was to compare teaching "methods" to see which was best. Often, a favored strategy was compared against what was labeled a "traditional" method; for example, the "part" method versus the "whole" method in teaching motor skills. This kind of research was very value-laden, in the sense that the researchers often set out to "prove" that the innovative method was better. Often the method labeled traditional was simply bad teaching. The methods strategy in teaching research was no more successful than the personality strategy. The methods were most often too rigid and too stereotyped to bear much resemblance to what went on in real classrooms, where teachers tend to use a variety of "methods" to achieve different goals. Pet methods tend to come and go, while the central task of the teacher remains fairly constant. If we have learned anything from the methods strategy, it should be to be very skeptical about magical methods for achieving teaching success.

All in all, the pre-1960 research on teaching does not constitute a striking series of successes. Instead, the failures were so consistent that many came to believe that teaching research could not possibly describe, analyze, and explain effective teaching. Indeed, during the 1960s many came to believe that a major reason for this continued failure might be that teachers simply don't make an important difference—that they are not sufficiently powerful influences to show up in measures of achievement and student growth. We now know that such pessimism is unwarranted. Teachers do make a difference! And it has been through teaching research that we have come to understand how they can make a positive difference in the educational lives of the students they teach.

The Turning Point: The Study of Teachers Teaching

It is most interesting that the turning point for teaching research—from failure to success—was the development of strategies for observing teachers as they teach in real schools with real students. Systematic observation of teachers, through the lenses of many different kinds of observational systems, finally provided the methodological tool through which teaching research began to understand the nature of teacher effectiveness. These were not special teachers, chosen for special reasons. They were ordinary, certified teachers, the kind one finds in schools throughout this society.

The observation systems developed were of many different kinds. Some of them, such as the systems developed from the Flanders Interaction Analysis tradition, used categories that explicitly valued some teaching styles more than others. In Flanders-type systems, teacher indirectness is valued. So too are student-initiated interactions. Other systems chose categories that were more value-free in the sense that the categories represented ordinary language descriptions of teachers doing their jobs—categories such as "instructs students," "gives directions," "reprimands students," and "asks questions" were simple, everyday descriptors of what goes on in classrooms. Some categories such as "reinforces appropriate student behavior," "cues student responses," or "punishes inappropriate behavior" were everyday occurrences familiar to most teachers yet also were traceable to theories of human behavior.

The era of 1960–1975 saw rapid development of observational systems and the techniques of securing good, reliable data through observation of teachers teaching. Some category systems fell by the wayside. Others survived. Much was learned about how to observe, how to be in schools as an observer without changing what went on in those schools, and how to develop and use reliable data about teaching and classroom processes. The result was a growing understanding of how things are, rather than romantic visions of how things should be. And the ability to describe things as they are was prerequisite to being able to analyze teacher effectiveness.

The Effective Teacher: The Beginning of Understanding

In the past decade, rapid strides have been made in teacher effectiveness research, enough so that a beginning picture of effective teaching has begun to emerge. The major strategy through which these findings have developed goes something like this. A large number of classrooms are identified through a sampling strategy that tends to account for variations such as the socioeconomic status of the children attending the schools, geography, and ethnic heritages. The identified classrooms are studied for an extended period of time, typically a school year. Throughout the year, the classrooms are observed systematically with observation systems that focus on teacher behavior, classroom processes, and student behavior. Achievement data are collected at the end of the research period. These achievement measures tend now to be content-valid (rather than standardized tests that might not be sensitive to local goals) and multidimensional. A useful measure of beginning performance also is collected so that the final measures can be adjusted according to entering abilities. Measures of students' personal growth, attitude, creativity, and problem solving are often included in the assessment battery. After the final data on achievement are collected and adjusted according to the entering abilities of the students, the high- and low-achieving classrooms are identified. The researchers then go back to examine the teacher, student, and classroom process data to discover patterns that tend to differentiate between the higher-achieving group of classes and the lower-achieving group of classes. Those patterns of teaching, classroom interactions, and student processes that are associated with the high-achieving classrooms become the elements from which patterns of effective teaching emerge. If similar studies, using slightly different approaches, in different parts of the country (or world), with different students, yield similar results, then one begins to have more confidence in that emerging picture of effective teaching.

Limitations on Our Present Understanding

The picture is not yet complete. The current status of research allows for cautious optimism and a beginning understanding of effective teaching. Hopefully, many of the current problems will be attended to in due course and our understanding will grow. But several points need to be at least mentioned because they do represent limitations.

First, far too many of the studies to date have focused on achievement in basic academic subjects such as mathematics and reading. There is a great need to extend the research using achievement in other subject areas. It must be said, though, that where other kinds of achievement data have been used, the results tend to be confirming.

A second limitation is that most of the research has been conducted in elementary schools. Far too few studies have examined teacher effectiveness in middle schools, junior high schools, and high schools. However, the research that has been done at levels above the elementary school has tended to be more confirming of the general picture than contradictory.

A third limitation, from certain points of view, is that recent research on teacher effectiveness has tended to adopt a rather standard view of the purpose of schools. These researchers, unlike many of the critics in the 1960s and 1970s, are not asking the question "What is school for?" They seem to have accepted the notion that school is primarily a place to learn the academic skills and knowledge valued in the culture—a place where the knowledge aspects of the culture are passed on to the next generation. Measures of attitude and students' personal growth have often been a part of the recent teaching research effort, and, as is explained more fully later in this chapter, the patterns of effective teaching sorted out through this recent research strategy have tended to affect those kinds of indices positively. But it is good to keep in mind that any kind of "effectiveness" research must define criteria by which effectiveness will be judged—and different criteria may produce a different notion of effectiveness.

Patterns of Effective Teaching

Despite the limitations just mentioned, the results of teacher effectiveness research from a number of different research programs have, in recent years, come together to form a fairly conclusive portrait of what constitutes effective teaching in today's schools, if academic achievement in basic skills and positive attitudes toward school and self are used as criteria by which to judge effectiveness. The amount of confirming evidence from different studies has grown sufficiently to begin to warrant the generalization of this pattern of effective teaching to different subject matters and different kinds of settings than the ones in which the results were originally determined.

The effective teacher is one who finds ways to keep students appropriately engaged in the subject matter a high percentage of the time and does so without resorting to coercive, negative, or punitive classroom techniques. Thus, the main ingredients of effectiveness in today's schools appear to be

1. High percentage of time devoted to academic content
2. High rates of on-task behavior among students

3. Appropriate matching of content to student abilities (success oriented learning)
4. Development of a warm, positive classroom climate
5. Development of class structures that contribute to Item 2 but do not violate Item 4

Notice that this overall description of effective teaching does not describe any particular "method" of teaching. An informally organized educational setting that has high rates of academically appropriate engaged time would be considered effective. A more formal but disorderly educational setting would be considered ineffective. The effectiveness is not in the method itself but rather in the degree to which the method produces high proportions of academic learning time.

It might be argued persuasively, in terms of today's schools, that certain methods of educational organization might more easily produce academic learning time (that is, academic in the sense of being related to criterion tests). In the research that has been done, the most common pattern associated with classrooms that have high rates of learning time has been labeled *direct instruction*. Rosenshine has described direct instruction:

> Direct instruction refers to academically focused, teacher directed classrooms using sequenced and structured materials. It refers to teaching activities where goals are clear to students, time allocated for instruction is sufficient and continuous, coverage of content is extensive, the performance of students is monitored, questions are at a low cognitive level so that students can produce many correct responses, and feedback to students is immediate and academically oriented. In direct instruction, the teacher controls instructional goals, chooses materials appropriate for the student's ability, and paces the instructional episode. Interaction is characterized as structured, but not authoritarian. Learning takes place in a convivial academic atmosphere. The goal is to move students through a sequenced set of materials or tasks. [Rosenshine 1979, p. 38]

This pattern of teaching, described most often as direct instruction, has been found in a number of independent research studies to be characteristic of classrooms where students achieve more and feel better about themselves and school. Conversely, the patterns of teaching that have been most often associated with open classrooms and informal education have been found most often to produce less achievement. Permissiveness, spontaneity, lack of class structure, and student selection of learning goals all seem to be *negatively correlated* with achievement and attitude. But it must be recognized that this is so because these patterns of teaching *do not usually produce high rates of academic learning time*. The lesson seems clear. It is not that open classroom techniques, informal education styles, or humanistic education methods in general are inherently deficient. But it does seem that they must be planned and controlled very carefully (if indirectly) in order to produce high rates of academic learning time.

The techniques of direct instruction appear to be easier to master, control, and use on a day-to-day basis in the complex world of today's schools. Thus, you should feel confident in using direct instruction as a realistically obtainable pattern of effective teaching. But you should not become so rigid as to suggest that it is the *only* effective pattern of teaching. There may be many, many effective patterns, many ways of producing a high proportion of total time in academic learning time within a generally positive climate. That is the main lesson of teaching research today.

What needs to be examined further, then, are techniques teachers use to achieve the main, overall ingredients described here. These techniques are described in the next section. The section following that examines some important situations in which modifications of the general pattern might be useful.

Strategies That Contribute to Effective Teaching

The main ingredients of effective teaching are keeping students appropriately engaged in the subject matter a high percentage of the available time, within a warm, nurturant climate. Therefore, it is useful to consider teaching strategies that contribute to that state of affairs. It should be emphasized again that our definition of effective teaching is framed primarily by what happens to students. As we consider useful teaching strategies, it is important to remember that they are judged to be useful *because* they contribute to higher percentages of appropriately engaged academic time, and, therefore, to achievement and good attitudes.

As early as 1971, Rosenshine and Furst (1971) identified five teacher variables that had been shown to be consistently related to achievement. These variables are (1) clarity of presentation, (2) enthusiasm of the teacher, (3) variety of activities during a lesson, (4) task-oriented and businesslike behaviors in the classroom, and (5) content covered by the class. It is clear that these teacher strategies tend to produce higher amounts of appropriately engaged learning time and also contribute to a nurturant climate. The variable of **clarity** means simply that instructions, demonstrations, and discussions are not only clear to the students but also take less time because of their clarity. Teacher **enthusiasm** contributes no doubt to the positive climate of the setting but also keeps things moving along at a brisk pace. Variety probably prevents boredom and contributes to the amount of content covered. The variable of **task-oriented behaviors** demonstrates that the major purpose of the educational setting is the learning of the subject matter, whether that subject matter is doing fractions, learning words, jumping rope, or playing soccer. Although other matters no doubt are attended to, it is clear that in the classrooms of effective teachers, learning the subject matter is the number one priority. The variable of **content covered** is another manifestation of this subject matter focus. The more time spent on the subject matter, the more of it can be covered in any total amount of time, be it one lesson, one unit, or an entire school year. For example, more volleyball skills and strategies are covered in a unit if there is clarity, enthusiasm, a variety of volleyball activities, and a clearly task-oriented volleyball setting.

Table 3-1 / *Differences Between Effective and Ineffective Teachers*

Area	Effective Teachers	Ineffective Teachers
Climate	Fewer teacher rebukes	More teacher rebukes
	Less criticism	More criticism
	More praise	Less praise
	Positive motivation	Negative motivation
Management of student behavior	Less disruptive behavior	More disruptive behavior
	Less time spent on classroom management	More time spent on classroom management
	More structure	Less structure
Management of learning tasks	More class time in "academic" activities	More class time in "nonacademic" activities
	Teacher works with whole class	More group and independent work
	Less unsupervised individual work	More unsupervised individual work

Source: Medley 1977.

In a large number of research programs during the past 15 years, these basic teacher strategies, and others like them, have been shown to be more evident in high-achieving classrooms than in low-achieving settings.

In 1977, Medley reviewed 289 research studies of teacher effectiveness. Using very stringent criteria (p. 5), he examined all the possible relationships among teaching strategies, student achievement, and attitude. Most of these studies were conducted in elementary schools and many of them with disadvantaged students. Nonetheless, the results point clearly in directions already established in this chapter. Using the model established in Chapter 2, the findings for climate, management of student behavior, and management of learning tasks are presented in Table 3-1.

The Medley review describes teacher strategies that create more appropriate learning time within a generally supportive educational climate. Another, interesting aspect of the Medley review was his examination of achievement *and* attitude gains. Medley found 54 studies in which data were collected not only on achievement but also on the students' attitudes toward school. In 72 percent of all those studies, the pattern of teaching that produced the best achievement also was associated with better attitudes toward school. In 36 studies, both achievement and attitude toward self were measured. Medley found that in 75 percent of these studies the teaching pattern that was associated with higher achievement was also associated with improved self-concept. Thus, from this review at least, it is clear that teachers do not have to sacrifice student attitudes toward school and student self-concept as they strive to improve student achievement. Indeed, it becomes more and more clear that achieving in school—improving at recognizable subject matter skills—is one major contributor to self-concept growth and to attitudes about schools.

These findings do not appear to be relevant only for the elementary school. Evertson and Brophy (1978) studied classroom processes, teacher behavior, student achievement, and student attitudes in the junior high school. Their conclusions sound very familiar and consistent with other studies:

Positive relationships for both math student ratings and achievement suggest that students may benefit from and may also like effective management, teacher leadership in the enforcement of classroom rules and organization, a generally task-oriented atmosphere, and a large proportion of time spent in class discussion and in whole class teaching. Certain personal and social teacher characteristics are also correlated for both criteria (achievement and attitude), those such as acceptance of student feelings, teacher enthusiasm, and academic encouragement. [p. 2]

What little research work has been done in the senior high school tends to confirm these results (Stallings 1980). Although it should be expected that there will be some differences in effective teaching of second- or third-graders as compared to senior high school students, it is also quite clear that similarities are also present, especially if the focus is primarily on how students spend time and the nature of the educational climate within which that time is spent.

It seems clear by now that effective teaching is strongly related to effective classroom management. The effective teacher is an effective manager of stu-

---

Plenty of Perfect Practice

The physical education program at the Adelaide College of Advanced Education in Adelaide, South Australia, uses the phrase "plenty of perfect practice" as a main guideline in its teacher education program. Plenty of perfect practice is realized when practice is

Pertinent: The lessons are appropriate for the abilities, interests, and experiences of students.
Purposeful: Children are kept on task in a climate that is both safe and challenging.
Progressive: Skills are ordered correctly and lead to significant learnings.
Paced: The learning space between one activity and the next in a progression is large enough to be challenging yet small enough for success.
Participatory: As many students are active as much of the time as is possible.

It is interesting that the notion of plenty of perfect practice is thoroughly consistent with research on teacher effectiveness; that is, a teacher who provides practice that is pertinent, purposeful, progressive, paced, and participatory will be an effective teacher. The program at Adelaide was not developed from research, but rather from institutions, experience, and just plain common sense of a group of teacher educators in physical education. They certainly have "hit the nail on the head" in a way that many of us would do well to emulate.

dent behavior in the best sense of that term. There are very clear indications about what kinds of strategies contribute to skillful management of student behavior. The most obvious finding from research is that effective teachers develop clear and unequivocal classroom structures and routines—that is, they take time to teach students how to behave in their particular educational setting, be it a self-contained classroom, an open classroom, or a gymnasium. Emmer and Evertson (1981) have determined that most of this management structure is taught during the first three weeks of the school year. This involves the teaching of rules for behavior, consistent reminders of these rules, contingencies for complying with or violating rules, and routines that enable students to get about the business of the class without disrupting the ongoing educational focus. Questions such as "How do I get the attention of the teacher?" "How and when is it all right for me to talk to my classmates?" "What do I do if I need more materials or equipment?" and "What do I do if I finish an assignment early?" are not only answered but made part of the class routine. Once these routines are learned and the class structure is developed, students can get on with the business at hand without incurring the displeasure of their teacher or their peers. Thus, the management of student behavior is built into the structure of the setting quite deliberately and quite early in the school year. After it is developed, there is much less need for the teacher to use current interactions to manage the behavior of students. This is why higher rates of managerial interactions tend to be associated with less effective teachers.

Once management structures are developed, the effective teacher then focuses on preventing situations from occurring in which disruptive behavior is more important for long-term achievement and attitude development than is the remediation of disruptive behavior. Kounin (1970) found that teacher techniques such as with-it-ness, overlapping, smoothness, momentum, group alerting, and accountability, were successful in the prevention of disruptive behavior and the maintenance of a task-oriented classroom. These concepts are defined as follows:

> **With-it-ness:** The degree to which a teacher communicates that he or she knows what students are doing at all times—that he or she has "eyes in the back of his or her head"
>
> **Overlapping:** The degree to which a teacher is able to deal effectively with two issues at the same time
>
> **Smoothness:** The degree to which the teacher is able to keep the lesson free from stops or breaks in the flow of activities
>
> **Momentum:** The degree to which the teacher is able to keep the ongoing lesson free from events that slow down its forward movement or hold back student progress in an activity
>
> **Group Alerting:** The degree to which the teacher is able to keep all children on task and "on their toes"
>
> **Accountability:** The degree to which the teacher holds students accountable for their task performances during a lesson

It is clear that these teacher strategies and characteristics are designed to keep the class on task and maintain a generally task-oriented atmosphere, but without a negative overtone. It is also clear that when a teacher does this more academic learning time is achieved and more content is covered—thus students tend to learn more.

Less Effective Strategies

When teaching is analyzed for its contribution to achievement and attitude gains, it is inevitable that less effective strategies begin to appear, if only as opposites to the more effective strategies. The research strategy used to analyze teaching effectiveness tends to sort many classrooms into those that have higher gains and those that have lower gains. The teaching patterns between the two groups are then examined. As a result, there is some evidence as to what constitutes less effective teaching in today's schools. It is helpful to examine these less effective strategies if you keep in mind that they are no doubt less effective because they do not produce high proportions of appropriately engaged academic time within a generally nurturant emotional climate.

The Medley review (1977) has already listed some teaching strategies that are generally associated with lower-achieving classrooms and gymnasiums, factors such as high rates of criticism of students, rebukes for disruptive behavior, more time focused on management, less structure, more reliance on current interactions to maintain discipline, less academic time, and less content covered within that time. Again, although the results reviewed by Medley were primarily for elementary schools, the results for other educational levels are confirming. Evertson and Brophy (1978), studying junior high school classes, found that class interruptions, student choice in assignments, teacher use of self-paced work, student lack of persistence, and higher proportions of serious misbehaviors were *negatively related* to both achievement and attitude measures. They concluded that the teachers probably did not have sufficient skills to individualize instruction and still keep all the students on task and that the general lack of control in the classroom no doubt led to student boredom and disinterest. Many researchers (Soar and Soar 1979, Stallings 1976, Evertson and Brophy 1978, Berliner 1979) have found that a negative emotional climate is usually associated with classrooms where students achieve less and like school less well. Although there is some disagreement about the degree to which a positive climate is necessary for achievement and attitude growth, there is strong consensus that a negative climate creates an educational situation where neither achievement not positive attitude development is likely to occur. The message seems clear—there is no evidence to support the "stern taskmaster" view of teaching. Managing through fear and punishment may produce good behavior, but it will be unlikely to lead to achievement and attitude gains.

As mentioned previously, the strategies generally associated with romantic views of open education or humanistic education have not fared well when examined closely through the lenses of teacher effectiveness research. Not only do children seem generally to achieve less in academic subjects in these educational settings, but there is a strong suggestion that they also grow less in the affective areas:

> Classrooms in which students chose their own activities and followed their own interests, were responsible for class planning, and were not dependent on the teacher were also classrooms characterized by rowdiness, shouting, noise, and disorderliness. Permissiveness, spontaneity, and lack of control in classrooms were found to be negatively related not only to gain in achievement but also to positive growth in creativity, skills in inquiry, writing ability, and self-esteem. [Rosenshine 1979, p. 41]

It seems clear that the kind of educational setting advocated by humanistic educators is extremely difficult to achieve in the real world of schools. It is no doubt also true that many have underestimated the degree to which achievement in regular school subjects contributes to growth in the affective domain. It is probably difficult for students to grow in self-esteem and improve their self-concepts if they do not also learn skills that are valued in the real worlds of the school and the community.

It is also abundantly clear that a strong subject matter focus must be established if achievement gains are to be made. This means quite simply that the teacher must be a skilled manager of time and must devote as much time as possible to the subject matter. Less effective teachers tend to devote too much time to "nonacademic matters," often in the form of informal conversation and discussion in the classroom. The analog for the gymnasium would be time devoted to "free play" or unsupervised, poorly planned kinds of experiences such as certain kinds of skill practice, warm-up time, or games that have no specific educational purpose. Starting late, finishing early, taking too much time for transitions, too much time for management, too much time for non-physical education matters all result in less time to learn the subject matter of physical education. The teacher needs to value achievement, expect students to learn, and try as hard as he or she can to arrange things in the physical education class so that those motivations are translated into high proportions of appropriate learning time for all the students. And this needs to be accomplished without resorting to a negative, punitive atmosphere or managerial style.

Some Variations on Direct Instruction

Although a general pattern of effective teaching appears to have validity and a degree of generalizability, that does not mean that it should be applied in the same way with all students and all educational settings. There are some important variations on the main theme that direct instruction leads to high proportions of appropriately engaged academic time within a nurturant emotional climate. This section describes briefly the nature and direction of the most important variations.

Four major variations on the main theme of direct instruction are sufficiently well documented to warrant consideration. As more is learned about effective teaching, we can look forward to an even better understanding of these and other variations. The four main considerations that deserve attention are (1) the developmental status of the learner, (2) the aptitude of the learners, (3) the socioeconomic status (SES) of the learners, and (4) the subject matter being studied.

Clearly, the nature of effective teaching changes as students grow older and move from childhood through pubescence and into adolescence. Younger children have not yet learned task persistence, how to delay gratification, or how to be self-controlled in a setting with other learners. They are also developing cognitive, emotional, and motor skills. They need to learn basic skills in each of these domains, and they evidently learn basic skills best when in a carefully structured setting such as has been described in this chapter as direct instruction. As they mature, as persons and as learners, they can better benefit from more cognitively complex kinds of learning settings, problem solving, and self-paced learning. Teachers can then effectively use higher-order questions, divergent teaching strategies, and more complex kinds of strategies. But even if students are more mature as persons in certain respects, they sometimes may still be immature as learners. If so, then direct instruction is probably the best form of instruction.

A second variation is based on the aptitude of the learner and ranges from low aptitude toward high aptitude. Low-aptitude learners tend to learn best when the setting is highly structured, requiring many academic responses, with useful academic feedback, all within a highly nurturant climate. High-aptitude learners can benefit better and more quickly from educational strategies that allow for individual work. Aptitude, of course, is often specific to the subject matter being studied. Therefore, a student who has low aptitude in reading might benefit most from a very controlled direct instruction format. In mathematics or physical education, the same student may have high aptitude and thus may be able to profit from strategies that more nearly allow for his or her aptitude to advance as quickly as possible.

A third variation is based on the socioeconomic status (SES) of the learner—the so-called educationally disadvantaged. It should be recognized that "educational disadvantage" does in no way imply "cultural disadvantage." Low SES students often come from rich ethnic and racial backgrounds with strong cultural emphasis. But in terms of the kinds of skills and behaviors necessary to achieve and grow in schools, they often are at a disadvantage. They tend to be less far along in terms of basic school skills such as paying attention, persisting at a task, and delaying gratification. They also may be less far along in terms of the language skills of the predominant mode of culture within society. Along with this they often bring poor attitudes toward school and low self-esteem as learners (this does not mean that they do not have high self-esteem in other aspects of their lives). The combination of poorer, less well developed academic skills, and less useful attitudes and self-esteem create the need for highly structured educational settings that are considerably more nurturant and supportive than for children who are a bit further along. Thus, the positive emotional climate of effective teaching seems to help to bring educationally disadvantaged students along most quickly, along with highly structured settings that require much academic responding and result in consistent, recognizable academic successes.

The fourth variation on the main theme is the subject matter itself. Certain subject matters—for example, mathematics, geography, history, volleyball—are learned primarily at school. Although children can learn about these activities in their daily nonschool lives, it is also true that most of what they know they have learned first in schools. There are other subject matters where much is learned outside the school. This is particularly true for reading and other aspects of literacy. In physical education, it may be true for basketball, soccer, or hockey. When children come to an educational setting with habits (good and bad) developed outside the school, it becomes particularly difficult to teach effectively. There is much greater heterogeneity in any group of students in these subject areas, including differing expectations about what is to be learned and what standards of performance are necessary. It is difficult to teach appropriate oral and written language to children who watch television from three to eight hours per day and who also acquire inappropriate language in their local neighborhoods before they come to school.

These four variations interact to make teaching even more complex. They obviously are not neat, clear distinctions, but tend to appear in clusters among students. But the variations tend to require similar strategies to maintain effectiveness. Notice that the low-aptitude, educationally disadvantaged, and less-mature students all require even stricter adherence to the direct instruction format and more attention to building a nurturant, positive climate. As students move along these channels toward greater maturity, away from their starting disadvantaged status, and toward higher-level skills despite their aptitude, they tend to profit from a gradually decreasing teacher-centered, controlled format and can benefit eventually from what is generally referred to as **heuristic instruction**—which can be described as more inquiry-centered, more discovery-oriented, and less formal instructional strategies. But until they are far along these channels (and this is true for "normal" students too), they tend to benefit most from forms of instruction, described here as direct instruction, that keep students appropriately engaged in subject matter a high percentage of the available time, all within a nurturant emotional climate.

CHAPTER 4

What We Know About Teaching Physical Education

Everybody knows something about teaching. For too long, however, expertise has been self-styled, dogma has gone unchallenged, and individual style has been the excuse for a plethora of dull, ineffective, and inadequate teaching behaviors. . . . Certainly, many different words have been used to identify teaching (*teaching, counseling, supervising, helping, intervening, change assisting*), which accounts for the great variety of approaches used in the (observation) instruments developed. Whatever the variables, however, systematic observation provided a formula whereby the teaching act could be placed under microscopic scrutiny for analysis, critique, and refinement.

John Cheffers, *Observing Teaching Systematically* (1978)

CHAPTER OBJECTIVES

To differentiate between levels of teaching research evidence in physical education and those in classroom research

To explain the major results from descriptive research of physical education teaching

To explain the major results from descriptive research on how student time is spent in physical education

To explain the major results from teacher effectiveness research in physical education

To explain the factors that might account for differences from the general results

To synthesize the research base to explain and provide examples of what constitutes effective teaching in physical education

Chapter 3 described and explained what is known about effective teaching in the real world of today's schools. All the strategies described and conclusions reached in that chapter were based directly on educational research conducted in schools with real teachers and real students. It would be nice if a companion chapter could be written describing the results of teacher effectiveness research in physical education. Unfortunately, no solid research base exists from which to draw conclusions. Teaching research in physical education has tended to lag behind its counterpart in education by as much as 10 years. Still, there is the beginning of a descriptive research base in physical education—a series of studies that describe the manner in which physical education teachers in today's schools actually teach and what happens to the students in their classes. As yet, we have barely begun to move beyond description—moving toward an analysis of effectiveness in a manner similar to what has been accomplished in classroom research over the past 15 years. Yet some studies are emerging, and their results can be compared to those detailed in Chapter 3. Most importantly, there is today more active teaching research in physical education than at any time in the past, and, if it continues, we should soon have a solid research base from which to compare and contrast physical education teaching with classroom teaching.

That, of course, is the big question—does effective teaching in physical education differ dramatically from effective teaching in the classroom? If we find that the answer to that question is no, then we can use the results cited in Chapter 3 and apply them directly to physical education and the preparation of physical education teachers. If, however, the answer is "Yes, there are important differences," then we face a considerably more difficult task in sorting out the exact nature of those differences so that physical education teachers can have guidelines similar to those now available for classroom teachers. Of course, one should not expect a simple yes or no answer to such a question. No doubt the gymnasium and the playing field and the pool are somewhat different from the classroom and therefore require slightly different kinds of teaching efforts to produce achievement and student growth. Just as obviously, there are some strong commonalities among the classroom and the various places where physical education is taught. What need to be analyzed and verified are the nature of the important differences, if any, and the degree to which they affect achievement and student growth.

The Scope of the Evidence

This chapter is based on systematic observation of physical education teachers in real schools with real students. The only analysis and conclusions reached within this chapter are based on actual research data collected in such settings. What is described here is how the real world of the gymnasium looks when viewed through systematic observation instruments that focus on teacher behavior, student behavior, and educational processes in the gymnasium. Each observation instrument provides a slightly different kind of lens through which this live, ongoing picture is caught and recorded. Through the careful integration of data collected from different kinds of "lenses," a fair, overall picture of the gymnasium can be analyzed and certain kinds of conclusions reached. It is important, therefore, to have some understanding of the scope of the evidence if you are to have faith in the conclusions to be drawn therefrom.

If one takes as a definition of teaching research in physical education only those studies in which the data are obtained through direct or indirect observation of actual instructional episodes (Locke 1977), then the research history from which this chapter is developed is barely 15 years old. Nonetheless, it has been a productive time and there are a large number of studies from

An Important Reminder

Research on teaching physical education is absolutely necessary. From it, someday, improved methods of instruction will develop, and use of those improved methods will result in a better physical education experience for students in schools. But better methods do not matter much if they are not used—knowing about better methods is different from using better methods! Larry Locke (1977) has reminded us all very clearly about the more important struggle that underlies teaching research:

> Improved methods of instruction are probably not the high payoff area, even though our pragmatic instincts may turn us in that direction. Whatever is inadequate with teaching in physical education lies much less in the domain of effective methods and hardware for use in public school gymnasia, and much more in the struggle for the teacher's soul. It is not inadequate teaching which bedevils us, it is mindless teaching; the non-teaching teacher. How to keep the teacher alive and struggling with the problem of doing good work, is now and will continue to be the question from which any great leap forward must begin.

which to draw. Just as importantly, several institutions have developed systematic research programs in teaching research in physical education and the cumulative contribution from these institutions has been quite important. Typical of colleges and universities where teaching research has been approached systematically are Boston University, Teachers College of Columbia University, Ithaca College, Ohio State University, University of Massachusetts, University of North Carolina at Greensboro, University of Wisconsin, Temple University, University of Montana, Florida State University, University of Laval in Quebec, University of Liège in Belgium, and the University of Victoria in Canada. Researchers at these institutions tend to study physical education teaching in their own regions; that is, the teachers and classes studied are likely to be drawn from their local schools. Thus, by the fact that these institutions are quite widespread geographically, the total research effort represents most kinds of physical education settings that one is likely to encounter. This is important because it gives one even more confidence that any commonalities found among the results from the various programs are highly likely to represent the status of physical education on a national and even international basis.

The number of studies that have been completed easily exceeds 100. Even if one assumes that each study focused on an average of 20 teachers, the total sample probably includes data from more than 2,000 separate teaching situations—and that is probably a conservative estimate. What this means, of course, is that if there are some common results from such a large sample, it is very likely that such results represent "things as they really are" in the teaching of physical education.

Describing Teaching Activities

What do teachers do in physical education? How much time do they spend at each of their various chores? What does the world of physical education look like when the lens is focused on the teachers? Results from a large number of studies tend to produce a fairly uniform picture of the typical physical education teacher. It appears that three major functions occupy most of the attention of physical educators as they teach. These functions are managing students, directing and instructing students, and monitoring students.

The term **managing** refers to verbal or nonverbal teacher behavior that is emitted for the purposes of organizing, changing activities, directions about equipment and/or formations, and taking care of classroom routines. Different studies define the managerial function somewhat differently, but in the definitions similarities are much more apparent than differences. The data suggest that managing accounts for at least 17 percent of a teacher's time, and estimates have run as high as 35 percent (these figures represent averages from separate studies—individual teachers would show percentages that were both lower and higher than the averages). From the many studies in which managerial data have been collected, it appears that 20 to 22 percent of a teacher's attention is devoted to managerial tasks. This, of course, is a startlingly high figure! Teachers manage the start and end of class, the transitions within a lesson, the moving of equipment, and other such things. These managerial episodes are usually devoid of learning time for students. This assumption is partially verified from those studies where teacher managerial behavior is subdivided into substantive and nonsubstantive, the former referring to behavior related directly to the subject matter and the latter referring to behavior related to social or procedural tasks (Morgenegg 1978). Teacher directions tend to be about 41 percent nonsubstantive, meaning that almost as many managerial instructions are given as instructionally related directions.

Physical education teachers also behave often in ways that are described as instruction. The term **instruction** refers to substantive verbal or nonverbal behavior such as lecturing, explaining, demonstrating, and otherwise communicating information about the subject matter. Instructional behavior does not include teacher responses to student skill attempts, nor does it include directions and instructions about nonsubstantive matters (these would be included in managerial behavior). Instructing, in its many forms, tends to account for between 14 to 37 percent of a teacher's time and behavior in the typical physical education class. The overall average is no doubt near 30 percent. It has been suggested (Pieron 1980) that physical educators probably spend a third of their time managing and a third of their time giving information. Those estimates are supported by the data collected so far. The style of instruction in physical education is very much teacher directed, in the sense that the teacher is the source of information, the controller of the movement of the lesson, and the director of activity. Although many "styles" of teaching are advocated in physical education (see Chapter 11), it would appear that in the real world of the gymnasium and playing field teacher-directed styles predominate to a marked degree. Over 90 percent of all the lessons observed in teaching research in physical education fit the teacher-directed format. This does not imply a value judgment. It merely states the fact that practicing physical educators have adopted a teacher-directed style. The only other style that appears with any frequency (perhaps 5 percent of the cases) is "task teaching."

The third major chunk of time and behavior that appears in descriptive research is teacher monitoring. The term **monitoring** refers to time teachers spend observing their students without interaction. Monitoring typically accounts for from 20 to 45 percent of a teacher's time and behavior. Researchers tend to agree that these figures *underestimate* the real amount of monitoring, simply because the observational systems tend to record only instances of monitoring that are at least 5 to 10 seconds long. Unfortunately, there is as yet no good in-depth analysis of teacher monitoring in physical education. As is explained in some detail in Chapter 10, there are several important functions that monitoring can serve. Monitoring can be useful. However, monitoring can also be unproductive. For example, teacher effectiveness work has shown conclusively that teachers who "supervise" individual work quite closely and actively are more effective. Clearly, when students know that a teacher is supervising a drill or practice activity closely, they probably tend to keep on task. Monitoring no doubt partially fulfills this supervisory function for group and individual practice. In physical education, because the spaces are much larger than in the classroom, supervising student work becomes much more of a problem and one that the teacher has to work at more carefully (see Chapter 11). The research to date has told us very little about what physical educators are doing when they are observed to be monitoring. We do not know the extent to which they are actively supervising or merely standing around occasionally glancing at their students while working on their plans for an after-school athletic practice. Until we have such evidence, it is difficult to interpret and evaluate this very large chunk of time (20 to 45 percent) that is devoted to monitoring.

Teacher-student interactions do not account for a very large percentage of teacher time in physical education. This does not mean that teachers do not interact a great deal with students. They do. It simply reflects the fact that interactions in physical education are typically of very short duration, usually lasting only a few seconds. Teacher-student interactions can take the form of praising appropriate behavior, reprimanding inappropriate behavior, providing feedback, criticizing, accepting student ideas and feelings, and so on. Research indicates that teachers devote anywhere from 3 to 16 percent of their time and behavior to these kinds of interactional behaviors.

How teachers interact with students about their social and organizational behavior is probably the largest single determinant of what I refer to as classroom climate (see Chapter 7). Educational climates can have a positive, neutral, or negative valence. As indicated in Chapter 3, it is clear that effective teachers most often develop and maintain positive climates in their classrooms. Negative climates are among the strongest predictors of less achievement and poorer attitudes among students. How teachers interact with students about their motor behavior no doubt also contributes to the overall climate of the gymnasium. Teachers can reinforce good skill attempts and well-executed strategy. They can provide corrective feedback to improve subsequent attempts. Or they can provide negative feedback—skill-oriented reprimands. Many descriptive studies in physical education have analyzed teacher-student interaction. Thus, the evidence is quite complete, and some conclusions can be drawn. The picture that evolves from the various research studies is not very positive—there is little evidence that many physical educators build and maintain what could be called a positive gymnasium climate. A sample of findings from some of the larger studies should serve to illustrate the point.

Cheffers and Mancini (1978) examined the large videotape data bank of physical education teaching that was collected at Columbia Teacher's College (Anderson 1978). An interaction analysis system was used to record instances of teacher-student interaction. In their conclusions (pp. 46–47), Cheffers and Mancini said that "By comparison with the total recorded teacher behaviors, virtually no acceptance of student feelings and ideas, praise or questioning behaviors were recorded . . . the use of sympathetic-empathetic behavior was almost nonexistent." Teachers did provide feedback at about the rate of 1.5 feedback statements per minute—approximately 45 feedback events for every 30 minutes of class. About 53 percent of all the feedback was evaluative, with no prescriptive or descriptive component—evaluative feedback would probably be statements such as "Nice going," "Good shot," or "Way to go."

In a group of studies in which over 100 physical education lessons were examined, McLeish (1981, p. 30) observed the following.

> Taking the 104 lessons as a group, the broad impression conveyed to this observer is that there is very little concern with that most basic principle of learning theory—that positive reinforcement (by successful performance in the first place and by encouragement, praise, and constructive guidance by the teacher) provides a guarantee that the desired behavior will be elicited in future performance. There is a noticeable absence of positive affect in these lessons.

McLeish's research employed two quite different kinds of interaction analysis system. The percentages of teacher behavior from each of the two systems are

Table 4-1 / *Teacher Behavior as Described by Two Systems*

Flanders System		McLeish System	
Accepts feelings	1.5%	Positive affect	1.7%
Praises	4.2	Negative affect	2.0
Accepts ideas	1.5		
Criticizes	.6		
		Compared To	
Lectures	25.0%	Commands	30.0%
Directs	25.0	Controls	22.0

presented in Table 4-1 to show the contrast McLeish found between teacher behaviors that produce a positive climate and those that might contribute to a less than positive climate. Although it is true that physical education teachers emit a lot of behavior during a 30- to 45-minute teaching lesson, it is also true that little of that behavior seems directed toward the establishment and maintenance of a positive climate. It needs to be reemphasized here that the meaning of an interaction is determined by its effects on the student. Thus, what acts positively for one student might work negatively for another. Generally, for example, patting a student on the head is a positive, nonverbal interaction. But some students do not like to be touched. For them, such an interaction might produce effects opposite to those intended.

A research program at Ohio State, with which I am associated, has divided teacher interactions with students into two major categories, those for skill and strategy behavior (subject matter-oriented or academic matter-oriented reactions) and those for class behavior such as organizing, keeping students on task, and other such managerial tasks and social behavior. These two major categories are further subdivided. The interactions based on skill attempts are categorized as positive, corrective, or negative. The interactions based on nonacademic class behavior are categorized as positives, nags, and nasties. A *nag* is a low-intensity reprimand such as "Keep that line straight," "Listen, over there," "John, be quiet," or "Sh'h." A *nasty* is a much harsher reprimand in which some anger and temper is shown by the teacher. In one study (Quarterman, 1977), we found the results shown in Table 4-2, and they tend to be quite typical of findings from other studies.

Clearly, the predominant method for reacting to skill and strategy behav-

Table 4-2 / *Teacher Reactions to Student Behavior*

	Skill Feedback			Behavior Feedback		
	Positives	Correctives	Negatives	Positives	Nags	Nasties
Rate per minute	0.28	0.67	0.06	0.03	0.57	0.03
Rate per 30 minutes	8.4	20.1	1.8	0.9	17.1	0.9

iors is to correct them. Clearly, the predominant way in which classroom behavior is reacted to is to nag. The combination of corrective feedback and nagging represents over 80 percent of the total interactions—what that means is that the teacher tends to react to what students do incorrectly. The environment does not appear to be a heavily negative one, but it just as obviously is not a positive one. Its main characteristics are correcting and nagging, at a combined rate of about 50 for every 30 minutes of class time.

In summary, from the teacher's viewpoint, the typical physical education class is one in which there is a great deal of managing, getting organized, moving from place to place, and getting equipment out and put away. The physical educator spends about a third of the time giving information—no doubt explaining skills, demonstrating, describing rules, and the like. The teacher also spends a great deal of time watching the students, with no interaction (monitoring). Interactions are typically of very short duration and typically show corrective skill behavior and nagging for classroom and social behavior. There is no evidence of a positive emotional climate. There is also no strong evidence of a punitive, coercive, strongly negative climate. Perhaps the best way to describe the climate, on the basis of research data, is that it is mildly reprimanding and corrective. When compared with the summary portrait of the effective teacher, presented in Chapter 3, the contrasts are clear in terms of managerial efficiency, a strong academic focus in which student responding is maximized, and a positive classroom climate.

Describing Student Activities

I have emphasized that, to be effective, what teachers do must translate into increased opportunities for students to learn. The picture of physical education teaching captured through the different lenses of descriptive research programs showed many commonalities—and the results were not very similar to the portrait of effective teaching described in Chapter 3. But the picture is not complete unless the same settings (the gymnasium, the pool, the playing fields, and so on) are examined with a focus on students rather than on the teacher. Although somewhat less research has focused specifically on students, there is enough to begin to make some generalizations. Moreover, the results are quite similar even though the research was conducted in different parts of the world, using different kinds of observation systems.

Perhaps the most startling aspect of the total evidence is the low percentage of time in which students are actually engaged in motor activity within the context of a physical education class. Naturally, students cannot be in motor activity 100 percent of the time. There are managerial chores to do, equipment to change, transitions from place to place to be made, and information to be given. But one would expect that, in a physical education class, students would be involved in motor activities a fairly large percentage of the time. In fact, seldom are they engaged in motor activity more than 30 percent of the time. What are they doing, if not engaged in activity? Probably they are waiting for something to happen!

The term **waiting** refers to time prior to, between, and after instructional and practice activities—time in which students are not involved as they wait for the next event to occur. When students are in "wait time," they are doing nothing that contributes to the goals of the lesson—and, far too often, they may be tempted to engage in off-task or disruptive behavior. Waiting seems to account for at least 28 percent of student time in physical education (see the summary chart on page 000). This amount of waiting represents an inability on the part of the teacher to organize and manage so as to keep students involved with the lesson. Given the importance of momentum and smoothness (see Chapter 5), it should be no surprise that most physical education lessons observed in descriptive research lack these two ingredients, which have been shown to be so important to preventive classroom management.

Students also spend a great deal of time involved in managerial tasks, from roll taking, to organization for practice, to choosing teams, moving from place to place, and changing activities within the lesson. Management typically accounts for from 15 to 20 percent of student time (it is difficult to estimate an average for management time, because different research programs define it differently). An effective teacher is first of all an effective manager. There is good reason to believe that many physical education teachers are not efficient managers. There is also reason to believe that the managerial problems in physical education are more difficult than in the classroom due to larger spaces, larger classes, and a subject matter in which people move around a lot. But the managerial chores are not insurmountable. What the data reflect clearly is the need for undergraduate teacher education programs in physical education to focus more specifically on managerial skills.

Students also spend a great deal of time in physical education receiving information—managerial directions, organizational information, skill descriptions, game information, lectures about rules and safety, and other such matters. Typically, over 20 percent of student time is spent receiving information. No doubt it is necessary for information to be imparted in order for classes to run smoothly and for students to learn. But, just as clearly, too much time devoted to that information process detracts from learning time in which students actually engage in the subject matter. A goal of reducing the amount of time it takes to impart information would lead to more effective teaching if the time savings were used to allow for more student motor responding. The notion of classroom routines (see Chapter 5) and building information into the environment (see Chapter 11) are particularly good strategies for reducing the amount of student time that is spent receiving information. Information can be imparted in other ways than through teacher talk. Finding creative ways to impart information while reducing teacher talk is one of the important challenges for improved teaching in physical education.

The fourth large chunk of student time is spent in engagement in the subject matter—motor engaged time. The term **motor engaged time** refers to

Does Physical Education Suffer from Overexposure?

How many times have you heard a physical educator say that his or her goal was to "expose" students to a game or activity? What is implied in such a statement is that the teacher doesn't really have expectations that students will learn a great deal or improve in the necessary skills and strategies of the game or activity, but will instead just "get to know it a little." Far too often, from my point of view, students get exposed to volleyball somewhere in the fifth or sixth grade, then exposed again to volleyball in the eighth or ninth grade, and then again in the senior high school program. Because each of the efforts is aimed at exposure, students never get beyond beginning skills and seldom can play at a level higher than that for "backyard" volleyball. I believe that this represents serious "overexposure."

One of the major lessons of recent teacher effectiveness research is that effective teachers hold high, yet realistic expectations that students will not only learn a great deal but will continue to learn and improve in whatever is the subject matter being studied. There is no thought to merely expose students to reading or mathematics. Students are expected to learn and to continue to learn and improve from day to day, month to month, year to year.

For effective teaching to occur in physical education, someone must *care* that students learn and improve. In many schools—far too many—the school administrators do not care as much as they should. Thus, it is clear that if the physical education teacher does not care about learning, then quite likely few others will.

Haven't we all "exposed" students long enough to volleyball, tennis, golf, and a host of other games and activities? And, how many games of kickball and bombardment need to be played before students are "overexposed"?

skill practice, drills, scrimmages, games, fitness activities, dance, warm-up, and cool-down. Research indicates that students spend about 25 percent of their time actually doing some physical education activity. This represents the *upper limit* of the time in which they might actually improve their skills. Naturally, not all motor engaged time leads to learning. Students may be involved in games, but not in such a way that they improve. Students may try physical education skills, but if the skills are too difficult for them, they will learn little. Also, students may be put to work doing simple, repetitive practice of things they already know how to do, thus not leading to further improvement. In other words, their involvement in physical activity can be too hard (in which case they don't learn), too easy (they don't improve), or appropriate (they can learn and improve). Twenty-five percent is not a very high figure.

Table 4-3 / *Student Time Data from Four Major Research Programs*

	McLeish	Pieron	Teachers College	Ohio State
Management	20%	6%	13%	22%
Waiting	22	32	25	24
Receiving information	22	23	25	15
Engaged motor time	26	30	27	21

For a 30-minute elementary lesson, that would mean 7.5 minutes of motor engagement. For a 45-minute secondary lesson, it would mean just over 11 minutes of motor engagement.

The data from four major research programs in physical education are shown in Table 4-3. The McLeish data were developed in western Canada (McLeish 1981); the Pieron data in Belgium (Pieron 1980); the Teacher's College data in the New York metropolitan area (Anderson 1978); and the Ohio State data in central Ohio (Metzler 1979, Rate 1980). The systems used to collect the data were slightly different. The waiting and motor engagement categories were fairly standard across the four programs. But the definitions of the management and receiving information categories differed somewhat. Therefore, events recorded as receiving information in one system might be recorded as management in another system. That, no doubt, accounts for the apparent differences in those categories. Still, the similarities are much more striking than the differences. It is also interesting to note that many of the subjects in the Pieron program had been taught by "master teachers." Teachers and classes in the other studies were selected with no purpose in mind other than that they represented a balance in terms of sex, years of experience, background, and school setting.

In summary, although descriptive research focusing on teachers gives the impression of much teacher activity, the descriptive research focusing on student time shows that teacher activity doesn't always translate into high proportions of learning time for students. There are two potential reasons why so little learning time accrues to students in physical education. First, teachers could have problems with the managerial and organizational aspects of teaching. Second, the design of the instruction itself could be inappropriate. The Ohio State research program (Metzler 1980, Rate 1980, Birdwell 1980) shows that managerial and organizational skills are the largest part of the explanation for small amounts of learning time. The evidence from this research program indicates that although teachers have the *group* supposedly involved in physical education activities about 70 percent of the time, individual students are engaged only about 35 percent of the time. The time lost between the intentions of the teacher and the realities of the experience for the student is given over to waiting, making transitions, and interim activity, such as chasing balls.

Once an individual student is actually engaged in motor activity, it is most often at an appropriate level of difficulty, one in which the student has a high probability of success. The only situations where this breaks down is in game play where students are asked to play a regulation game before they have sufficient skills and game strategies to play it effectively. Costello and Laubach (1978, p. 18) reached a similar conclusion from their examination of the Teachers College videotape data bank:

> The organizational ability of the teachers probably also contributed to the large percentage of time that students waited. For example, during the coding of student behavior for almost 300 clock hours, it was evident that some teachers had trouble organizing groups for an activity, making maximum use of available equipment, and moving groups from one area to another.

Effective Physical Education Teaching

There is now a descriptive research base from which to evaluate effective teaching in physical education. Physical educators also must depend on companion research done in the classroom and must ascertain the degree to which they feel that results from classroom teacher effectiveness research generalize to the gymnasium (see Chapter 3). The beginnings of teacher effectiveness research in physical education have tended to confirm what has been found in classroom research.

McLeish's (1981) analysis of 104 lessons into best ($n = 18$), average ($n = 48$), and poor ($n = 38$) indicates that the major determining factors for the analysis were higher rates of appropriate learning time and lower rates of waiting time. These two factors accounted for the largest part of the differences between the good and the poor lessons. The good lessons were high in appropriate learning time (what McLeish calls task-practice-motor-easy or TPME) and low in waiting time. The poor lessons were low in TPME and high in waiting time. The academic learning time-physical education instrument (ALT-PE) was used in the assessments (see Chapter 2). As was suggested in Chapter 2, ALT-PE proved to be a useful criterion variable for determining effectiveness.

Another interesting result of the McLeish study was that time spent in a knowledge focus (students receiving information) did not discriminate among the good, average, and poor lessons. In fact, each group had almost identical amounts of knowledge focus. Thus, the imparting of information, although obviously necessary, does not seem to distinguish among different levels of effectiveness in teaching physical education. Probably most physical education teachers spend too much time imparting information. Clearly, time spent on a knowledge focus should be shifted to more practice time. McLeish (1981, p. 29) reached the following conclusion concerning the learning time model:

> The theoretical basis of the ALT-PE system is what is now conventionally referred to as *learning theory*. By this we mean that we accept as established fact certain

basic principles: (1) that learning is maximized in direct proportion to the number and type of opportunities to learn; (2) we learn best by concentrating on practicing the motor, cognitive, or psychomotor skill by actual doing; or (3) by observing others performing the skill. There is (4) no advantage to be gained in practicing the skill at a difficulty level which results in a level of failure rate greater than 10 percent. Effective teaching means structuring the lesson to maximize the amount of time in direct practice by each individual at a level which at once ensures a continuing development of the skill compatible with the minimal number of mistakes.

These results are very similar to those found in classroom research. They should give us confidence in using the results of classroom research as we search for improved effectiveness in the gymnasium.

Pieron (1981) conducted a more controlled experiment to determine effective teaching, using skill in the handstand rollover as the task. He, too, found that time spent in receiving information (knowledge focus) did not distinguish between the groups in which students learned the task better and the groups in which students learned less. What did differentiate between the groups was the amount of time spent practicing the actual criterion task. The most effective groups spent 22 percent of their time practicing it, while the students in the less effective classes spent only 7.7 percent of their time practicing the task. In actual number of learning trials, the students in the more effective groups made more than three times the number of skill attempts made by students in the less effective groups. Pieron (1980, p. 11) concluded that the "teacher's effectiveness in producing learning gains was dependent upon his ability to transform time allocated to practice into individual student activity." These results confirm classroom research and support the learning time model as a useful way to evaluate teaching effectiveness in physical education.

Variations on the Main Theme

A few important points must be made concerning factors that may cause variations in the major themes of teacher activity and student learning time. These two themes seem fairly consistent across many physical education research studies.

1. Very few studies have found any differences in teaching behavior between male and female teachers. Male and female teachers in physical education teach with essentially the same patterns of behavior, devoting their attention and teaching behavior to similar functions.

2. There appear to be no differences in student activity in classes taught by male or female teachers. Again, the gender of the teacher does not seem to make a noticeable difference in terms of student behavior and student learning time.

3. Experienced teachers usually have somewhat different patterns of

teaching, especially in that they appear to give more feedback than do less experienced teachers, and that feedback is more substantive.

4. Physical education teachers who are more knowledgeable, skilled, and have better attitudes toward teaching tend to show patterns of teaching behavior that are closer to those shown by effective classroom teachers (Oliver, 1978). These teachers tend to be more experienced.

5. Enormous differences in student learning time appear on the basis of what activity is being taught. This is a common finding, and not too surprising. Activities such as gymnastics are taught in such a way that individual students have very low amounts of learning time. Activities such as volleyball and soccer tend to produce higher amounts of learning time. Certain activities such as swimming and exercise dancing can produce very high student learning time figures. This finding needs to be treated seriously and considered both in terms of selecting activities (a curriculum decision) and planning how to teach different activities (an instructional design decision).

CHAPTER 5

Preventive Classroom Management

Effective classroom management consists of teacher behaviors that produce high levels of student involvement in classroom activities, minimal amounts of student behaviors that interfere with the teacher's or other students' work, and efficient use of instructional time. These criteria have the advantage of being observable.

Edmund Emmer and Carolyn Evertson,
Effective Classroom Management (1981)

CHAPTER OBJECTIVES

To distinguish between positive and punitive management strategies

To explain the relationship between effective management and instruction

To explain the concepts of managerial interaction, managerial time, managerial episode, transition, classroom routine, and disruptions to the flow of lessons

To distinguish among managerial time, transition time, and wait time in observations of teaching

To distinguish classroom routines that are based on structure from those controlled by current managerial interactions

To explain and provide examples of techniques for improving managerial effectiveness

To develop a managerial game to meet the needs of a specific situation

To distinguish between smoothness and momentum

To explain and provide examples of overlapping, thrusts, magnetization, dangles, flip-flops, overdwelling, and fragmentation

To explain and provide examples of ways in which managerial effectiveness might be assessed

Chapter 2 presented a model that distinguished among the emotional climate of an educational setting, the management of student behavior, and the management of learning tasks. I argued that each of these factors has different dimensions and that the realities of teaching are considerably more complex than traditional stereotypes would lead one to believe. For example, it is clearly not true that strongly structured teacher control of student behavior is always associated with a negative emotional climate. Indeed, the research summarized in Chapters 3 and 4 gives every indication that there are classrooms and gymnasiums everywhere in which teachers structure and control things quite closely, yet do so within a warm, nurturant emotional climate. Those classrooms and gymnasiums have been most often associated with higher achievement and better attitudes among students.

Of all the lessons to be learned from teacher effectiveness research, none is more clear than that effective teachers develop and maintain management systems that prevent disturbances, thus allowing them to devote most of their attention to the learning of the subject matter. Effective teachers are, perhaps first of all, effective managers. And they accomplish these managerial tasks without resorting to coercive, punitive forms of control—indeed, their classrooms and gymnasiums have been consistently identified as warm, nurturant, and accepting. The purpose of this chapter is to identify skills and strategies through which physical education teachers can develop smooth and effective management structures for their educational settings. This is not to suggest that smooth and effective management structures will prevent all disruptive behavior. They will not. It is important, however, to distinguish between preventive management techniques and remedial management techniques. When misbehavior does occur, or when students are consistently off task, teachers need a repertoire of useful techniques for improving things quickly. These techniques are described and discussed in Chapter 6. The purpose of this chapter is to describe strategies that prevent disruptions and off-task behavior.

Some Dangerous Assumptions About Teaching

Teachers often make assumptions about the conduct of a class. Teaching interns are especially prone to making unwarranted assumptions concerning the behavior of students. Interns spend time carefully planning lessons and approach the teaching experience with anticipation. But they spend less time examining the assumptions that underlie any lesson plan.

Common assumptions are that students will enter the gymnasium quickly; that they will be eager to begin the lesson that has been planned; that they will be attentive to instructions and demonstrations and will attempt later to imitate demonstrations, that they will organize and change activities quickly, and that they will make an honest effort to engage in the planned learning activity and will generally behave in a manner that is consistent with accomplishing the goals of the lesson. When any one of these assumptions is violated, it tends to disrupt the flow of a well-planned instructional experience. When several of them are compromised during the same lesson, the well-planned instructional experience fails—not because it was poorly planned or executed, but because the teacher had not paid enough attention to the behavioral assumptions that underlie a positive learning environment. Too often this kind of experience creates tension between teacher and students, and if it happens frequently it is one of the main ingredients in a teacher's growing dissatisfaction with his or her job. Many teachers feel that they are trained to teach and are paid to teach. If honest and sincere efforts to teach well fail because of student disruption, inattention, or lack of effort in organization or practice, then the learning environment can quickly deteriorate into a battleground where teachers go to war with students.

Teachers have traditionally relied on parents to raise their children in such a manner that the children come to school with certain behaviors already fairly well developed, and other behavioral predispositions solidly entrenched. Traditionally, it is in the home that children have learned to pay attention, to respond to instructions, to respect an adult authority figure, and to approach school with the clear expectation that these ways of behaving will also occur at school. Parents not only helped develop these behaviors at home but also made sure that the child was exhibiting these behaviors when he or she went to school. If the child did behave differently at school, it was usually quite easy to change this by threatening some punishment or by hinting that a note would be sent home or the parents asked to come in to discuss the problem. In many schools this situation still exists to a large degree, but in many others it is increasingly dangerous to assume that children come to school equipped with these behavioral tendencies. The result is that classroom management has assumed more importance in teaching.

A common assertion in the educational literature is that discipline is inherent in good teaching; that is, if you teach well you will have no discipline problems. The implication is that the right choice of activity combined with the right teaching method will automatically produce learners who behave well and try hard. No one would disagree with the proposition that discipline is less problematic when activities are chosen and taught well. But this does not ensure that all students will suddenly turn into eager learners. To assert such a relationship between teaching and discipline is at best simplistic. Teachers should strive to improve their programs and teaching methods, but they can also attack the problems of classroom and gymnasium management directly.

Classroom management skills are essential to good teaching. This is true in every classroom and in every subject. It is true in the open classroom. It is true in a classroom where the children sit in neatly arranged rows of desks. It is also true in the gymnasium, on the playground, and on the playing field. The result of the positive application of management skills is that students learn self-management. Once students have learned self-management, it becomes easier for the teacher to proceed with good teaching. It is a mistake to ignore the management function or to assume that students will exhibit the behaviors necessary for a positive and effective learning environment. The goal of this chapter is to provide you with the skills necessary to manage your classes effectively and positively.

Some Useful Perspectives from Which to View Management

The development of structures and routines that result in skillful and efficient gymnasium management can be viewed from several important perspectives. These perspectives are (1) managerial time, (2) managerial episode length and frequency, (3) transitions, (4) gymnasium routines, and (5) disruptions to the flow of the lesson. Each provides a way of viewing the development of managerial skill and the evaluation of those skills. What needs to be emphasized is that to the casual observer, skillful management is difficult to actually see, especially during a brief visit or observation session. You might observe a teacher in physical education and see a great deal of obviously useful learning time, quick movement between activities, high rates of on-task behavior, and few disruptions—without actually seeing the teacher engage in managerial interactions. In fact, if you see a lot of managerial interactions

---

Are Your Students too Dependent on You?

Situation. The teacher is doing a movement education lesson with second-graders. The lesson involves solving movement problems that are structured around a rope lying on the floor. Each child has a rope in his or her own space. The teacher has the students sit down in a line. The teacher then walks about placing the ropes on the floor. The children are instructed to disperse to find their own spaces. There are at least six instances of two children on one rope. The teacher takes one child from each pair and directs him or her to a vacant rope. The lesson proceeds. After the lesson, the teacher has the children sit down while he or she puts the ropes away.

Results. Far too much time is spent in management, and a very high rate of managerial behavior is emitted by the teacher.

Analysis. The students have everything done for them. They are not learning to manage themselves within the context of the gymnasium and the movement education curriculum. Second-graders are perfectly capable of learning how to put away equipment and how to find their own spaces quickly without further prompting from a teacher. If this situation continues, the students will not learn self-management. All evidence indicates that "sitting in lines" is an opportunity to misbehave. After all, why shouldn't a student misbehave when there is nothing to do but watch a teacher walk around placing ropes on the floor!

Prescription. This lesson offers a perfect opportunity to teach self-management skills. Students can be taught how to place the equipment. Students can be taught how to find their own places. They need to practice these skills, and they need feedback and positive interactions when they perform them well. The major point is that it is perfectly legitimate to teach these as separate, identifiable skills and not merely as ancillary aspects of the movement education lesson.

from a teacher, you probably are not seeing a skillful manager! The term **managerial interactions** refers to verbal and nonverbal teacher behavior aimed at organizing, moving from place to place or activity to activity, giving directions about equipment or formation, placing or replacing equipment, prompting nonacademic student behavior, or reacting to nonacademic student behavior.

Managerial Time

An important perspective for viewing management is the amount of total time spent in management. The term **managerial time** refers to the cumulative amount of time students spend in organizational, transitional, and nonacademic tasks. It is time when no instruction is given, no demonstrations are made, no practice is done, and no observation of performance is made. It is devoid of opportunities for students to learn the subject matter. Roll taking, getting equipment out, waiting, organizing teams, moving from one site to another, and discussing an upcoming school event all contribute to total management time. Chapter 4 noted that physical educators tend to spend too much time in managerial activities. Teaching research also supports the commonsense notion that disruptive student behavior is more likely to occur during management time than during instruction and activity time. Thus, reducing the amount of management time tends to reduce the likelihood of disruptive behavior. This is probably most true for time students spend waiting for something to happen. Again, data in Chapter 4 show how much time physical education students spend *waiting*—waiting for a game to begin, waiting for another turn, waiting for equipment to be placed, and waiting for roll to be taken. A primary goal for improved preventive gymnasium management is the overall reduction of managerial time.

Managerial Episode Length

A second important management perspective is that of the managerial episode, which is a single unit of management time. A **managerial episode** begins with a managerial behavior emitted by a teacher (or a predetermined signal) and continues until the next instruction or activity event begins. The total time of individual managerial episodes plus the total time spent waiting should equal the total managerial time of a lesson. Focusing on managerial episodes allows a finer analysis of where and how management time is being accumulated. The following are examples of managerial episodes:

1. The class comes from the locker room and awaits the first signal from the teacher to begin the class (time from official beginning of period to time when first instruction begins).
2. The teacher blows a whistle and tells the class to assemble on one side of the gym (time from whistle until class is assembled and first instruction or demonstration is given).
3. The teacher, having explained the lesson or game or drill, signals for

the class to go to their proper places and begin the activity (time from the signal to disperse until the activity actually begins).

4. The teacher signals a halt in activity to provide some feedback or further instruction (time from the signal until the feedback or instruction begins).
5. The teacher signals a halt in one activity and signals for change to another activity (time from the signal until the next activity begins).
6. The teacher, having given instructions inside the gym, sends the class outside to begin an outside activity (time from the end of instruction inside until the beginning of activity outside).
7. The teacher takes roll (time from signal for beginning roll taking until next activity or instruction begins).

The time taken to accomplish any or all of these managerial tasks is time that could be used for instruction, practice, or play. How much time do you spend in managerial episodes? Have you had baseline measurement yet? Many teachers are surprised at the large amount of time lost in these episodes. The time can be reduced significantly. The following data are from three physical education majors who were student teaching in a middle school (Siedentop, Rife, and Boehm 1974). The length of the physical education period was 35 minutes. Times are given in minutes:seconds.

	Baseline	Intervention
S_1 Average total management time	10:37	1:46
Mean time per managerial episode	1:49	0:23
S_2 Average total management time	11:36	2:03
Mean time per managerial episode	1:37	0:25
S_3 Average total management time	13:33	1:23
Mean time per managerial episode	1:38	0:13

Each of these student teachers saved approximately 10 minutes per class session when they began to focus on reducing managerial time. The classes moved more quickly and more smoothly. There was substantially less trouble between student and teacher.

A useful goal for improved effectiveness in teaching physical education is the reduction of the average time per managerial episode in a lesson.

Time Spent in Transitions

Another important aspect of total management time are the several transitions within and between activities in any physical education lesson. A **transition** is a managerial episode within or between activities. Transitions occur when teams need to change courts, when students move from one activity station to another, when students move from one drill to another, when substitutions are made in game settings, and other similar situations. Transitions are a natural part of almost every physical education lesson from kindergarten through the senior high school. In fact, quite often several transitions exist within any one activity in a lesson, and several exist between the activities that together comprise the lesson. Although any one transition may not seem overly long, the accumulated time in transitions can become a fairly large part of the total time available within a lesson. Clearly, a reduction in the average length of transition episodes would improve the managerial efficiency of the physical education setting.

Structure for Classroom or Gymnasium Routines

One of the more important managerial perspectives, the structure for classroom routines, is often quite difficult to judge and quite easy to miss when observing physical educators teaching. A **classroom** or **gymnasium routine** is any frequent student behavior that, unless structured, has the potential for disrupting the ongoing flow of a lesson. Examples of such routines important in physical education are how a student gets the attention of the teacher when he or she wants it, how a ball is retrieved once it leaves the field of play or the area of a drill, how children are to react when a ball and/or player from an adjacent game or drill enters their space, how students are to respond to teacher directions, when a student can get a drink of water or leave to use the bathroom, and other such frequent daily events in the physical education setting. Effective teachers teach appropriate ways of behaving in important gymnasium routines early in the school year. Such teachers point out how each of these situations is to be handled, allow for practice, and provide relevant feed-back and/or contingencies which develop student behavior in these areas quickly, so that it becomes habit. Once the initial teaching is done, the routine of the gymnasium, pool, or playing field runs according to that structure and does not depend on current teacher interaction, thus preventing the disruption of the flow of teaching. In this sense, observation of frequent current teacher interaction in order to control routine events is probably evidence of inefficient management in that the important structures have not been developed. An important goal for improved effectiveness is the definition of important gymnasium routines for a specific situation and the deliberate teaching of appropriate forms of student behavior relative to these routines so that eventually classes can run smoothly and routines can be accomplished without constant attention from the teacher and without disrupting the teaching and learning process.

Disruptions to the Flow of the Lesson

A smooth lesson in which momentum is established and carried forward without breaks quite simply creates fewer "time gaps" in which disruptive and/or off-task student behavior might occur. On the basis of a series of research studies, Jacob Kounin (1970) concluded that preventing situations in which student misbehavior might occur was much more important to successful teaching than were specific techniques to remedy misbehavior. Disruptions to the flow of a lesson occur when events stop or break the activity flow or slow it down unnecessarily. Such events may involve students intruding on what a teacher is doing with the class or a group within the class; how a teacher reacts to unplanned events; starting an activity and stopping it before it reaches its appointed conclusion; stopping one activity, then starting another, and finally returning to the first activity; breaking activities into unnecessarily small parts; having one member of the class do something when the whole class could have done it; and other such situations. Sometimes disruptions to the smoothness and momentum of a lesson are teacher initiated; for example, a lengthy, drawn-out explanation of a rule that could have been done quickly. In other situations, the smoothness or momentum is disturbed because another event occurs to which the teacher must attend but which is not dealt with in a way that maintains the flow of the lesson. Establishing and maintaining smoothness and momentum is an important goal for managing so as to prevent inappropriate and off-task student behavior.

Techniques for Improving Managerial Effectiveness

If students have been taught appropriate gymnasium routines and are on their way toward self-management within the established structure, then they can also learn other organizational behaviors that will improve the overall effectiveness of the educational setting. This section explains and describes some important techniques that can contribute to that goal.

Control the Initial Activity

The momentum of a lesson should be established when students enter the gymnasium. Too often, that momentum is simply never established. The amount of managerial time typically accumulated at the beginning of a lesson is far too much. One way to get things started smoothly and to reduce the initial managerial time is to post information about what students should do when they enter the gymnasium.

Post the first activity of the day on a bulletin board or chalkboard, or simply tape a paper on the wall next to the gymnasium entrance. The information should include where students are expected to be when class begins and what activity will be pursued. For example, if it is a gymnastics lesson and you are using squads, then you might include information about where each squad should be for the first activity. Posting the activity and where students are expected to be at the start of class avoids the chaos of having to get the attention of students and organize them for the first activity of the day. With younger children, large diagrams of the formation and location work well. For example, the diagram might indicate a circle formation near the stage.

Begin Class at a Definite Time

The beginning of class should not be whenever you get things going. There should be a definite time set for the beginning of class. Setting a time works in combination with posting the first activity to effect a smooth beginning to the class session. Students who get to the gym early can check the

---

Getting Started on the Right Foot

Research has indicated clearly that teachers who spend time in the early part of the school year—the first several weeks—teaching specific classroom and gymnasium routines not only have an easier time of managing and disciplining throughout the school year but also have students who learn more. Teachers who take time to specifically teach routines such as how to contact the teacher, use equipment, and move around the available space have fewer problems. Gymnasium routines become part of the content that is taught, which has a high payoff.

Hayman and Moskowitz (1975) found that what junior high school teachers did on the very first day went a long way toward determining their overall effectiveness for the year. Before patterns of inappropriate behavior can develop, the teachers taught specific patterns of appropriate behavior—laid down the ground rules for getting along together in the class. According to Emmer and Evertson (1981), "All classroom management systems, good, poor, or in-between, have a beginning. The way in which teachers structure the first part of the year has consequences for their classroom management throughout the year."

---

posted message and then engage in some preliminary activity if they choose to do so, knowing that they must be at a certain place at a certain time; that is, at the time marked as the beginning of class. You have a responsibility to be there and ready to go at the beginning time. Don't expect students to be punctual if you are not.

Use a Time-Saving Method for Roll Call

Calling roll takes time. Time spent in roll taking could be better used in instruction, practice, or play. Inappropriate student behavior is more likely to occur during roll taking. After all, how much fun is it to stand in line while a teacher checks attendance? If you must record daily attendance, find a way to do so that does not detract from instructional time.

One method is for students to sign in when they arrive at the gym. By having them sign their name and time of arrival, you get an attendance record and a tardiness record. This is a form of behavioral self-recording (see Chapter 11), and it will be reliable if you make an occasional spot check to ensure that students are reliable in their sign-in. This kind of public signing in can decrease tardiness (McKenzie and Rushall 1973).

A second method is to have a gym aide take attendance as the first instructional activity begins. This method allows for more teacher control of attendance records but does not use student time. If you feel that student time must be used for attendance purposes, find some method of numbering or lining up that will use the least amount of time. If you spend more than one minute taking attendance, you probably are not using student time effectively. If the class begins routinely with warm-up exercises or activities, a useful strategy is to assign each child or student a specific "spot" in the gymnasium. While the children are doing their initial movement routines, it is easy for the teacher to identify absent students—their "spots" are vacant.

Transferring daily attendance data to permanent records should be done outside class. Although record keeping is important, it should in no way diminish your opportunity to teach or interact with students. Do not yield to the temptation of using class time for administrative purposes. Every minute you spend standing on the sidelines working on attendance records could be spent giving instruction, feedback, and encouragement to your students. During class, you should be a teacher.

Teach a Signal for Attention

A great deal of time is wasted and tempers too often flare when a teacher attempts to gain the attention of the class and fails to do so. Most teachers use a whistle. Many elementary teachers use a single clap of the hands. Whatever the signal, you can teach students that it means you want their attention for purposes of instruction, feedback, or management. To teach students to respond properly to the signal, you should first identify it clearly and explain why you use it. When you use it, you should provide feedback to students on how well they did; that is, on how quickly they responded. In terms of quantitative feedback, you can simply tell them how many seconds elapsed from the onset of the signal. You can compliment students who respond quickly. Or you can compliment the group as a whole when the group response is quick. At the outset, you should probably be willing to compliment them even though you fully intend to have them respond much more quickly. Once you make students aware of the need to respond to the signal, you can gradually reduce the amount of time you think qualifies for a complimentary response.

You should remember that in this text there is constant emphasis on the use of positive interactions with students. Teaching students to respond to a signal is one of those times when teachers tend to harass students. Don't react to children who respond slowly; react to those who respond quickly. Unless there is serious disruption, you should ignore those who don't respond quickly. If you do this for a time, while saying some nice things to students who respond quickly, you will achieve your goals. Following is a list of reaction statements you might use in management situations.

Sample General Reactions

Good job, Bill.
Way to go!
Thanks, the whole class did well.
Terrific!

Sample Reactions with Specific Information Content

Thanks for paying attention so quickly.
Great job of listening for that signal.
Good, nine seconds and we're ready for a demonstration.
Hey, that's a quicker job than you've ever done.

Sample Reactions with Information and Value Content

Thanks, only 8 seconds and now we can change stations.
That's the way to quiet down—now you can hear me.
Terrific job of getting quiet—now we can watch Sally.

Once students learn what signal you want to use to gain their attention, you will have reduced management time.

Use High Rates of Feedback and Positive Interaction

You can't forget that you are teaching your students to organize quickly and change activities quickly. As in any teaching situation, these goals are best accomplished with high rates of feedback and positive interaction. Unless they become a serious problem, you should ignore those in the class who are not learning to manage themselves quickly. If you have patience with them and respond positively to the students who are doing well, the "slow" managers will gradually begin to speed up.

With young children, it is most often sufficient to use a combination of quantitative feedback and a compliment. Letting children know that they took only 22 seconds to find their own space and complimenting them for this tends to make a game out of it. Children usually respond well to this kind of treatment.

With older students, it is better to explain the purpose of good management habits (more time to practice and play) and occasionally to draw their attention to the time factor and compliment them. At this point, you may imagine yourself interacting positively with a younger child but may not be able to see yourself running around complimenting senior high school students. Methods for interacting with students of different age levels are discussed in Chapter 7. With older students you do not need quite as high rates of positive interaction; also, the variety of verbal interactions is somewhat restricted and the method of delivery is different. Obviously, you can't interact with a 17-year-old in the same manner that you interact with an 8-year-old, but this does not mean you can't find ways to interact positively with the older student.

Post Records of Management Performance of Students

A simple way to emphasize the importance of organizing quickly and effectively is to keep some records about the management time spent in each class and to post records on the gymnasium wall. You can keep a fairly accurate record of management time with a wristwatch and jot down the length of each managerial episode on your clipboard or record book. At the end of each class, you can add up the episodes to get a total managerial time, and this time can be posted. If all classes are listed on the same record sheet, it is easy for students to compare their class to other classes. This kind of public posting of records and the competition it engenders motivates students to reduce management time. This technique is useful in the elementary and junior high school situation. It may be effective in the high school situation and should be attempted, but there it should be monitored carefully to see if it is indeed achieving the desired results.

Use Enthusiasm, Hustles, and Prompts

It has already been pointed out that enthusiasm is consistently related to effective teaching. One of the best ways to show enthusiasm is through verbal and nonverbal behavior that maintains the momentum of the lesson and prevents slowdowns. A **hustle** is a verbal or nonverbal behavior that is used to energize student behavior. Hustles are not necessarily reactions to lack of student initiative—they are a form of communicating to students the need to keep the lesson moving, to keep trying hard, and to continue to put forth an effort—in short, to hustle! Teachers can be said to show "hustling behavior" when they use verbal statements (in a positive way) such as "Let's go," "Keep it up, keep it up," or "Hustle, hustle." They show it nonverbally with hand-clapping and other such gestures or by moving themselves in ways that are energetic.

A **prompt** is a teacher verbal behavior that acts as a reminder of appropriate ways of behaving within the framework of the lesson. Prompts tend to keep students "on their toes" and keep the group alert as to what should be going on. Prompts are especially useful early in a learning situation when new behaviors are being acquired. Prompts can relate to skills, strategies, activities, or simply appropriate ways of behaving. When framed positively and given enthusiastically, these "reminders" tend to prevent disruptions and off-task behavior. But prompts should be given frequently and with some consistency, rather than only when student misbehavior has occurred. Too many teachers remind students (prompt them) only after a misbehavior. To be effective, prompts should not be tied to misbehavior cues, but should, instead, be given in some regular, positive fashion.

Use a Management Game for Quick Results

In certain situations, students have been behaving disruptively and managerial time is far too high. Although management skills still need to be taught in such situations, quick action sometimes is also required to reduce the management time so that instruction may begin to take place. A **management game** is a behavior change technique where students are rewarded for achieving managerial goals within a game format. Management games can help to bring an out-of-hand situation under control quickly so that a teacher can begin to teach management routines.

Management games are quite effective in physical education classes at the elementary and middle school levels. They are less likely to be effective at the senior high school level, but they should be attempted and judged by their effectiveness. A management game provides some extrinsic motivation for achieving certain management goals. The extrinsic motivation is usually free time that can be earned and then used for a variety of activities in the gymnasium. The following steps are necessary to implement a management game:

1. State the rules of the game clearly and post them or remind students of them regularly.
2. State the rewards to be earned and their precise relationship to the game.
3. Emphasize that each individual or team can win the game.
4. Be absolutely consistent in your application of the rules of the game.

A management game is usually best played by using a group contingency. A **group contingency** means that the reward is given on the basis of the group's performance. If one member of the group does not meet the rules, the group loses the reward. The group may be defined as the entire class, or it may be defined as squads or teams. If squads are used, then it should be emphasized continually that each squad can be a winner; that is, the groups are not in competition against one another but all are in competition against the standards of the game.

If free time is used as a reward, you should make sure that a variety of activities are available during the free-time period. The nature of the activities will depend on the kind of unit you are involved in and the preferences of the students. It is best to have a minimum of three or four activities available, and students should be free to choose among them and switch from one to another during the free-time period. It is always advisable to consider "sitting around and talking" a legitimate free-time activity. The following is a description of the management game used to produce the data shown earlier on page 71 (Siedentop, Rife, and Boehm 1974). This game was a group contingency, and the entire class had to meet the criterion to win the free time.

Rules and Related Free Time Earned

1. Read posted opening activity when entering gym and be at assigned station and attentive by 8 minutes after the hour. (2 minutes free time for each successful class beginning)
2. If during an activity the teacher blows the whistle for attention, the class is attentive within 5 seconds. (1 minute free time for each successful instance)
3. When moving from instruction to activity or from one activity to another, the class will begin the next activity within 15 seconds. (1 minute free time for each successful instance)

The teachers kept records of the free time earned by each class, and this free time was accumulated and spent on Friday of each week. During free time, students could work on the minitramp, play basketball, or sit in the bleachers and talk. Other possibilities would be to spend the earned free time at the end of each class, or accumulate free time until enough for one class period is earned and then devote one period to free-time activities.

Managing the Flow of Activities in a Lesson

Teachers who manage lessons so that they run smoothly and keep the momentum moving forward at an even pace have done a great deal to prevent disruptive and off-task behavior from occurring. This is especially true for managing transitions and dealing with unpredictable events that intrude on the lesson.

Researcher Jacob Kounin (1970) has provided a set of interesting and useful concepts to explain the importance of this aspect of preventive classroom and gymnasium management. One set of concepts is used to describe the kinds of situations that can detract from the smoothness of a lesson. The concept of **smoothness** refers to the absence of stops or breaks in the flow of activities in a lesson. Other concepts refer to events that disturb the momentum of a lesson. The concept of **momentum** refers to the rate of movement within and between activities and the absence of slowdowns to that rate of movement. These concepts are overlapping, thrusts, magnetizations, dangles, flip-flops, overdwelling, and fragmentation. They are described in greater detail in the following sections. It should be remembered that research has tended to verify that good preventive management is more important than being able to remedy misbehavior. Being an effective manager is more important than being a skilled disciplinarian!

Overlapping: Dealing with More Than One Event at a Time

A teacher is giving feedback to a small group, and another student comes over and interrupts with a question. A teacher is giving instructions to the entire class, and a visitor comes into the gym. A teacher is providing a demonstration, and several children are disrupting with some minor misbehavior. Each of these situations presents a two-issue situation to the teacher. The teacher can continue with what he or she was doing and ignore the intruding event, can stop what he or she was doing and focus entirely on the intruding event, or can deal with the intruding event while still maintaining the momentum of the original activity. The term **overlapping** refers to the ability of a teacher to deal successfully with the intruding event while maintaining the momentum of the original activity. Teachers who cannot overlap successfully obviously have breaks in the activity flow or lose momentum (slowdowns). The teacher who can deal with the intrusion with a direction, a remark, or a quick look, while still paying attention to the main event, has maintained smoothness and momentum.

Managing
the Flow of
Activities
in a Lesson

79

Thrusts: Bursting in on an Ongoing Activity

When should a teacher interrupt an ongoing activity to give some feedback to a group or the entire class? How do you decide when to stop a drill and move to another drill? At what point should you interrupt a game? The term **thrusts** refers to badly timed interruptions when a teacher bursts in on an ongoing activity on the basis of his or her own purposes and without regard to the students' involvement with the activity. Smooth teachers time their point of entry into an activity on the basis of the activity's flow. Frequent thrusts break up the flow of an activity and destroy the momentum of a lesson. Waiting for a moment until an activity has a natural break pays off in the long run.

Magnetizations: Being Captured by an Irrelevant Event

Teachers plan lessons. The purpose of the activities within a lesson should be to achieve the goals of that lesson, which, in turn, contribute to longer-range goals. Sometimes, however, teachers turn away from their plans and get caught up in events that bear little relationship to their goals—they get magnetized by such events. When a teacher becomes **magnetized**, he or she is reacting to a minute or irrelevant event in such a way that he or she is pulled out of the main activity flow. Occasionally something does happen in a class that deserves to be attended to even though it wasn't planned for—what has been called a "teachable moment." It is just as true, however, that much more often teachers get magnetized by some small or irrelevant event and follow that event even though it takes them away from the lesson they had planned. They behave almost as if they had no strong goals or, at least, no strong will to make sure that goals are achieved. As you will recall, effective teachers have been shown to have a strong "academic focus" in that they devote a lot of time to learning the subject matter and are not easily distracted from that goal—that is, they do not often become magnetized!

Dangles and Flip-Flops: Not Completing Planned Activities

Learning activities are always whole units. They have identifiable beginnings and identifiable termination points. The term **dangling** refers to the interruption of an activity before it reaches its natural or appointed conclusion. For example, students are engaged in a drill that has a specified conclusion. The teacher interrupts to get them started in another activity; and the students are left dangling. The term **flip-flopping** refers to interrupting one activity, starting another, and then returning to the first activity. The teacher may think it to be an opportune moment to switch to another activity, but the flow of the activities themselves indicate that it is not the right moment at all. Activities should be completed as planned unless they have been planned so poorly that students cannot do them successfully. Dangling destroys the smoothness of a lesson. Flip-flops slow down the momentum so that it is difficult to recapture.

Overdwelling: Teacher Overkill

Teachers need to give instructions, place and replace equipment, organize students, and give feedback. These ought to be done quickly and efficiently. The term **overdwelling** refers to teacher's engaging in a chain of actions or talking that goes well beyond what is necessary for students to understand. A teacher who spends 30 seconds nagging a group of students about their organization is overdwelling. A teacher who spends twice as much time as necessary to explain a simple rule is overdwelling. A teacher who spends three minutes helping students find their own spaces for a movement lesson is overdwelling. A teacher who "lectures" students well beyond the point where the message has been received is overdwelling.

Overdwelling destroys the momentum of a lesson. A teacher can't establish a brisk pace to a lesson and expect to maintain it if slowdowns due to overdwelling occur too often. A major outcome of overdwelling is that students spend far too much time waiting. As shown in Chapter 4, students spend too much of their physical education time waiting for something to happen. Teachers who overdwell on off-task behavior, fine points of a skill, or organizational events make the majority of students in the class wait. Students who are waiting often find ways to entertain themselves—and those ways are often troublesome to the teacher.

Fragmentation: Choosing the Wrong Unit for Activity

Physical education teachers often have one child (or small group) doing something when, in fact, the entire group could be doing it, resulting in group fragmentation. The term **group fragmentation** refers to having a student do something singly and separately when the larger group could be doing it at the same time. Group fragmentation results in waiting on the part of the audience students, and waiting is clearly up near the top of any "enemies" list for effective teaching. Teachers sometimes do not have an entire group active at the same time because they believe that control is more difficult that way. Instead, they choose to have one student perform at a time (or several students, one from each group) while others wait for their turn. This strategy is clearly inefficient in terms of learning time per child. It also produces group fragmentation—which produces waiting—which increases the opportunity for misbehavior.

Teachers also sometimes commit the error of **activity fragmentation**: making the focus for an activity something that is not a meaningful activity unit in itself. Sport skills are often broken down into very small units for purposes of practice. Teachers understand that these units are eventually put together into meaningful wholes for use in game play. Students do not always understand that. A focus for a drill or a learning activity should be a meaningful unit of behavior in and of itself. If the activity is not meaningful to the students, they soon tend to slow down and lose momentum.

Assessing Preventive Management Skills

The effectiveness of a physical education teacher in developing and maintaining efficient structures for management can be assessed in several important ways. It must be remembered that the purpose of more efficient gymnasium management is to provide more learning time for students in order to increase the amount of content covered and to improve their skills and strategies in the subject matter. Therefore, an overall way to judge improvements in managerial skills is to periodically assess the learning time that accrues to students in classes taught by the teacher. It is also important to make sure that managerial improvements are being made through primarily positive techniques so that the climate of the educational setting does not become negative. It does little good to become more efficient if the manner in which it is done turns the students off the subject matter and the setting. Therefore, using primarily positive techniques to improve managerial structures that result in more learning time for students represents the best long-term method for assessing managerial skills.

It is also useful to consider assessing the managerial skills directly, especially for providing feedback to the teacher as he or she tries to improve. The following kinds of assessment are useful for direct evaluation of managerial skills:

1. *Regularly monitor the total amount of time spent in management per teaching lesson.* Goals can be set either in terms of minutes or in terms of a percentage of total time, such as no more than 15 percent of total available time spent in management.

2. *Develop an observation system to monitor the individual managerial episodes.* Goals can be set in terms of the average time per managerial episode. Episodes can be identified as related to organizational, transitional, equipment-related, and other pertinent types of events.

3. *Develop an observation system to monitor transitions.* Transitions, when focused on specifically, often can be improved quickly and result in great time savings. A system to identify and monitor the length of transitions can be useful for assessment and feedback purposes. This kind of system can be further subdivided to differentiate between transition time (actual time to make the transition) and wait time (time from when the transition is actually completed to when the next instructional or practice event begins).

4. *Develop a checklist or rating scale (or keep anecdotal records) to monitor the degree to which gymnasium routines are carried out without dependence on current interactions from the teacher.* The first task here is to identify a limited, yet important list of gymnasium routines (specific to the age group, local needs, and teacher's purposes). The second task is to observe the degree to which these get carried out quickly and

efficiently by students without the constant supervision of the teacher and without constant prompting or reacting by the teacher to students who behave inappropriately as regards the list of routines. One element of such a system could be doing frequency counting of teacher reactions related to gymnasium routines, assuming that a high frequency of interactions is evidence of need for improvement in this area.

5. *Develop an observation system to monitor the smoothness and momentum of the lesson.* This kind of system is based on frequency counts of errors related to smoothness and momentum (evidence of inappropriate overlapping, thrusts, dangles, flip-flops, group fragmentation), and other ways in which the movement of the lesson is disrupted or delayed. Rating systems can also be used for this purpose.

Further information on instrumentation techniques for observing, assessing, and evaluating these and other teaching skills can be found in Chapter 14.

CHAPTER 6

Discipline Techniques

The mastery of classroom management skills should not be regarded as an end in itself. These techniques are, however, necessary tools. Techniques are enabling. The mastery of techniques enables one to do many different things. It makes choices possible. The possession of group management skills allows the teacher to accomplish her teaching goals—the absence of managerial skills acts as a barrier.

Jacob Kounin, *Discipline and Group Management in Classrooms* (1970)

CHAPTER OBJECTIVES

To define discipline in reference to appropriate student behavior

To distinguish between discipline and punishment

To describe why discipline is important for teaching

To describe basic strategies for changing behavior

To suggest techniques for developing appropriate gymnasium behavior

To suggest techniques for decreasing inappropriate gymnasium behavior

To describe alternative ways to formalize behavior change strategies

In this text, **appropriate behavior** is defined as student behavior that is consistent with the educational goals of a specific educational setting. Different settings often require differing definitions of appropriate behavior, yet each setting requires a high percentage of appropriate behavior in order to achieve whatever educational goals have been set. Therefore, I will say very little here about what kinds of student behavior ought to be defined as appropriate. Eventually, that will be up to you. Is always being quiet appropriate? Is wearing the prescribed physical education uniform appropriate? Is keeping in a straight line appropriate? Ultimately, schools, departments, and teachers decide these things based on their own convictions and their interpretations of the concerns of local parents and administrators. However, a basic assumption is made here that high rates of appropriate student behavior are universally sought after by teachers. I have some opinions about what should be considered appropriate, but when I cite or discuss them they will be clearly delineated as opinions rather than as universal "do's" and "don'ts."

Teachers make decisions every day about what is or is not appropriate for the classroom and gymnasium. Whenever a teacher reprimands a student, he or she is helping to delineate the boundaries of acceptable behavior. Every educational environment has rules of behavior. Sometimes they are made public, but most often they are unwritten and students learn them as they go along. And all too often they learn by violating one and being the target of a negative interaction. Most unwritten class rules are negative; they come across as "don'ts" rather than "do's."

The term *discipline* has always been important in a teacher's vocabulary. In today's schools, many teachers are judged primarily by their ability to maintain good discipline. Discipline is an important component in education, but discipline can be approached from a positive as well as a negative viewpoint. Many people, if asked to define the characteristics of a well-disciplined class, would probably respond with a definition close to the one used here for appropriate behavior; that is, "behavior consistent with the educational goals of the specific situation." That constitutes a positive approach to discipline.

But many people define discipline by the absence of inappropriate behavior; to them, *discipline* means "keeping the troops in line," and the military analogy is not used without reason. For many teachers, maintaining discipline amounts to developing and maintaining a rigid, military atmosphere in the gymnasium. If you value that kind of atmosphere, you will have great difficulty with the positive approach to discipline advocated here.

The crux of the matter can be seen by examining the following two definitions of **discipline**: (1) training to behave in accordance with rules, and (2) punishment carried out by way of correction. The first definition allows for a positive approach, for teaching students to "behave in accordance with rules" can be done through a positive or a negative approach. But the second definition allows no room for anything positive. Indeed, when used as a verb (*to discipline*) the term implies an act of punishment.

It is important that you understand my perspective on discipline from the outset. Punishment is a behavior management technique. Several punishment techniques are discussed later in this chapter. Punishment is used in schools and is sometimes an extremely valuable technique in a teacher's overall repertoire of management skills. But, the sole purpose of punishment should be to redirect disruptive or otherwise inappropriate behavior into more useful and productive forms of behavior. Punishment techniques should be used skillfully and without emotional overtones, such as angry outbursts at students. Punishment should not be used in retribution or merely to "flex your muscles."

Punishment is a much overused discipline strategy that is usually of short-term benefit only and is fraught with potential problems. There is too much punishment in schools! The main reason for this is quite simply that too few teachers have and use the skills necessary to maintain discipline through positive strategies. Appropriate behavior is important, but it also is more than the absence of inappropriate behavior! The basic task of discipline is not only to reduce forms of disruptive and inappropriate behavior but also to develop the kinds of appropriate behavior through which students can learn and grow.

Why Is Discipline Important?

Why should a teacher maintain adequate discipline? Why is a teacher's ability to teach judged partly by the rate of appropriate behavior in his or her classes? One simple answer is that teachers have traditionally been held responsible for teaching and maintaining appropriate behavior in schools. Today that expectation is as strong as ever. There seem to be two basic reasons why the teacher has always been held responsible for good discipline. First, school has always been considered a place where students learn more than the three R's. At school, children are supposed to learn appropriate ways of getting along in a group and interacting with group members. They are supposed to learn respect for adults (teachers), respect for property (school materials and materials of other students), proper ways of cooperating and competing, proper work habits, and a host of associated behaviors. Of course, the definition of what is "proper" changes from time to time and from place to place. A student who has not learned some or all of these proper behavior patterns is considered a discipline problem. With the mobility of modern families, and the breakdown in some traditional family patterns, the teaching of proper behavior patterns has assumed more importance in many school situations.

A second reason for maintaining classroom and gymnasium discipline is that it sets a proper climate for learning, which has always been considered the primary function of the school. It has always been assumed that the student who is well behaved will learn more than the student who misbehaves. That assumption has never received adequate research testing and may or may not be true. Ferritor and his colleagues (1972) found almost no relationship between rates of appropriate behavior and academic performance in an elementary school. They suggested that appropriate behavior and achievement were both important, but they should be approached as separate motivational problems. In other words, you should consider it important to maintain good discipline in your classes, but you cannot assume that by doing so you have ensured a high rate of learning. The discipline and learning problems may be only marginally related. There are many gymnasiums across this country (perhaps you have been in one) where there is very adequate discipline, but very little is learned.

There is another important reason for maintaining good discipline. If you are going to have a career in teaching, you will want it to be as satisfying as possible. Nothing is more detrimental to personal satisfaction in teaching than having to battle constantly with students about discipline. Teaching cannot be a pleasant and rewarding vocation if it is based primarily on negative interactions with students. To be happy and successful in teaching, you should take seriously the problems of maintaining appropriate behavior, and you should consider doing it through positive rather than negative approaches.

Definitions of Appropriate Behavior

Usually you will decide what is appropriate behavior for your classes. However, during student teaching you may have to accept certain standards that you would not personally advocate. For example, school rules or the rules of the cooperating teacher may differ from those you would establish. If this is the case, it would be useful to discuss these differences and attempt (as far as possible) to establish definitions of appropriate behavior that are consistent with your values.

The definition of appropriate behavior advocated here was not chosen without some real purpose. That purpose was to have you examine what you think are the educational goals of your situation and to further examine student behavior in light of those goals. There are very few educational situations in which silence in a gymnasium is consistent with the goals of physical education. Although most of the task of providing definitions in this category is left to you, I would be remiss if I did not suggest that classroom and gymnasium climates characterized by rigidity, quietness, and docile students are not consistent with sound educational goals. I do not believe that "discipline for discipline's sake" is a defensible educational position.

Although it is necessary to consider the question of inappropriate behavior, I hope that you will spend real effort on appropriate behavior. Too often, appropriate behavior is thought of as nothing more than what occurs when a student is not misbehaving. Realistically, your goal is twofold. You must define those behaviors that are detrimental to your educational goals; those are the inappropriate behaviors. You must also define the behaviors that are conducive to your educational goals; these are the appropriate behaviors. Often you can take care of the inappropriate behaviors by focusing on appropriate behaviors that are incompatible with the inappropriate ones.

Williams and Anandam (1973) have suggested a very simple yet inclusive four-category system for rating student behavior. They suggest the following categories and definitions:

Student Behavior Rating Categories

1. *Task-relevant behavior*: All student participation in activity relevant to the lessons (for example, looking at the teacher during demonstrations or instructions; participating in the activity in an appropriate manner; participating when he or she should be participating; following instructions in an appropriate manner)

2. *Appropriate social interaction*: Any student-student or student-teacher interaction that does not disrupt the educational activity (for example, laughing, cheering, talking to other students, helping other students)
3. *Time off task*: Any nonparticipation that occurs when an activity has been assigned (for example, standing around or gazing). The student is not distracting or disrupting another student by his or her inattention
4. *Disruptive behavior*: Any behavior that disrupts the educational activity (for example, pushing a student while standing in line, preventing a student from appropriate participation, talking while the teacher is demonstrating or instructing), or any act of aggression that is not part of an activity

It should be pointed out that these behaviors are very specific to what is going on in the class. Most of the time we want to encourage students to laugh and generally have a good time interacting with their fellow students; however, this kind of interaction is considered disruptive if it occurs when the teacher is demonstrating or when another student has the floor for demonstration or instruction. What you are teaching is that there is a time and place for these behaviors.

Huber (1973) developed the following definitions for his work with mentally retarded youngsters in physical education. You should notice that the definitions are somewhat rigid because of the specific needs of working with retarded students in a physical education setting.

Appropriate Behavior

1. Attends to teacher's explanations and demonstrations
2. Complies with teacher's directions within 2 seconds from the time the directions are stated
3. Moves from place to place as assigned
4. Remains in his or her own space
5. Practices tasks as instructed
6. Uses equipment properly
7. Does not interfere with practice of others

Inappropriate Behavior

1. Looks away from teacher or makes unnecessary noises or actions while teacher is demonstrating or instructing
2. Does not comply with teacher's directions or does so too late
3. Does not go to proper station when asked to do so
4. Uses unassigned equipment
5. Mistreats assigned equipment or moves equipment from station to station
6. Disrupts the practice or attention of another student

As you can see, retarded students need to learn some very specific kinds of behaviors to function effectively in a physical education setting, such as persistence at working at a task, the ability to follow directions, the capacity to practice without interfering with the practice of others, the proper use of equipment, and how to pay attention to a demonstration or instruction. Your students may also need to learn such behaviors.

Basic Strategies for Changing Behavior

Discipline, viewed properly, often requires behavior change. Some behaviors need to occur less frequently. Other behaviors need to occur more frequently. Again, good behavior is seldom merely the absence of bad behavior, especially if you are trying to achieve some educational goals rather than simply to provide custodial care for groups of students.

Certain basic strategies apply to all behavior change situations. These principles, if followed carefully, form the basis for a teacher's repertoire of discipline skills.

1. *Be specific.* Make sure that you and the student(s) understand what behavior is to be changed. Don't expect that saying "Stop fooling around" will work often if students aren't told specifically what it means. Also, defining the target of behavior change specifically and carefully prevents the possibility that you will change more behavior than you want or less than you want. For example, you might want to use a punishment technique to stop an inappropriate behavior but you don't want the student to think that you don't like him or her. Likewise, you might want to increase the likelihood that a student will ask a question, but you don't want to create a situation of nonstop questioning on the part of students.

2. *Define the change contingency carefully.* A contingency is the statement of relationship between a behavior and a consequence. It should be defined carefully; for example, "If you do X, then Y will happen." "If you are late to class again, you will be sent to the office." "If you stay on task for 25 minutes, you can pick an activity to end the class for the final 5 minutes."

3. *Think small.* Don't try to change the world in a day or the entire personality of a student in one week. Start with a small, but significant behavior problem, define it specifically, provide consequences for it carefully, and then observe it as it changes. Then move on.

4. *Move gradually.* Be satisfied with small, consistent improvement, especially if you are working with small rewards and punishments. If you can generate some large consequences, then you can move ahead more quickly. But don't expect enormous amounts of change for trivial consequences.

5. *Be consistent.* Stick to your contingency and apply it in the same manner all the time. Nothing confuses students more, or makes them more

The Show-Off

Situation. A student tends to be a show-off. The student acts up just enough to get some snickers and glances from the rest of the class. The teacher tries to stop the behavior with some reprimands.

Result. The misbehavior continues.

Analysis. The behavior pattern is probably controlled by the attention provided by the peer group. If this is the case, a teacher reaction that might be effective in another situation will not work here. In order for a teacher reaction to change this behavior pattern, it must be stronger than the attention provided by the peer group.

Prescription. The choice here is rather clear. A very strong reprimand will usually desist this kind of behavior; however, it will not replace the positive strokes that the student received from the peer attention. If a negative interaction is used, then the teacher must find a way for the student to receive peer attention for some more appropriate behavior pattern. Because the cooperation of the peers will be beneficial anyway, it might as well be used from the outset. When the student is away from the group, the teacher can ask the rest of the class not to provide attention for the kinds of behavior he or she wishes to eliminate. The teacher may also ask them to try to interact with the student more often when he or she does other things.

distrusting, than to have contingencies change from day to day without being told. If you want consistent behavior, then establish clear contingencies and stick to them. You will get only what you arrange.

6. *Start where the student is.* Don't expect miracles of good citizenship from a student who has been in constant trouble for years. Define an immediate problem. Change it. Then, build on success gradually. Continued success should allow for larger and larger chunks of behavior change as you go along. You have to get students to school before you can teach them. You have to get them on time and on task before they can learn.

The basic rules just described apply both to decreasing misbehavior patterns and increasing appropriate behavior patterns. Small, specific improvements in behavior are achieved by applying contingencies consistently, by using effective consequences, and by gradually moving to larger, more expanded, and more appropriate forms of behavior. But remember that the absence of misbehavior does not, in and of itself, constitute good behavior

When a student misbehaves, the immediate tendency is to eliminate the misbehavior as quickly as possible. That is OK—all teachers share that tendency. Yet we should also remember that a student misbehaves for some reason (which means simply that he or she is getting some reinforcement from some source, which is sustaining the misbehavior). If peer attention is reinforcing misbehavior, then teacher punishment will reduce it momentarily but a student who so badly needs the attention of peers will do it again. Good discipline consists of reducing such misbehaviors and at the same time beginning to build a pattern of good behavior through positive behavior change techniques.

It should also be noted that being specific, providing consistent consequences, and maintaining other principles of behavior change usually require that a teacher keeps a record of the behavior, to make sure that it is changing. Keeping records of behavior is also useful for assessing exactly how much change is called for and noting when it has occurred. "Things seem better" is just not adequate as an evaluation, even though it may be comforting. The many ways of monitoring student behavior suggested in this text should provide a sufficient number of alternatives so that teachers can actually know what is going on in their classes.

Techniques for Increasing Good Behavior

A teacher can't build good behavior without focusing on it in a specific and systematic way. Teachers tend to be far too stingy about focusing on good behavior. That observation is not only a fact of my own experience in schools but is also well documented in classroom and gymnasium research. Typically, teachers tend to react negatively or correctively to students when they misbehave. The gymnasium is far too full of "Be quiet," "Pay attention," "Listen," "Straighten up that line," "Sh-h," and "That's enough, over there." There is far too little "Thank you," "Jack, you have been very good today," "That's the way to get that drill started quickly," or "I appreciate the way the class really worked hard today."

Don't expect to build good behavior and have a warm, nurturant gymnasium climate without focusing on good behavior and finding ways to recognize it and reinforce it. Enough is known about the nature of effective teaching in today's schools to be absolutely sure that high levels of achievement and on-task behavior, and warm, nurturant gymnasium climates are not only compatible, but indeed may actually depend on one another.

Let's be very clear about what the research says and what this text advocates. The "hard-liner" and "stern taskmaster" will find no comfort in these pages—not, at least, if those descriptions include a harsh and punitive gymnasium climate developed mostly through an overreliance on punishment and the threat of punishment. You don't have to be an unlikable, hard-nosed punisher to develop and maintain good discipline. However, the teacher who be-

**Shouldn't Students Behave Well Without
Having to Be Rewarded?**

There is no good answer to this question. When teachers use behavior change techniques, they are often criticized by people who assume that students should always behave well just because that is "expected" and the "right thing." That may be good enough for mature adults who behave properly because they have been taught to do so and value the acceptance that society provides for these ways of behaving. It is seldom enough for students who are not very far along to adulthood. No teacher should feel that using specific behavior change techniques is inappropriate. However, teachers need to use the techniques skillfully and wisely. Far too often, teachers use large consequences (rewards or punishments) where small ones would do nicely. An important principle of behavior change programs is referred to as the "principle of least intervention." What it means, quite simply, is that you do as little as possible to get the job done! If you can teach young children to behave appropriately by using social praise and positive feedback, then special privileges or material rewards would be unnecessary. But in some situations, privileges and rewards are much more useful because systematic social praise is ineffective or not powerful enough. Eventually students should behave well without always being rewarded.

lieves that all that is needed for good discipline is to teach the subject matter well is also in for a rude shock. It is my contention that the former view tends to be self-serving and often downright cruel, while the latter view is naive and romantic. And neither stands much of a chance to achieve any important educational goals. The techniques described in this chapter (along with those for preventive management, described in Chapter 5) can be learned, perfected, and used to produce good discipline, high proportions of learning time, and a warm gymnasium climate.

Make Your Class Rules Clear

Students cannot behave appropriately unless they know what behavior is expected of them. To assume that they know how you want them to behave is folly. Their other teachers may expect different kinds of behavior, and the students will transfer that behavior to your class until they learn that you want them to behave differently. Class rules for behavior are the basis of effective classroom management. Rules should be made clear to students. They probably should be posted in a conspicuous place so that students are reminded of them. You might consider discussing possible rules with your students and using the input in deciding what the rules should be.

Tardiness

Situation. Tardiness is a problem in a junior high school physical education class. The teacher decides to make each student who comes in after the tardy bell run two laps of the gym.

Result. No change. Tardiness does not decrease.

Analysis. The imposed punishment is not effective; it does not decrease the rate of tardiness, because the students do not consider it a punishment at all. Moreover, it is unwise to use an activity (running) as a punishment and then in another situation to try to sell the students on it as a good activity. The problem can be viewed as one of attempting to eliminate tardiness or one of attempting to strengthen the habit of coming to class on time. The results would be the same, but the methods would be drastically different.

Prescription. Are there positive reasons why students should attempt to get to class on time? Is the first activity promptly started and fun to do? Do students who come on time ever get complimented? The best strategy would be to ignore those who are tardy and provide some positive interactions for those who come on time. It would be especially important to target the students who are often tardy and compliment them when they come on time. Having a prompt and pleasurable first activity would also help. Severe or chronic tardiness may need a punishment that would indeed serve as a punishment.

Children who are too young to read posted rules can understand posters with stick figures showing the behaviors. Young children relate well to bright posters with the class rules clearly written. Older students relate better to a simple posting of a typed or written list of class rules. Following are some guidelines for initiating the use of class rules (Madsen and others 1968). Application of the guidelines will differ slightly according to the age of your students.

1. Make the rules short and directly to the point.
2. Use no more than seven rules so students do not forget them.
3. Wherever possible state rules in a positive manner.
4. Keep a tally in your record book of the number of times you review the rules during the initiation period.
5. Remind the class of the rules at times other than those cued by a breaking of the rules.

6. Write and discuss the rules in a language appropriate to the age level of your students.

A few short rules written in language that students relate to stand the best chance of being remembered, understood, and followed. At the outset you should remind students of the rules fairly frequently, and it is a good practice to mark a tally each time you do so. Try not to get into a situation where the only time you mention rules is after a student has misbehaved. It is just as easy to have a positive rule ("Listen and watch the teacher when he or she is demonstrating or instructing") as a negative rule ("Don't talk when the teacher is demonstrating or instructing").

The best check of whether your rules are adequately posted and clearly written is how well your students understand them and are aware of them. This is best measured by asking a student to explain one or more of the rules.

Class rules should be developed and taught early in the school year. Time must be devoted to teaching them, especially with younger children. If students are seen only once per week, then special reminders need to be made available so that after three or four such weekly meetings the rules have started to become routines. Once the students internalize the rules, productive gymnasium routines will have been developed and subsequent classes can run smoothly without constant attention from the teacher. At this point, the classes operate on the basis of established structure (see Chapter 2).

Motivate Appropriate Behavior Through Positive Interactions

The best way to motivate your students to behave appropriately is to interact with them in a positive manner when they are showing appropriate behavior. This is probably an entirely different way of interacting from what you are accustomed to. It is a different way of interacting from what you have experienced. Most of you are accustomed to interaction only after a misbehavior. That is the standard way of teaching, but it is not the best way.

Classroom and gymnasium climate is an important factor in education. One of the clearest developments in education in our time is that too many students dislike being in school. Sadly, this is as true sometimes for physical education as for any other content area. This issue cannot be avoided. When you receive feedback on your baseline performances in the negative and positive behavioral interaction categories, you will probably be surprised by the results. Unless you have already made some effort to relate in a positive way to your students, the baseline data may well indicate a 0.0 rate of positive interactions. This would not be unusual for physical education teachers.

Several studies observed teachers for weeks and showed baseline rates of 0.0 per minute (Hughley 1973, Rife 1973, and Hamilton 1974). A recent effort to examine research data about school performance from a host of educational studies came to a rather startling conclusion. Many of the things we consider to be crucial to good education, such as facilities, equipment, and class size, were not found to be significant factors in differences in achieve-

Fooling Around

Situation. Two high school students tend to disrupt class with their fooling around and do not take part in activities in a manner conducive to learning and the smooth functioning of the group. The two students are always together and create the disturbances as a pair. A series of reprimands seems only to discourage them temporarily, and no permanent change is seen.

Result. No long-run change occurs, and the two students tend to become enemies of the teacher.

Analysis. It is virtually impossible to know exactly why this kind of behavior pattern occurs. The two students provide attention for one another, regardless of what is going on in the class. To break them up would take away their source of enjoyment but would not by itself be a solution. Indeed, it would probably produce further hostility and perhaps more serious misbehavior.

Prescription. The students are asked to come in for a conference where the situation is discussed. The students are asked, as a pair, to desist from certain behavior patterns and are encouraged to behave in some specifically different ways. In class, the teacher has frequent, private positive interactions with the pair when they are engaged properly. If any improvement occurs, they are privately thanked outside of class. The bond between the pair is respected, and their standard of behavior is turned toward more positive outcomes.

ment or in the degree to which school was a satisfying experience. Indeed, the authors indicate that "the primary basis for evaluating a school should be whether the students and teachers find it a satisfying place to be" (Bane and Jencks 1972, p. 41). A climate that is characterized primarily by negative interactions is not a place students or teachers will find satisfying. Research is also quite clear that a negative classroom and gymnasium climate is most often characteristic of less effective teachers—of settings where students achieve less well and like school less well than in settings where a positive climate prevails.

Following are some examples of positive behavioral interactions. They are divided into general interactions, nonverbal interactions, interactions with specific information content, and interactions with a value content. Examples appropriate to various age levels are included. Obviously, the interaction must be consistent with the age level of the student and delivered in a sincere manner that is not perceived by the student as phony. Questions related to developing interaction skills that are perceived to be sincere are dealt with in Chapter 7.

General Positive Behavior Interactions

Yes.	Thank you.
Good.	That's the way to do it.
Nice job.	I appreciate the way you did that.
Excellent.	You're doing a lot better.
Exactly.	I'm very proud of you all.
Beautiful.	That was done very nicely.
Terrific.	That's the right way to do it.
Way to go.	The entire class did well.
Nice going.	That was great.

Nonverbal Positive Behavior Interactions

Smiling	Signaling thumbs up
Nodding	Touching a child and smiling
Clapping hands	Shaking hands
Making an OK sign	Applauding
Patting a student on the back	Winking
	Circling hand in air (to continue)
Putting an arm around a student	Laughing
	Scruffing the hair of a student

Positive Behavioral Interactions with Specific Information (Can Be Combined with Any Nonverbal Interactions)

Squad 2 really did a job getting organized that time.
Thanks for paying attention, Jack.
Did you all see that way Jane helped Billy?
That was a very good answer.
The entire class worked hard at that drill.
That was a heck of an effort, Marcus.
This squad (pointing) was quiet right away.
Great job of getting ready; it took you only 12 seconds.
I appreciate the way you're following instructions this week, Mary.

Positive Behavioral Interactions with Value Content (see Chapter 11)

That's the way to get quiet, now we can get on with the game.
Thanks, Bill, when you make an effort the other guys seem to also.
Squad 3 watched me closely, they will know exactly what to do now.
That was a good answer, you must have been listening very closely.
Ann, you did a good job all week and I'm sure the class was more fun for you.
Hey, nice effort today, if you continue that way you're going to really learn a lot in here.

Positive behavioral interactions can be delivered in three ways, each of which has a different purpose. First, an interaction can occur privately between you and an individual student. The purpose is to motivate individual appropriate behavior in a private manner. A quiet word. A frank and open compliment delivered privately. A wink or nod of the head. Each kind of interaction is private and individual. Second, there is the individually directed interaction that is public, in the sense that the other students are aware of it. This kind of interaction is responsible for what is referred to as the *modeling effect*, because students tend to imitate behavior they see approved of. Third, there can be interaction with a subset of the group or with the entire group. Here, each individual may derive some satisfaction from the interaction and group standards of behavior are also strengthened.

Vary Methods

The effective teacher uses several ways of interacting. This means diversifying the kind of verbal interaction, using frequent nonverbal interactions, spreading interactions among many individual students, using occasional group interactions, and varying the delivery of the interaction. Varying delivery means using different voice levels, different degrees of enthusiasm, and different physical characteristics in the nonverbal interactions.

When you begin to be a positive interactor, you may well find that you fall into a predictable pattern of verbalization, what has been referred to as the "global good" (Hughley 1973). You may run around saying "Good job," "Good job," "Good job"; or "Way to go," "Way to go," "Way to go." This should not disturb you, as it is a normal development. You should not expect to become an accomplished positive interactor overnight. If you continue to work at it and get feedback about your progress, you will develop a larger repertoire of positive interaction modes.

Nonverbal interaction can be very powerful. You are no doubt familiar with the commonly used negative nonverbal interactions: the finger to the lips; the teacher standing with hands on hips, staring down a class in order to get them quiet; the menacing look that tells a student that something inappropriate has been done; and the even more subtle cues that indicate displeasure or disapproval. Just as negative nonverbal communication can be powerful, so too can positive nonverbal interaction.

Nonverbal interaction is very important because students often feel that the message conveyed in nonverbal communication is more "real" and "true" than that conveyed in verbal communication.

> Pupils assume that nonverbal cues are more consonant with the actual feelings and thoughts of a teacher; therefore, those detecting a contradiction between a teacher's verbal and nonverbal behavior will accept the nonverbal as being more valid. [Galloway 1971, p. 70]

Generally, you should attempt to spread your interactions among many students. If one or two students are particularly bothersome in terms of misbehavior, then it would do well to focus many of your positive interactions on them for a while until their appropriate behavior becomes more stable. This is often referred to as "catching them when they're good." Your baseline data can reveal the degree to which your interactions are group or individually directed. If there is a wide disparity between these directions, you should work to balance the interactions. Often teachers do not make sufficient use of group interactions. This is one of the best ways of establishing group standards and group expectations about appropriate behavior in the gymnasium, locker room, or playing field.

Initiate Positive Interactions Without Misbehavior Cues

When you first switch to a positive interaction style, you will find that you are cued to emit a positive interaction with a student when another student behaves in some inappropriate manner. The scenario will probably go something like this:

You are giving some instruction or demonstration.
You notice that Bill and Jack are talking and fooling around instead of watching you.
You look for a student who is paying attention.
You say, "John will be able to do this because he is paying attention."

The interaction is entirely appropriate, and this is a legitimate method of getting Bill and Jack to desist from their inappropriate behavior. However, you don't want your positive interactions to occur only in connection with instances of misbehavior. If that were the case, your rate of positive interaction would increase or decrease in direct relationship to the level of inappropriate behavior in the class. There are many reasons to interact positively with students (many are covered in Chapter 7), only one of which is to motivate appropriate behavior. Don't be surprised if you depend on misbehavior cues for initiating positive interactions when you first start to develop a positive teaching style. Gradually you will be able to respond to appropriate behavior without needing a cue of misbehavior. This will occur as you learn how to focus more on what students do right and well than on what they do wrong or poorly. Interactions initiated solely on the basis of appropriate behavior will occur as you begin to feel more comfortable "looking for the good" in your students.

Techniques for Decreasing Inappropriate Behavior

It is often necessary to stop disruptive behavior quickly, before it spreads and interferes with a lesson. This is occasionally true even when a positive program for developing and maintaining good behavior has been initiated. When disruptive behavior does occur, teachers should have alternatives for dealing with it effectively—and then clear and effective strategies for redirecting the student into more productive patterns of behavior. Remember, it isn't enough just to eliminate bad behavior. Instead, strategies for eliminating bad behavior need to be combined with strategies for building good behavior. The following strategies have been tested and proven to be useful in a wide variety of school settings.

Ignore Inappropriate Behavior When Possible

The development and continued motivation of appropriate behavior in school is normally considered to be a function of three basic strategies: (1) clear rules, (2) the use of positive interactions to support appropriate behavior, and (3) ignoring inappropriate behavior unless it is seriously disruptive or harmful to other students. I have suggested that you may have some problems adjusting to the use of the first two strategies, and it may also be difficult for you to ignore inappropriate behavior. Many teachers feel very awkward about ignoring misbehavior that they have previously reprimanded. Most of you have experienced teachers who emitted high rates of reprimands (negative interactions), and you have probably used this technique yourself. Often during a class you may cast a knowing glance at a student who is talking when he or she shouldn't be, say, "Let's get quiet," ask a student to "Stop that," tell a squad to "Hurry up," chide a lagging student by saying "Come on, Billy," react to a noisy class by saying, "I'm not going to start until you're quiet," or tell a student to "cut it out." None of these negative interactions is necessarily made in anger, and no one of them alone would be sufficient to create a negative classroom climate. But if you emit these at a rate of 2.0 per minute, you would have 70 such reprimands and chides in a 35-minute class: that would be sufficient to create a negative atmosphere. The major points are (1) Does this method of negative interaction do any good? No. (2) Isn't there a better way to accomplish your goal? Yes. (3) When should you reprimand a student? The answer to this question is discussed in the next section.

All evidence indicates that constantly reprimanding students is not a useful method of maintaining appropriate behavior and may indeed be harmful. First, it is possible that your reprimands may be supporting a pattern of inappropriate behavior in a student (Madsen and others 1968). For any child who is reinforced by attention from the teacher and the group, a mild reprimand may indeed provide the needed attention and therefore support the misbehavior rather than stop it. Second, a positive classroom climate cannot be established or maintained if most of the interaction between teacher and students is concerned with inappropriate behavior. This produces a nagging, slightly repressive kind of climate in which it is very unlikely that good human relations can be developed. Third, much evidence suggests that a mild reprimand does not produce better behavior. Thus it is a monumental waste of time and should be cast aside as a major strategy for dealing with students.

A high rate of positive interactions for appropriate behavior combined with ignoring inappropriate behavior will usually produce the level of behav-

The Pest

Situation. A second-grade boy always seems to be causing minor disturbances. In a parachute activity, he is often doing the opposite of the directions. The teacher calls numbers to run under the lifted parachute and the boy goes on someone else's number. The teacher says, "Run under," and the boy crawls. The teacher says, "Lift and pull out," and the boy lifts and ducks under. After each of these occurrences, the teacher gives the boy a "Come on, get with it" look, provides a mild verbal reprimand, puts the boy back in the right place while going on with further instruction, or gives some combination of these reactions.

Result. The boy continues to misbehave mildly.

Analysis. This behavior is typical of a child that most teachers would consider a "pest" type. He is not a real problem; in fact, he is well liked by his teacher and peers. He wants attention and is getting all he desires. The teacher assumed that the verbal and nonverbal negative reactions would reduce the "pesty" behavior when, in fact, they actually encourage it. This is a dangerous strategy, not only because the teacher is unwittingly encouraging inappropriate behavior but also because other children may imitate that behavior in order to get similar attention. What the teacher assumes to be a punishment is actually a reward to a child who badly wants some attention.

Prescription. Such behavior should be ignored if it is of no harm to other children. The boy should receive attention when he behaves in a manner that is more consistent with educational goals. Attention must be given to this kind of child because he or she needs it, but the key is *when* to give attention, verbal and/or nonverbal. Ignoring the misbehavior without giving the child attention for more appropriate behavior is likely to produce outbursts of temper. This kind of child is accustomed to getting attention and won't like it if it is taken away. If pestiness is going to be ignored, the child must receive attention when he or she is behaving well.

ior you consider necessary for smooth functioning of the class and also provide an environment conducive to learning. It will not happen overnight, but with some patience on your part you should see some changes within a week. Remember, your goal is to foster a particular kind of classroom climate: one that is conducive to learning, to fun, and to good human relations. Obviously, this kind of climate cannot occur if the rate of inappropriate student behavior is high. The goal is not to punish students, but rather to develop and maintain a level of appropriate student behavior. The point here is that this goal can be accomplished without high rates of negative interaction.

Use Verbal Desists Effectively

The most common form of punishment in American schools is the verbal reprimand—what I refer to as a **desist**. Verbally desisting a misbehavior is a useful skill, particularly if it is done effectively. Research (Kounin 1970) has shown that some methods of desisting are better than others.

A desist should be clear. A clear desist is one that contains specific information telling the student exactly what was wrong. Instead of merely saying "Stop that," a clear desist would be "Stop sitting on the basketball; that ruins its shape."

A desist should also be delivered with firmness. The word *firmness* refers to the degree to which the teacher follows through on the desist, in order to let the offender know that what was said is indeed meant. Eye contact for a moment is a good way to follow through. So too is moving a bit closer to the offender. Desists that lack follow-through simply occur in a moment and then are gone, and their effectiveness is limited.

An effective desist is well timed; that is, a misbehavior is desisted immediately when it is recognized and not allowed to spread before the desist is delivered. Bad timing occurs when a misbehavior occurs and spreads before it is desisted by a teacher. Similarly, effective desists are properly targeted; that is, the desist is directed toward the original offender and not toward some second or third party to the misbehavior. Targeting errors also occur when a serious misbehavior is not desisted and a less serious misbehavior is desisted. When students learn that your timing and targeting is accurate, they then know that you know what is going on in the class—that you are "with it," seemingly having eyes in the back of your head.

A desist does not have to be punitive to be effective. Firmness does not mean harshness. You don't have to get rough to be effective. In fact, research shows that roughness is counterproductive and does not help reduce misbehavior. A harsh or rough desist seems to have one typical outcome: It makes all the students uncomfortable. In Kounin's research program, he found that "rough desists did not make for better behavior in the watching children—they simply upset them" (Kounin 1970). Desists should be clear, firm, well timed, and well targeted, but they should not be rough or harsh.

Use Specific and Effective Punishment Strategies

By definition, punishment means achieving a decrease in a particular behavior by applying a consequence to it. Punishment should be used carefully and skillfully, as should any other professional teaching skill. The following behavior change strategies have been shown to be effective in school settings for reducing misbehavior.

1. *Omission training:* With this strategy, the teacher rewards the student for *not* engaging in a particular behavior. Thanking a student for not talking out during an explanation is an example. Another is a child earning one point for each gym period in which he or she does not argue with peers. After five points are accumulated, the student earns some privilege or access to a favored activity.

2. *Positive practice:* With this strategy, a student is required to engage in an appropriate behavior a specified number of times each time he or she engages in an inappropriate behavior. The two kinds of behavior are usually opposites. For example, a student does not put equipment away properly. As a result, that student must get out the equipment and put it away properly five consecutive times. The result is that improper treatment of the equipment decreases in frequency.

3. *Time out:* With this strategy, a student loses a specified amount of time from physical education activity for an infraction. For this strategy to work, obviously, participation in physical education must be rewarding to the student. A time-out strategy is analogous to a penalty box in ice hockey. The time-out, typically no more than 2 minutes, is of short duration and tied specifically to rule violations. The time-out space should be such that the student is fairly well cut off from social contact with peers for the brief period of the penalty. Time-outs should be timed. Egg timers or clocks in the time-out space should be available.

4. *Reward cost:* With this strategy, a student loses something as a result of misbehaving. For example, a student loses time in the time-out strategy. Students could also lose accumulated points, privileges, or access to other activities such as intramural events. Reward costs are the most common form of punishment in society; violations of many rules in society (such as traffic rules) result in loss of money.

Punishments should always fit the nature of the misbehavior in a fair, balanced manner. Just as the use of overly strong rewards should be avoided, so too should the use of overly harsh punishments. Simple rules violations should result in simple punishments. This reflects the tradition in our society, and it also reflects the principle that the least intervention necessary is the most effective.

Formalizing the Behavior Change Strategy

Teachers can do much to reduce misbehavior and to build and maintain good behavior simply by using their own teaching behavior skillfully and systematically. Establishing class rules, prompting students frequently, using hustles, using higher rates of positive interactions for good behavior, ignoring pesty behavior that is not disruptive to the class, and desisting skillfully can improve and maintain good behavior and a warm, nurturant gymnasium climate. But there are times when more drastic strategies are called for, when things have gotten sufficiently serious or out of control that they need special and immediate attention. In such cases, it is useful to consider making the basic behavior change strategy more formal in order to give it even greater power and specificity with one offending student, a small group of students, or even an entire class. What follows are some ways in which behavior change strategies have been formalized in school settings and resulted in important behavior changes among students.

Behavior Proclamations

A **behavior proclamation** is a formal statement of contingencies that might apply to an individual student, a group of students, or even to an entire class. The proclamation states the behavior to be achieved (and perhaps the behavior to be avoided) and the rewards that can be earned for fulfilling the contingency. The teacher decides both the level of behavior necessary and the amount of reward to be earned. The behavior is monitored frequently, and the reward is earned when the specified amount or length of behavior has been achieved. An example of a behavior proclamation is found in Figure 6-1.

Naturally, the behavior must specify, clearly and understandably, what the

Figure 6-1. *Example of a Behavior Proclamation*

```
                    G O O D    B E H A V I O R


        Betsy Smith          will (1) take part in all games

                                  (2) not argue with

                                  classmates for four (4)

                                  weeks in Phys. Ed.


        For this good behavior   Betsy          will get to

        help Mrs. Jones after school 15 minutes a day

        for two (2) weeks


                                        Mrs. Jones
                                        Physical Education Teacher
```

students are to do or not to do. Also, the reward specified must be sufficiently strong so as to motivate the good behavior.

Behavior Contracts

A **behavior contract** differs from a behavior proclamation in that the student (or students) has a role in defining the behaviors, deciding on a reward, and establishing the precise contingencies (how much, for how long, and so forth). Teachers should not use behavior contracts unless they are willing to negotiate with students on these matters. From a learning and development point of view, the behavior contract is an important step forward from the behavior proclamation and starts students on the road to self-control. The elements of the contract are the same as for the proclamation. It is important that all parties sign the contract. Many teachers who use contracts successfully also have a third party sign the contract, thus underlining the importance and seriousness of having each party fulfill his or her side of the bargain. An example of a behavior contract for an individual student is shown in Figure 6-2. It should be emphasized that contracts can also be written for groups of students.

Good Behavior Games

One of the quickest ways to "turn around" a group of students who are misbehaving too frequently is to use a **good behavior game**. Behavior games have been used successfully in many different kinds of elementary physical education settings (Young 1973; Huber 1973; Siedentop, Rife, and Boehm 1974; McKenzie 1976). Many different kinds of behavior games can be developed. What follows is a description of the most common game format used to reduce inappropriate behavior quickly.

1. The class is divided into four groups. Groups are allowed to choose a name for their team.
2. It is emphasized that each team can win and that teams are competing against a behavior criterion rather than against each other.
3. Four to six behavior rules are explained thoroughly (see the section on rules in this chapter).
4. Rewards are discussed and decided on by the group.
5. The game is explained. Points will be awarded each time a signal goes off (the students won't know when the signal will occur). The teacher will check each group when the signal occurs. If all team members are behaving according to the rules, the team gets one point. If any team member is breaking any of the rules, the team gets no point.
6. A cassette audiotape is preprogrammed with a loud noise to occur periodically (a bell or a buzzer works well). Eight signals are programmed. The intervals between the signals vary. Several tapes are preprogrammed. When class begins, the teacher simply turns on the

BEHAVIOR CONTRACT

Sarah Caldwell and Mr. Roman agree that the following
plan will be in effect for the next four weeks.

Starting date <u>January 6</u>   Ending date <u>February 3</u>

Sarah will

1. Remember to bring her gym clothes for each PE day

2. Not disturb the class by talking or fooling around
    with Melanie

3. Participate in all activities and try hard to
    improve skill

Mr. Roman will

1. Give Sarah individual help on the balance beam

2. Count one point for each day Sarah meets the three
    points stated above

3. Let Sarah help with the 4th-grade class for two
    weeks if Sarah earns seven (7) points during this
    contract

Signed *Sarah Caldwell*

Mr. Roman

Mrs. Sylvia, Principal

Figure 6-2. *Example of a Behavior Contract*

tape recorder with the volume up (often he or she doesn't know when
the signals will occur).

7. When the signal occurs, the teacher quickly glances at each team and
makes a judgment on their behavior. Teams that win a point are
praised and told about their point. Teams that do not win a point are
told why. (After doing this for a few days, the teacher can usually

manage this kind of behavior game easily, not taking more than 15 or 30 seconds at each signal to record and announce points.)

8. At the end of the period, the teacher totals the points and posts the scores for the day.

9. At the end of a specified period (ranging from one day to as long as 8 weeks), the rewards are earned by each team that has met the criterion.

10. If one player on a team loses more than two points for his or her team two days in a row, the team meets and decides whether this player should sit out from gym class for a day (this "doomsday" contingency very seldom needs to be used).

11. With each consecutive game played, it is possible to reduce the number of signals per class and increase the length of the game. As good behavior becomes the norm for the class, the game can gradually be phased out.

With eight checks per day and a three-week game for a class that meets twice weekly, a team might have to accumulate 42 out of 48 points to earn a reward. The extra gymnasium time is combined with access to favored activities and is usually sufficiently powerful to motivate good behavior. With a particularly unruly class, the contingency might have to begin as a daily game where the reward is five minutes of free gym time at the end of the period (if they don't win, they return to their classroom five minutes early). Once good behavior has been achieved, the game contingencies can be stretched out.

The criterion for winning the game can also be made progressively more stringent, thus allowing the teacher to get continually better behavior for the same amount of reward. The number of behavior checks programmed on the cassettes can be reduced gradually so that less time is taken to manage the game.

Behavior games can also be played as "management games," with the outcomes defined in terms of managerial and organizational behavior. An example of a management game was presented in Chapter 5.

Token Systems

The most fully developed, formalized system of behavior change is known widely as the token economy. A **token system** is a formal program including academic, organizational, and managerial outcomes with a clear and specific exchange system in which students earn and accumulate "tokens" that can be exchanged for a number of different kinds of rewards. Our society operates on a massive token economy system where the tokens are different denominations of money. People earn "tokens" (money) and can exchange them for the goods and services the society offers. A small version of this system could be developed for a physical education program or even for a single physical education class.

To develop a token system, teachers must define very carefully all the behaviors they would like included in the system (or work this out with students). Then rewards are developed. The best way to do this is to ask students to rank the available kinds of rewards in terms of their attractiveness. The most attractive (highest ranked) is the most powerful reward. The least attractive probably won't motivate much behavior.

Typical rewards used in physical education have been public recognition (start a name board, list a player of the week, post a photo on a bulletin board in the hall), choice of activities (develop a reward time when students who have accumulated a sufficient number of points get to choose from among attractive activities), extra physical education time, field trips (to a local university or professional game), or privileges (such as being gym aide or a tutor for a younger class). Once the behaviors and the rewards are defined, then the most important phase of the development occurs—deciding how much behavior is necessary to earn "tokens" and how many tokens are necessary to earn the different rewards.

In physical education, it is best to use points as tokens rather than some physical object like a chip or paper money. The "point system" then becomes the "rate of exchange" in the small token economy. The system can be changed from time to time to reflect changes in the definition of behaviors, the kinds of rewards available, and the exchange system. Readers interested in more information about token systems should consult Rushall and Siedentop (1972) or any of the many books on school applications of token systems.

The Ultimate Goal of a Discipline Strategy

Discipline strategies have both short-term and long-term goals. Clearly, the major short-term goals have to do with reducing inappropriate behavior, preventing disruptions, and building good behavior to achieve the immediate goals of a daily lesson or a unit. Longer-term goals are more likely to include (or should) some notions about self-development, self-control, and self-direction. In the longer term, physical education should contribute to a student's growing ability to make decisions wisely, to behave responsibly toward his or her peers, to accept responsibility for his or her own actions, and to be able to do all this and persevere in it without constant supervision or the need for frequent reinforcement.

In summary, the longer-term goals should be to bring students into a responsible, mature relationship with their peers, the subject matter they are studying, and the small society of the school. This will not happen overnight. It takes time, patience, and careful instruction, just as does the acquisition of any important behavior habit. There is also the danger that it may not happen at all. Too often students are brought into a pattern of conformance and then left there, never to grow beyond it into a more mature, self-directed status. To take students beyond the stage of conformance, teachers must give them progressively more responsibility and more freedom to exhibit responsible behavior. To become truly self-directed, students must be weaned gradually and carefully from the normal kinds of behavioral supports that the school provides for them as they are learning how to become responsible people. Teachers must take some risks to do this, but it is necessary if the longer-term goals are to be achieved. The same principles of specificity, consistency, and gradual change apply to achieving these goals as they do to reducing off-task behavior and to increasing cooperative behavior. Also, goals won't be achieved unless they are striven for directly and systematically.

CHAPTER 7

Interpersonal Interaction Skills

What makes us human is the way we interact with other people. In *humanizing* relationships, individuals are sympathetic and responsive to human needs. It is positive involvement with other people that we label *humane*. There is nothing more important in our lives than our interpersonal relationships. The quality of our relationships, as well as the number, depends on our interpersonal skills. It takes skills to build and maintain fulfilling and productive relationships.

David W. Johnson, *Reaching Out: Interpersonal Effectiveness and Self-Actualization* (1981)

CHAPTER OBJECTIVES

To summarize the research evidence on interpersonal interactions in physical education

To explain the relationships between effective teaching and good interpersonal relations

To explain and provide examples of messages conveyed through various approaches to teaching

To describe the characteristics of effective interactions

To describe the characteristics of enthusiastic teaching

To explain the primary elements of communication

To define and provide examples of sending and receiving skills

To define and provide examples of roadblocks to communication

To explain the characteristics of a helping relationship

One of the overriding concerns of educators during the past twenty years has been the development of humane classroom environments that promote individual and group development in the affective domain. The term **affective domain** refers to the attitudes, values, and feelings of students. This humanistic goal in education has been particularly difficult to achieve. There would be little problem if one could assume that every person who enters the teaching profession is both motivated by a desire to serve students humanely and equipped with the skills necessary to do so. But this is not the case. Many teachers are concerned, but do not have sufficient skills to put their concerns into action successfully. The purpose of this chapter is to identify the most important interpersonal interaction skills that should be used in developing a humane educational environment.

In Chapter 3, I indicated that effective teaching is not possible in negative, coercive settings. Teacher effectiveness research has found that effective teachers not only promote academic growth, but tend to do so within a warm, nurturant educational climate. Thus, the search for a humane educational setting is consistent with the search for an effective academic setting. The two can go hand in hand.

The Evidence from Physical Education

Positive teaching styles in physical education are hard to find in the descriptive research that has been done. That sad fact needs to be restated here. Cheffers and Mancini (1978) used an interaction analysis system to examine the junior high and high school teaching episodes in the Columbia videotape data bank (Anderson 1978). They concluded that "by comparison with the total recorded teacher behaviors, virtually no acceptance of student feelings and ideas, praise, or questioning behaviors were recorded . . . the use of sympathetic-empathetic behavior was almost nonexistent" (pp. 46–47). Were these data simply a fluke? Unfortunately, it appears that they were quite similar to what every other investigator has found no matter where the data have been collected.

Quarterman (1977) described the teaching behavior of 24 physical educators teaching kindergarten through eighth grade. Eighty-five percent of all their feedback interactions with students were negative or corrective. Ninety-five percent of all their behavioral interactions were negative or corrective (a behavioral interaction is a teacher response to student behavior other than academic behavior). Physical educators in a different part of the country were studied by Stewart (1980), who concluded, "If we are to accept the notion that high rates of positive behavior and low rates of negative, monitoring, and managing behavior are desirable, one is led to conclude that teachers in this study were not performing very well" (p. 81).

McLeish (1981) reported results of a large study in which 104 teaching episodes were examined from various perspectives, one of which dealt with interpersonal interactions by teachers. He felt compelled to conclude that "there was a noticeable absence of positive affect in these lessons."

Thus, the evidence from research in physical education is consistent, but not very encouraging. This evidence makes the content of this chapter and that of Chapter 8 quite important—at least if we are to someday change the picture that is described by teaching researchers. The notion of change allows us to end this brief review on a hopeful note. A series of experimental research studies at the Ohio State University (Siedentop 1981) shows that physical education teachers and student teachers *can* change their interpersonal interaction-skills and *can* create positive educational settings. They can also improve related teaching characteristics such as their enthusiasm (Rolider 1979) and can also help their students to relate better to each other (Wescott 1977). The established fact that teachers can change, and often very quickly, is a very positive finding, one that lends a hopeful note to this chapter and the next.

Tension Between Good Teaching and Good Interpersonal Relations

A survey asked students and teachers to place in rank order what they felt to be important in their educational experience (Cohen 1970). The teachers were asked to rank the list in terms of what they thought their students wanted out of the educational experience, and the students were asked to rank the list in terms of what they did in fact want. The teachers picked items such as commitment to students, ability to communicate, and closeness of teacher-student relations as the most important factors, and ranked specific learning objectives last. The students ranked specific learning objectives first and tended to rank interpersonal relations items last. The message was clear. Students were most interested in what they were learning, while teachers thought students were most interested in good student-teacher relations. Cohen (1970) labeled this discrepancy the "cult of personality in teaching," and he suggested that too many teachers view their own personality as the most important variable in the educational environment.

Teachers are responsible for learning. They have an important educational function to fulfill. This can and should be accomplished in a manner that also fosters the kind of interpersonal relations that help students grow as individuals. The teacher who attempts to win students with his or her personality and whose teaching success hinges entirely on a "nice guy" reputation does not fulfill the teaching function.

Several chapters in this text are aimed directly at execution of the teaching function, and the positive teaching styles advocated in those chapters can go a long way toward fulfilling the educational function as well as developing good interpersonal interactions. Positive instruction and positive management techniques contribute to good interpersonal relations and good teaching.

In the final analysis, good teaching should not be inseparable from good interpersonal relations. The skills to be developed through this chapter should not be thought of as necessarily different from other teaching skills. Just as good management and teaching techniques contribute to better interpersonal relations between teachers and students, so too do good interpersonal relations skills contribute to good management and instruction.

The Message of the Gymnasium

Whether you are teaching in a multipurpose room, a cramped half gym, a playground, or in the best physical education facility imaginable, you must come to view it as a total learning environment. This is not an easy task, but those who claim that teaching is an easy profession are not aware of the complexities involved. Your students will learn what you teach them, but they will also pick up subtle messages from you and the environment. They will learn movement skills, dribbling, headstands, bump passes, and lowered heart rates; they will also learn some things that you may be much less aware of. A few of the many possible messages that your students will gather from the learning environment are the following:

1. Learning physical education is primarily an active or a passive experience.
2. Risk taking is good, or one should follow all directions and not rock the boat.
3. Physical education is fun, or it is a drag.
4. Physical education teachers are open, consistent, caring people, or they are rigid, uncaring authoritarians.
5. School can be fun, or it can be boring.
6. Physical activity is enjoyable, or it is too much of a hassle.

You could easily double the list of subtle messages that will be conveyed to students by your teaching manner. This is why you must look at what you do in terms of its total impact on your students. Two teachers could teach from identical lesson plans for a volleyball unit and even use similar teaching methods, but the results would be different because the hidden messages conveyed would be entirely different. The impact on one group of students could be negative, while another group could get excited about learning physical education skills.

Conveying a message to students through your teaching manner underlies many of the techniques suggested in this text. The messages meant to be conveyed through the techniques advocated in this text are that physical education is fun, learning is enjoyable and challenging, physical educators are good people, and school is a good place to be. Whether you are involved in planning for instruction or managing your class, you should be thoroughly aware of the hidden messages emanating from everything you do.

This chapter attempts to deal with some of the more important hidden messages conveyed to students, including the messages that you value them as people, that they can accomplish things in physical education, and that you care about their lives beyond the classroom. The skills to be developed here should be integrated with management and instructional skills so that one message conveyed to all who observe you is that effective teaching, good discipline, and strong interpersonal relations are not distinct but can be skillfully interwoven into what would be described as good teaching.

Implementing Interpersonal Relations Skills

It might seem odd that this text approaches interpersonal interactions in a manner similar to other teaching skills such as lesson planning or providing learner feedback. Many would suggest that interpersonal relations are opti-

"Teacher, What's My Name?"

"Hey, you over there—get back in line!" Have you ever been called "Hey, you?" Do you remember what it feels like to think that a teacher with whom you interact on a daily basis doesn't even know your name? The *personal* in interpersonal must at least mean that you know the name of the student with whom you are interacting.

Try to use students' first names in interactions. There is no evidence indicating that using first names results in a more effective interaction, but experience and logic support the contention that nothing is more devastating for a student than doubting that the teacher even knows who he or she is. The use of first names should add a personal touch to the interaction. The extent to which first names are used in interactions can easily be measured via event recording.

It might be assumed that as time goes by the teaching intern would naturally learn the names of students and come to use them more and more frequently. Unfortunately this is yet another invalid assumption. Research indicated that student teachers in physical education hardly ever used first names, whether they were in the first or the fourth week of a ten-week student teaching experience (Darst 1974, Boehm 1974, Hamilton 1974). When, in the same studies, a terminal objective was set that 50 percent of interactions include first-name use and when regular feedback was provided, all student teachers began to use first names regularly. This is one of those "little" interaction skills that may seem not to warrant such attention. In fact, however, this skill may not develop unless a specific goal is set and sufficient feedback is provided to gauge progress toward the achievement of that goal.

Some interns learn names by using name tags for the first week. Others ask students to help them by providing feedback on how they are doing; that is, they try to remember the student's name and have the student say immediately whether the correct name was used. If an intern teaches four classes and each class has 30 students, he or she has 120 students and learning their names is no easy task. This is why some systematic effort to learn names is helpful and why feedback about using those names helps development of this skill.

mal when the teacher "is him- or herself." The common instruction would be "Just be yourself." The assumption is that when people are themselves, all has been done that can be done in the area of interpersonal relations. There are several problems with this approach.

First, a "be yourself" approach to this important area tends to be static: it implies that a "self" adequate for teaching is already developed. But it is clear that in many schools today relations between teachers and students are not all they should or could be. Part of the problem is that teacher education programs have never paid sufficient attention to the development of interpersonal interactions skills. The assumption in this text is that teachers can learn to be more effective in their interpersonal relations and that development of specific skills will improve teacher performance in interpersonal relations.

A second problem is that our perceptions of ourselves and our actual behavior may differ. There is ample evidence that although student teachers in physical education see themselves as interested and concerned, they actually interact with students in a negative manner (Hughley 1973, Rife 1973).

Fortunately, there is also ample evidence that teachers can change, can adjust their own teaching behavior so that it is more congruent with their images of themselves as caring, humane teachers. This is especially true of their abilities to change their interaction styles from negative and corrective to positive (Siedentop 1981). They have also been shown to be capable of changing seemingly permanent behavioral characteristics such as their enthusiasm (Rolider 1979). These changes were accomplished primarily by bringing to the attention of the teacher his or her behavior, as revealed by systematic observation, providing helpful hints about how and what to change, and continuing the observations to provide regular feedback about the degree to which they were changing. It does work! You can change your own teaching behavior with just a little help and, most of all, by really wanting to do it!

A third problem is that a person may be perfectly well integrated in his or her own personality and still not help students grow. A teacher has an impact on students, and there is no reasonable way to judge teaching without focusing on that impact. This problem is compounded by the fact that adult perceptions of what constitutes good interpersonal relations may differ considerably from student perceptions. Each of us has a concept of what an ideal teacher should be, but that idea may be based on factors that students would consider irrelevant to their needs.

Interpersonal interactions are approached here on the assumption that there are skills and techniques that can be learned and will help to make a teacher a more effective person. I do not claim that the skills outlined in this chapter represent all there is to know about interpersonal relations, nor is it suggested that the sum of the skills presented here equals a totally effective teacher. Much is not understood about the specifics of human interactions. What are presented here are some "tools of the trade" for improving basic abilities in the interpersonal relations area.

Be Consistent in Your Interactions

I hope that this entire text will help teachers become effective, positive interactors. An important corollary to that development is that the positive interaction be perceived by the student as sincere and caring. Interactions will have a detrimental effect if they are perceived to be phony. Many teachers experience difficulty when first learning how to interact positively. Their repertoire of positive interaction modes is limited, and they sometimes feel phony and uncomfortable due to the newness of the approach and their limited capability. Not all aspects of sincerity can be pinpointed, but certain aspects of interactions do indicate that they are sincere or phony. One such aspect is the consistency of interactions.

Suppose, for example, that a student attempts a comic stunt in a gymnastics lesson or does a trick shot in a basketball lesson and you show some approval in the form of laughing and smiling. The next day the student tries the same stunt or another trick shot, and you frown and express disapproval. Has the student changed? What is the message he or she receives? Will the student perceive you to be sincere? Probably not! Nothing is potentially more devastating to your relations with students than inconsistency. Students are very sensitive to inconsistency, and in their developing value systems inconsistent treatment from adults ranks among the worst of all sins.

To be consistent, you must do two things. First, you must give some thought to the behaviors you want to approve, the behaviors you want to ignore, and the behaviors you want to desist. It might be helpful for you to list the general classes of behavior that you would put in each of these categories. Once you know how you want to react to certain classes of behavior, you can monitor your performance simply by being aware of what class of behavior you are reacting to.

Consistency has yet another meaning. Do you treat all students similarly? If you seem to favor some students by interacting differently with them than with others, you will be considered insincere. This does not mean that all students should be treated the same. Nor does it mean that you won't find yourself liking some students better than others. It does mean that in each specific behavior category all students should be treated similarly unless you discuss with the class the reasons for differential treatment. Is it all right for one student to try trick stunts, but not for another? For one student to swear, but not another? If you interact differently in a single behavior category with various students, you will probably get some adverse reactions unless you take the time to explain why you are operating that way. If students are provided with a reasonable explanation they are usually quite willing to tolerate differential treatment, but if they think you just don't act consistently you cannot expect your interactions to be effective.

Direct Interactions Toward Significant Student Behavior

A warm, sincere interaction based on a trivial aspect of student behavior may be perceived as phony. In terms of developing interpersonal relations, an interaction will be most effective when it is based on a significant aspect of the student's behavior. How do you determine what are significant student behaviors? One way is to examine what behaviors are considered valuable in the educational context. You might decide that following instructions, making an effort, completing a difficult task, and other such matters are of significance. The problem with this approach is that it reflects your view and that of the educational establishment. Although it is important that you attempt to have the student view these behaviors as significant, that is more a task of instruction than of developing interpersonal relations. For purposes of interpersonal relations, the significance of student behavior should be viewed more from the student's point of view. If you want to relate better on a personal basis, the way to do it is to interact with students on matters that are important to them.

The development of this aspect of sincerity requires a keen and sensitive eye. There is no need to guess at what students consider important. Most often you can learn what students value by watching them. What do they do on the playground or at lunchtime? What do they read on their own? What do they like to talk about? What group of students does a student relate most to, and what characterizes this group? This approach means meeting students on their own turf and interacting with them about whatever interests them most.

If you interact with students on the basis of their interests, you will begin to develop good personal relationships with them. Having done this, you can begin to extend the interaction into areas that you consider significant, and you can do so assured that your efforts will be perceived as sincere. I am not suggesting that you "con" students. Interaction is a matter of give and take. It is important that you interact with students in terms of what they value, but it is also important that you attempt to help them appreciate what you consider significant. It is a matter of timing and trust. You must start on their terms and develop the relationship so that eventually you can help them come to know what you consider significant in the educational environment. Without making any effort to interact with students to find out what they consider important at their particular stage of development, teachers expect students to adopt the values of the adult education establishment. The teacher who is considered sincere and caring is often the one who takes the time to learn what a student values and to interact with the student about the activity or interest.

Match the Interaction to the Task

Matching interactions to the task is another aspect of interaction skill that contributes to the degree to which the interaction is perceived as sincere. An extravagant, flowery interaction based on a relatively minor student behavior or task will be considered phony, especially if the excessive manner is applied to several students. A student who is told, "That's the best headstand I've ever seen," will probably be suspicious. The student will be even more suspicious if he or she hears you react similarly to a headstand performed by another student.

Likewise, there are times when understated interactions can adversely affect the degree to which students perceive you to be sincere. If a student struggles with a difficult, risky stunt (such as a flip on a trampoline) for some time, and when he or she finally achieves it your reaction is merely "Way to go," the student may wonder how much you really care about his or her development.

This chapter makes it seem that developing effective interaction skills that are considered sincere and caring by students is a difficult and touchy business. It appears that way because that's the way it is! Being perceived as a sincere and therefore effective interactor with students is no easy task. There are indeed some teachers who do not have to develop this skill, for they have it well developed when they start teaching. They are fortunate. They have had experiences that have helped them become positive people and sensitive to the interests and values of those with whom they work. But many of us have not had sufficient opportunity to develop this skill to its fullest potential.

A single thread runs through these first three suggestions for implementing interpersonal relations: all three depend on a sensitivity to students. Just as directing interactions toward significant student behavior depends on what students feel is significant, interacting in a manner commensurate with the

---

The Elitist Teacher, or
"Don't Bother Me with Any Average Kids"

Situation. A teacher interacts well with the highly skilled students in class, but interacts with poorly skilled students only to correct errors. Observations show that the teacher interacts in terms of feelings and nonschool factors only with the 7 most highly skilled students (there are 26 in the class). Interactions directed at these 7 students account for 63 percent of all interactions in the class.

Result. Seven students perceive the teacher to be a sincere, caring teacher. Nineteen students have no feeling about the teacher or else doubt his or her sincerity. They feel no sense of personal relationship with the teacher.

Analysis. The concentration of interactions with so few students shows a real imbalance. The teacher will be viewed as one who has no time for anybody but the best students, or as one who plays favorites. The students who are not highly skilled will not react favorably to the teacher and will learn that physical education is a good activity only for highly skilled people.

Prescription. Goals should be set to disperse interactions over a more representative group of students. Interactions with low-skill students should be more positive, and there should be interactions based on nonschool factors and on feelings.

task depends on what students feel is the importance of the task. This is yet another area where the imposition of adult value systems sometimes works against effective interpersonal relations. What seems a small task to you might be an enormously significant accomplishment for a student. Some things you consider to be important might be shrugged off by students.

A good guideline is to have interactions relate precisely to the task. This can be accomplished by having the interaction contain specific information. If you say, "That's a fine headstand, your feet are very straight," you run little danger of being too flamboyant or not concerned enough. The specific information tells the student not only that you appreciate the skill demonstrated but also that you cared enough about the performance to watch it carefully, as shown by the fact that you can respond to some detail of the performance. This kind of interaction combined with a nonverbal component such as a smile or a pat on the back can be potent without being effusive.

Interact with Students on the Basis of Nonschool Factors

The term *interpersonal* includes the word *personal*, and thus suggests that good interpersonal relations must be based on personal factors. Teachers often go for weeks and months without interacting with a student on any basis other than school-related matters. Such teachers know the student only as a student and not as a person.

It is particularly difficult for teaching interns to interact with students on a personal basis, because the teaching experience is of short duration and there is no reason to expect that there will be continued contact with the students. Nevertheless, beginning effort can be made. It is unreasonable to suggest that a physical education teacher will really get to know all the students with whom he or she comes in contact during the teaching day. Unlike the classroom teacher in the elementary school, the physical educator sees a different group of students each hour. This does not allow him or her to get to know the students intimately. There are too many students, and the physical educator sees them too seldom. At the high school level, the physical educator has the same opportunity as other teachers, but depends somewhat on how often the student is required to take physical education in order to graduate. Regardless of the institutional factors that encourage or prevent the development of closer personal relationships, you can begin to develop a capacity to interact with students by occasionally doing so strictly on the basis of nonschool factors.

The development of strong interpersonal relations is a two-way street. The teacher cannot do it unless the student is willing. The student will be much more likely to enter into that kind of relationship if the teacher is perceived to be someone who cares about him or her in a personal as well as an educational sense. This kind of perception is encouraged when teachers interact with students on nonschool matters. The interaction can be a simple reaction such as commenting on a new dress, or it can be a teacher-initiated contact such as asking the student about experiences during a vacation period. Such an interaction provides the teacher with information that can be used for further interactions, and it lets the student know that the teacher cares about what he or she does outside class.

It should be remembered, however, that these personal interactions should, for the most part, take place outside of the main academic time. Chapter 3 indicated clearly that effective teachers have high rates of academic feedback, a strong academic focus, and high proportions of learning time. Although this does not mean a teacher should avoid personal interactions during a lesson, it does suggest that they should take place before the lesson, during lull moments, and after the lesson. If they are infused into the lesson, they should not detract from the mainly academic focus.

This aspect of interpersonal relations requires sensitivity. It would be inappropriate for a teacher to begin to interact with students on very intimate nonschool factors when he or she doesn't really know them all that well. It is far better to begin by relating to a nonschool factor that is reasonably unimportant. The idea is to let the student know that the teacher cares about his or her outside life as well as his or her student life. Once this message is received clearly, then the scope of the interaction can gradually be broadened into more sensitive and important areas.

Sustain Enthusiasm to Improve Instruction and Interpersonal Relations

Few would argue with the assertion that enthusiasm in teaching is important. A teacher's enthusiasm about the subject matter, the students, and the act of learning provides an important vehicle for communicating many of the messages listed earlier in this chapter. A teacher can teach volleyball in a manner that communicates to students that this activity is OK, a drag, a really enjoyable recreational activity, or an enjoyable, highly skilled competitive sport. Part of the message is communicated directly through talk about the activity and through the instruction itself, but much of it is communicated through the teacher's enthusiasm or lack thereof.

Research indicates that enthusiasm is an important quality in teaching (Rosenshine 1970). Studies that have manipulated enthusiasm as an independent variable or correlated it as it occurred naturally have shown that it is often strongly related to student performance. Gage (1972) feels that the evidence is sufficiently strong to discuss enthusiasm as one of the very few characteristics of teaching that can be identified as important in helping students achieve.

There are three fairly distinct areas toward which your enthusiasm can and should be directed. First, you should be enthusiastic about the content of what you are teaching, be it basketball, gymnastics, or movement education. Second, you should be enthusiastic about learning or improving in the skills that comprise the activity. Third, you should be enthusiastic about your students, be they highly skilled or awkward.

You might reasonably interject at this point that it is easy to discuss enthu-

On Smiling!

Do physical education teachers smile often? Does it matter? The answers seem to be "No, they don't smile much" and "Yes, it can matter a great deal."

Amos Rolider (1979) experimented with physical education teacher enthusiasm. He asked 1,000 students, over 100 teachers, and several teacher education experts to list the main characteristics of an enthusiastic physical education teacher. Most of those characteristics are described in this chapter. One of the characteristics most often mentioned by students was that enthusiastic teachers smiled a lot.

Rolider then experimented with physical education teachers. Through a workshop in which they discussed, role played, and videotaped, the teachers learned how to use their nonverbal gestures to convey enthusiasm and to smile more often. They then went out and tried to do more of this in their teaching. Systematic observation revealed that they had indeed improved (increased) their nonverbal gesturing and their smiling. Did the students pick it up? Yes, indeed they did. A questionnaire given to students after each class session had several questions about enthusiasm imbedded within it. When the teachers smiled more often, the students rated them as more enthusiastic.

Now, smiling isn't all that hard, is it? It could be that a little more of it in your own teaching will convey to students the enthusiasm you actually feel for them and for teaching!

siasm and suggest its importance, but it is difficult to describe it precisely. You're right. A major problem with the research just cited is that there was no consistent definition of the components of "enthusiastic teaching." Enthusiasm is one of those qualities that each of us has some ideas about, but that none of us can define completely and adequately. Several approaches to enthusiasm are suggested here.

One aspect of enthusiasm is certainly a positive teaching style. Focusing on appropriate student behavior and providing more feedback on what students are doing right help create a learning climate that is much more enthusiastic. Positive approaches to behavior interactions are discussed in Chapter 5, and positive feedback is discussed in Chapter 11. A well-developed positive interaction style that includes a variety of interaction modes is without question the primary component of enthusiastic teaching.

A second component of enthusiastic teaching is the "message" that you send out about the activities you teach. Do you take part in any of the activities? Do your students perceive you to like the activities? Have they ever seen you participate? A great deal of enthusiasm can be generated through your participation. If you enjoy activity, then participate with your students, and the enjoyment will be more meaningful than it would be if you only talked about the activity.

A third component of enthusiasm relates to starting points and change points in a lesson. A quick start and changes made with eagerness and anticipation help promote general enthusiasm for what is going on. If you drag in several minutes late and dally around before getting the lesson started, your students will rightly perceive that you are not all that thrilled by the entire venture.

A fourth component of enthusiasm is your expectations for students. If you expect them, as a group or individually, to perform poorly or learn very little, it is likely that they will be dull and listless. If you expect them to have no fun, they may well have none. The evidence is abundant that teacher expectations are important in setting gymnasium climate. If you expect students to learn and have fun while they are doing it, it is more likely that they will do so.

A fifth component of enthusiasm is found in the target of your enthusiasm. It is perfectly legitimate to be enthusiastic about good performance, and students who perform well should know that you feel enthusiastic about their skill. But a portion of your enthusiasm should also be directed at learning. Performance is always relative and is often judged against a group norm. Those who can spike, do flips, swim fast, and play good defense will always receive their share of attention from teachers and peers. It is less likely that someone who, although still far from the top in performance, has improved will receive the same kind of attention. This kind of student should know that you are enthusiastic about the improvement (that is, the learning) and that you value that improvement and recognize its importance.

This section on enthusiasm is not meant to convey the notion that you approach class each day as if you were selling used cars. Phoniness and a façade of enthusiasm will be detected quickly by students. The quality of enthusiasm that is being discussed only rarely involves a rah-rah approach to teaching. Such an approach is very hard to sustain from day to day, and most of us simply don't feel that way about what we do. Enthusiasm can be as quiet as a kind word and a nod of the head. It can be as subtle as always being on time. It can be as loose as a game of pick-up basketball. What is being discussed is an approach to teaching that has positive expectations and gives evidence of those expectations through interactions with students.

Base Interpersonal Interactions on Students' Feelings and Emotions

Good interpersonal relations between teachers and students cannot be based solely on the regular curriculum. It is my view that learning skills is the most important aspect of a physical education curriculum, that skill in sport, gymnastics, dance, and other activities remains the major goal of physical education. But it need not be the only goal. A teacher can influence the whole life of a student, but this won't happen if the teacher does not establish a lasting relationship on a personal basis, and the latter cannot be done unless there is some interaction based on the student's feelings.

Many leading proponents of the humanistic education movement have emphasized the need to shift from an exclusive emphasis on the regular curriculum to an equal emphasis on the affective content of what transpires in schools and in the lives of students (Weinstein and Fantini 1971). This is another aspect of teaching that is usually taken for granted; it is contended that when a teacher is sensitive and cares about students, emphasis on student feelings will take care of itself. This may not be so. One survey indicated that teachers in the study devoted less than one-half of 1 percent of their time to student feelings (Myrick 1969).

The goal here is to interact with students in a manner that enables them to feel free to express their feelings and perceive you as someone who sincerely cares about those feelings. The major skill to be developed is that of interacting positively with students who express feelings in one manner or another. Often feelings are expressed nonverbally. A child jumps up and down excitedly. An older student has a look of satisfaction after winning a match. Another student shows signs of accomplishment after making a difficult physical effort. Teachers must look for such nonverbal cues and show approval of the underlying feelings. Following are examples of such interactions:

I'm glad you feel good about your progress.
It feels good to win, doesn't it?
I'm glad you feel happy about getting that stunt right.
I think it's fine that you feel satisfied with the good effort you made.
I'm really pleased that you get a feeling of satisfaction from helping those students.

Notice that in each case the interaction is based directly on the feelings underlying the behavior in question. The behavior is indirectly referred to, but the object of the approval is the feeling.

Many students experience great difficulty verbalizing their feelings. Students should be encouraged to express feelings. More importantly, they should be encouraged to express positive feelings. The more a student can learn to express his or her positive emotional reactions openly, the more that student will appreciate the positive aspects of affective behavior. It is important that students learn to express their feelings in different situations. It may be one matter for a student to express a feeling in private with you but an entirely different matter for that student to express the same feeling about the same matter in front of his or her peers. Appropriate interactions might be "I'm pleased that you feel you can share that with me," or "I'm pleased that you shared that feeling with us."

Encouraging openness will bring increased expression of positive and negative feelings. Even though an emphasis on positive feelings is most important, this does not mean that all negative feelings will disappear. Students feel badly when they are defeated. They feel anxious when called on to perform in front of their peers. They feel angry if they are inadvertently slighted in some way. They feel frightened when learning a skill that involves physical risk.

In dealing with positive feelings, your goal is to accept and encourage those feelings in the hope of increasing the experience of positive feelings and the ability to share them with others. In dealing with negative feelings, your goal is to alleviate and relieve the feeling. This is not an easy task, because many students who experience anxiety or fear do so because of previous experiences, and these just cannot be erased. Nonetheless, the goal should be to convey to the student your acceptance of the negative feelings and your willingness to help him or her overcome this feeling.

In cases where student anxiety and fear are related to the educational environment, the instructional sequence can be arranged so that students ease into difficult learning situations gradually, thus reducing the chances that the situation will cause the student to feel anxious or fearful. Above all, it is imperative that no student be ridiculed for feelings of fear or anxiety. When a student is ridiculed or made fun of due to his or her fear or anxiety, there is a high probability that the student will come to really dislike the environment (the physical education class) in which such punishment occurred.

One word of caution: sometimes, when students are encouraged to be open in the expression of feelings and emotions, one or two students will be encouraged by the attention they receive to verbalize endlessly about their feelings, to the point where one may suspect that they are reporting feelings that are trivial or irrelevant or even inaccurate. This is fairly common among younger students, and it is not confined to the expression of feelings. For example, if you encourage children to help one another there will inevitably be several children who, in order to get attention, will try to "help" even when the situation does not call for it. Students who overreact in this manner should not be punished or even considered in a bad light. They have not yet learned to distinguish between situations in which it might be legitimate to "help" or express feelings and those where it is uncalled for. The best strategy is to ignore all instances where you feel the expression of feeling is inappropriate (see the discussion of extinction strategy in Chapter 6). If you encourage the appropriate expression of feelings, students will quickly learn to differentiate between the two. But if you penalize an inappropriate expression of feelings through ridicule or some other form of social punishment, the student will almost certainly be less likely to express any feeling.

Interpersonal Interaction as Communication

Another useful perspective from which to view teacher interaction skills is that of communication. When communication takes place, it always has three primary elements. First, there is a **sender**, the person who communicates the message. Second, there is the **receiver**, the person to whom the message is directed and who will later respond to it. Third, there is the nature of the **message** itself. The message can be sent in words, expressions, or gestures, or in some combination of each. Obviously, it is important for a teacher to be an effective communicator. When messages are not sent clearly—when there is **miscommunication**—the result is often confusion and misunderstanding. Such situations often lead to trouble, both for the teacher and the students.

More specifically for purposes of this chapter, teachers need to communicate certain kinds of messages effectively if a humane educational setting is to develop. Messages such as "I value you as a person," "I want you to succeed in here," and "I accept you" are crucial for establishing a humane climate. If teachers do not pay attention to these messages and are not aware of their own interpersonal communications, no such climate is likely to develop. Effective, humane communicating is not likely just to happen by chance. Nor, indeed, does it occur just because a teacher wants it to occur. Skills are involved, which need to be developed and then systematically used if the goal of a humane physical education setting is to be achieved.

Sending Skills

Effective communication exists when a listener interprets a message in the way the sender intended. The skills described in this section can ensure clearer, more accurate sending.

1. *Take ownership for what you say.* It is important that people communicating messages speak for themselves. Using pronouns such as *I, me, my,* and *mine* help to establish ownership. Beginning a message with "I think," "I feel," or "I need" identifies clearly whose idea, feeling, or need that will be expressed in the message. Vagueness occurs when messages are sent by saying, "Someone thinks . . ." or "Wouldn't it be nice if . . ." When you take ownership for what you say, you invite a sense of trust and convey a sense of openness to those who receive the message.

2. *Describe rather than judge.* Messages sent to students should describe the content of the message clearly but should do so without being judgmental. Being judgmental stifles communication. If you persist in being judgmental about students, you will be unlikely to affect them in ways that contribute to their personal growth. For example, telling a student he or she is a terrible defensive player (a judgment) has a different effect from telling the student that he or she has trouble executing defensive strategies (a description).

3. *Try to incorporate the student's viewpoint.* Each of us tends to see the world from a limited perspective—our own. If you are trying to influence the personal growth of students, it is important that you begin to try to take their perspectives into account when sending messages to them. To what are they sensitive? How do they react to certain things? What is their nonverbal behavior like? What are the major forces that

affect their perspectives? The more the sender (the teacher) can take such factors into account, the more likely are the messages to be received well.

4. *Be sensitive to feelings.* It is very helpful to be sensitive to feelings, both your own and those of the receiver. Each of us feels differently from day to day and often differently within the same day. Those feelings quite often are expressed in our messages, *even though they may have nothing to do with the communication.* For example, you may have had some disappointment. You then communicate with some students during the next class. The students may receive a message that shows that disappointment even though it had nothing to do with them! If you are more aware of your own feelings, they are less likely to intrude into your messages. The same sensitivity and awareness should be applied to messages you receive from students. They too have factors that affect their lives and get mixed up in their messages.

5. *Be aware of your nonverbal cues.* It is virtually impossible not to emit nonverbal behavior and to have that behavior become part of the message you are sending. Often the receiver reacts more to the nonverbal components of the message than to what the words themselves convey. Effective communicators tend to have direct eye contact. They look at the person(s) to whom they are talking. Their facial expressions tend to express messages that are similar to those expressed in the words they are saying. Body movement and alignment also communicate messages. A relaxed position with a slight lean toward the listener conveys warmth. A rigid body position tends to stifle communication. Far too few of us are sensitive to the messages we send through our posture and body movements.

Receiving Skills

Although each of us no doubt could stand to improve our sending skills, it is in the area of receiving skills that most of us are really in need of practice and improvement. More communication is probably ruined by inadequate receiving skills than by inadequate sending skills. Far too few of us are good listeners! Skilled communicators need to be as involved in listening as they are in sending. Some important skills for improving your receiving skills are described as follows.

1. *Paraphrase to clarify messages received.* The term **paraphrasing** means restating, in your own words, what the sender has just said to you, including what you perceive to be the feeling and the meaning conveyed by the sender in the message. For example, a teacher might say to a student, "Am I correct in thinking that you are feeling a lack of confidence about the skills in this unit?" Paraphrasing has several benefits. First, it helps to get the message straight. Second, it provides good feedback to the sender concerning how clearly the message was delivered. Third, it makes absolutely clear to the sender that you were listening. Fourth, paraphrasing helps you to gain insight into the perspective of the person from whom the message was delivered, helps you to see his or her point of view.

2. *Use effective attending skills.* When you listen to someone, you emit a lot of behavior, particularly nonverbal behavior. Eye contact, posture, body alignment, and facial expressions all contribute to your attending behavior. Obviously, these behaviors tell the sender how you are attending and from this the sender tends to infer how much you care about the message.

3. *Attend to the nonverbal cues of the sender.* Often a message in words needs to be interpreted in terms of the nonverbal cues that accompany the words. Nonverbal cues give hints about the involvement of the sender, how much emotion is involved, how much it means, how angry or happy the sender might be, and a host of other possibilities. Just listening to the words, and even the tone of voice, is seldom sufficient to gauge the full meaning of the message. The nonverbal cues add the extra dimension and allow you to interpret the full meaning of the message more accurately. For example, a student might send a verbal message that he or she does not want to be on a particular team, but the emotion and stress the student displays nonverbally might cause you to consider the message much more seriously than if no emotion were shown.

4. *Take into account your own feelings and how they affect the message.* If you are nervous or preoccupied, you may not hear all of a message. If you are angry or frustrated with the sender, you may infer incorrect meanings from the message. Misinterpretation is likely when the receiver is emotionally involved with the situation or is distracted, thinking about other things. To avoid this, the sender must be sensitive to his or her own feelings, especially as they apply to the message conveyed. For example, if you are having a bad day for some reason, you might want to paraphrase more often just to make sure that you are responding correctly to student messages rather than reacting incorrectly because of your own concerns.

Roadblocks to Communication

Communications experts and counseling experts agree that efforts toward communication are often blocked and thwarted by responses from one party that tend to produce negative reactions in the other party. Sometimes the intensity and severity of the block is such that communication is completely shut off. At other times, milder blocks simply slow down communication and inhibit one or both of the communicating parties. Teachers sometimes slow down or completely block communication between themselves and students, often without even being aware of what they are doing. A sensitivity to these blocks is the first step toward eliminating them from your interaction style. Here are some examples of the more common blocks (Johnson 1981).

1. *Ordering, commanding, and directing:* "You quit complaining and just pay attention!"
2. *Threatening:* "If you guys don't stop messing around, I'm going to have to put you on report!"
3. *Preaching or moralizing:* "You girls know better than to behave that way!" "Is that any way to behave?"
4. *Offering advice or solutions prematurely:* "You'll just have to have your mother help you to get your gym clothes ready on time."
5. *Judging, criticizing, and blaming:* "You are just lazy!" "You two are always causing problems in this class!"
6. *Stereotyping or labeling:* "Don't act like a fourth-grader!" "You are acting like a baby!"
7. *Interrogating or cross examining:* "What in the world did you do that for?" "How come you didn't ask me first?"
8. *Distracting or diverting:* "Why don't we talk about it some other time?" "Now just isn't the time to discuss it."

Each of us has no doubt blocked communication by using these kinds of responses with students. If your goal is to communicate more clearly and effectively and through communication to help students to reach effective solutions to problems, then you should avoid such blocks. To avoid responding in this way takes patience and sensitivity—and the skill to eliminate such responses from your interaction patterns.

The Helping Relationship

Effective communication and interpersonal interaction skill used in the service of students is often referred to as the **helping relationship**. To help means to facilitate, not to solve problems for students but to help them to learn to solve their own problems. The goals of the helping relationship in educational settings should be to create learning conditions within which students learn to behave appropriately, to mature, to grow in independence, to approach and solve problems rather than to avoid them, and to communicate effectively with others in the setting.

The helping relationship was developed for counseling and therapeutic goals in the human services professions. But the helping approach is also applicable to educational settings where teachers are often called on by students to help to solve problems. There is widespread agreement concerning the four major conditions for effective helping: they are empathy, respect, warmth, and genuineness.

Empathy, respect, warmth, and genuineness are not a set of abstractions that are mystically developed by some teachers and not others. In counselor education, these characteristics have for years been approached as if they were skills to be learned, developed, practiced, refined, and maintained. Clearly, it is not enough just to want to be an effective helper, just as it is not enough to want to be a good basketball player or a good teacher: skills must be learned, practiced, and refined.

1. *Empathy:* The term **empathy** refers to the skill of perceiving a problem from the viewpoint of the person who has the problem. Empathy is not sympathy. When a teacher empathizes, he or she does not feel sorry for the student. Rather, the teacher tries to see the problem through the eyes of the student, understanding it from the student's perspective. Empathy is necessary for accurate detection of the problem, without which no useful solution is likely to arise.

2. *Respect:* In the helping relationship, **respect** means that the helper behaves as though he or she believes the student can solve the problem, that the student has it within him- or herself to achieve a satisfactory solution. Few problems are solved by imposing a solution on the person who faces the problem. Respect means supporting the student as he or she attempts to arrive at a solution.

3. *Genuineness:* The dimension of **genuineness** refers to the honesty with which the helper deals with the student. How a teacher talks and behaves needs to be honest and as congruent as possible with what the teacher really believes. Students become quite skilled at detecting phoniness in teachers. When a student suspects a teacher to be acting in a phony way, the chances of further communication are seriously impaired.

4. *Warmth:* The characteristic of **warmth** in the helping relationship is quite similar to the manner in which that term has been used to describe the classroom climate. Warmth is typically a result of consistent, positive interactions, both in the academic and behavioral aspects of the educational setting. Personal behavior such as smiling, enthusiasm, eye contact, and other such nonverbal behaviors also contribute to the establishment of a warm relationship between teachers and students.

CHAPTER 8

Maintaining a Humane Physical Education

This bias toward humanism allows me to define the good teacher—the effective teacher—as not only a teacher whose students learn but whose students perceive themselves to be learning (the student not only improves, but he also sees himself as improving) and whose students feel good about that learning experience.

Donald Hellison, *Humanism in Physical Education* (1973)

CHAPTER OBJECTIVES

To distinguish between educational and therapeutic settings

To help you develop your own view of the humanizing contribution of physical education

To explain how sex stereotyping occurs in physical education

To describe methods through which teachers can promote sex equity

To describe methods through which teachers can promote racial equity

To characterize teacher behaviors that promote racial stereotypes

To suggest ways in which teachers can promote cultural pluralism

To define and provide examples of student self-growth skills

To describe methods through which teachers can enhance student self-growth

To describe methods through which teachers can promote responsible student behavior

What does it mean to be humane? What does it mean to be a humanist? Does anybody sane really set out to be *in*humane? The answers to the first two questions would occupy hours of debate, but the answer to the third is clearly no. People who actually intend to be inhumane are often defined by society as "mentally ill," which implies that nobody in his or her right mind would actually *intend* to be inhumane.

Yet there are as many different versions of what it means to teach humanistically as there are humanistic teachers. And simply labeling oneself as a humanistic teacher is no guarantee of anything. It is beyond the purpose and scope of this text to enter into an involved philosophical discussion of humanistic teaching or what constitutes a humanistic physical education program; for a discussion of humanistic physical education, see Siedentop (1980). Generally, most educators agree that educational experiences should facilitate growth in students as individuals and in the society to which they belong. That is, humanistic teaching has both an *individual* focus and a *collective* focus. Humanistic teaching is concerned with the optimal development of the individual student, as well as with the development of the society within which the student lives and grows. To those ends, humanistic educational settings should be challenging, growth enhancing, supportive, and free from threat and coercion.

Educational and Therapeutic Settings

It is important to distinguish between settings whose primary goals are in academic achievement, broadly conceived, and those settings whose primary goals are in individual self-growth. I refer to settings in which achievement goals are primary as *educational* settings. I refer to settings in which self-growth and self-development goals are primary as *therapeutic* settings. This, of course, is not to suggest that educational settings can't or don't achieve goals in the affective domain. Nor, indeed, is it to suggest that therapeutic settings can't or don't achieve goals in the academic areas. But a distinction can be based on the *primary* goals of the setting—and the distinction is an important one.

It is important for teachers to be quite clear as to whether their goals are primarily educational or primarily therapeutic. Likewise, it is important that schools make clear what their positions are relative to this distinction. For most of the 1960s and 1970s, many educators in this society moved toward a therapeutic model, especially for the elementary school; there is less evidence that parents and communities fully supported such a move. It is important that a teacher's goals be reasonably consistent with the goals of the school and community in which he or she teaches.

In Chapter 3, a review of research indicated that teachers who were most effective in achieving academic goals for students also tended to be most effective in reaching attitudinal and self-growth goals for students. It needs to be consistently emphasized that having academic growth and achievement as a primary goal does not rule out the possibility of achieving important gains in affective goals. Indeed, a strong argument can be made that achievement in academic areas enhances self-concept and self-growth and, when done within a nurturing educational climate, leads to positive attitudes toward self, school, and the subject matter being studied. The point is that this is not an either/or situation. The effective teacher can achieve goals in each domain.

However, there is some reason to question whether goals in each domain can be achieved as well if therapeutic goals are made primary. When self-growth and self-development are sought after, independent of academic achievement, the risk is high that academic performance will suffer. And there is reason to question seriously the humaneness of sending students into the real world without having reached substantial academic goals.

Developing People as Players—Our Primary Humanizing Contribution

We should never lose sight of the fact that our primary contribution to the humanistic education of students we serve is to help them to gain skill in and an affection for our subject matter—physically active motor play. Although it may not be apparent on first examination, a strong and compelling argument can be made for the notion that helping students to be good at and to like basketball, gymnastics, rapelling, diving, skiing, running, and dancing is a

---

Learning Interpersonal Skills, or "Are Your Listening Skills as Good as Your Dribbling Skills?"

Physical educators understand what needs to be done for skill development—understand what is to be done, practice it, get some feedback, keep practicing it, have success with it, and so on. This text has made the argument that teaching skills (feedback, reinforcing appropriate student behavior, asking questions properly) should be approached in the same way. Can interpersonal relations skills also be viewed in this way? Yes. Not only do I consider that possible, but so does David Johnson, whose book *Reaching Out: Interpersonal Effectiveness and Self-Actualization* (1981) is one of the leading books on developing interpersonal relations. Johnson suggests the following steps for learning and improving interpersonal skills. They should sound familiar simply because they are nearly identical to the steps suggested in Chapter 1.

1. Understand why the skill is important and how it will be of value to you.
2. Understand what the skill is and the component behaviors you have to engage in to perform the skill.
3. Find situations in which you can practice the skill.
4. Get someone to watch you and tell you how well you are performing.
5. Keep practicing.
6. Load your practice toward success.
7. Get friends to encourage you to use the skill.
8. Practice until it feels real. [Johnson 1981, pp. 11–12]

There is no mystery about becoming better skilled in interpersonal relations, just as there is no mystery about improving your tennis game. The skills must be learned, practiced, and perfected until they are virtually automatic.

strongly *humanistic* outcome. To teach people how to play and to want to play is to enhance their potential for humanistic experience. To develop a society of players and a culture devoted to play is to contribute to a civilized, humanistic future.

In *The Joy of Sports* (1976), Michael Novak has offered the most complete argument for the humanistic nature of physical education outcomes.

> Sports are the highest products of civilization and the most accessible, lived, experiential sources of the civilizing spirit. In sports, law was born and also liberty, and the nexus of their interrelation. In sports, honesty and excellence are caught, captured, nourished, held in trust for the generations. Without rules, there are no sports. Without limits, a sport cannot begin to exist. Within the rules, within the limits, freedom is given form. Play is the essence of freedom: "The free play of ideas." Play is the fundamental structure of the human mind. Of the body, too. The mind at play, the body at play—these furnish our imaginations with the highest achievements of beauty the human race attains. [p. 43]

The basic argument to be derived from such an analysis is that education is humanizing if it is carried out within a challenging, nurturant setting that is free from threat and coercion. Thus, the teacher who strives for primarily academic goals, within a warm, nurturant climate, is involved in a humanistic enterprise. So too, perhaps, is the teacher whose main goals are therapeutic rather than educational. But the tendency in recent years has been to label the therapeutic orientation as humanistic and to assume that humanistic goals cannot be achieved in settings where primarily academic goals are sought. This latter argument simply does not ring true if one considers humanism in the broad sense of fostering useful human development.

Therefore, the general view taken here is that physical educators who help students to develop skill, to understand play, and to develop an affection for play forms such as games, sports, and dance are contributing to humanistic outcomes. If they teach so that the educational climate is challenging and nurturing, then the humanistic nature of their teaching is further enhanced, and they have every right to describe what they do as humanistic physical education.

Promoting Human Relations in Physical Education

Although teaching the subject matter of physical education in a challenging and nurturant climate can be considered to be the primary feature of humanistic physical education, it is most certainly not the only feature. There are many ways in which physical educators can promote good human relations in physical education and, in so doing, contribute both to the development of humane individuals and the growth of a humane society. The subject matter and its concerns may be the direct and primary focus of teaching, but there are many, many other lessons to be learned within physical education. Many of these other lessons are learned indirectly, as a result of the manner in which the teacher interacts with students, helps the students to interact with one another, and directly or indirectly espouses or reinforces values and behaviors associated with issues such as sex equity, racial equity, ethical behavior, sportsmanship, cultural pluralism, and human relations in general.

As indicated in Chapter 7, the physical education program and, more specifically, the physical education teacher send certain *messages* to students. These messages are sometimes sent directly through direct verbal reference or through calling the attention of students directly to an issue. But, more often than not, the messages are conveyed indirectly through the behavior of the teacher and the manner in which the teacher reacts to the behavior of students. The purpose of the remainder of this chapter is to call to your attention some important kinds of messages that teachers convey to students, particularly messages that, if properly sent, can contribute to the development of humanistic individuals and a more humanistic society. The basic assumption underlying what follows is that specific humanistic goals for teaching can and should be developed and approached systematically in a manner similar to which one approaches the achievement of subject matter goals. You may disagree somewhat with the goals chosen to illustrate humanistic teaching in physical education, but the basic thing is to understand that you will be teaching values and value-laden behavior to your students. At the very least, you ought to understand what values you are promoting and then try to make your teaching as consistent as possible with the value structure you want to convey to students.

Sex Equity

Sport and physical education do not have good records in terms of discrimination against women. Many of the limiting stereotypes that girls learn about themselves are learned on playgrounds and in game situations. For many years, girls and women were systematically denied the opportunity to learn and to participate in physical education. In other cases, the opportunities were restricted to those thought to be *appropriate*. Girls and women who dared to venture beyond what was considered to be appropriate did so at some risk.

> This risk involved is, of course, that associated with concepts of femininity and masculinity. Masculinity too often means tough, assertive, and hard. Femininity too often means yielding, nonassertive, and soft. Boys play football. Girls are cheerleaders. The girls' role is supportive and noncombative. Girls who step outside their prescribed roles too often are the objects of curious glances and off-color comments. The same phenomenon is true for the boy or man who participates in dance. [Siedentop, 1980, p. 213]

The segregation of girls and women in sport and physical education was specifically prohibited in Title IX of the Educational Amendments of 1972. But eliminating illegal sex segregation does not necessarily abolish sex inequity. Griffen (1981) has suggested several ways in which sex inequity is apparent in physical education teaching:

**Promoting
Human
Relations in
Physical
Education**

133

1. In team sports, boys dominate games regardless of the skill differentials between boys and girls.
2. Teachers often group students for games through public selection in which girls are typically chosen last.
3. Teachers tend to provide more academic feedback for boys than for girls.
4. When class leaders or demonstrators are chosen, they typically are boys.
5. Teachers sometimes make sex-stereotyped statements to students ("She does well for a girl." "The boys will put the mats away." "The girls will not be able to do as many pushups as the boys.")
6. Teachers seldom intervene to correct sex-stereotyped interactions among students (such as saying, "Billy, Jane doesn't run 'like a boy,' as you said. She runs like a girl who has practiced hard and is skilled.")
7. Teachers often (inadvertently many times) role model sex-stereotyped activity patterns.

These examples occur in gymnasiums everywhere. Obviously, they could be corrected if teachers would pay more attention to them and even work specifically to achieve sex equity goals. Teachers need to be aware of how they distribute their attention. They need to make sure that all students have equal opportunity to learning and playing time and that the quality of that learning and playing time is equal. And teachers need to be sensitive to the messages conveyed in their language and interactions with students. Teachers need to avoid the sex stereotyping of activities, such as labeling certain things as "girls'" activities and certain things as "boys'" activities.

The humaneness of the setting will be improved if teachers specifically try to break down sex stereotypes. This can be done in three ways: through teacher prompting, teacher interventions on student behavior, and role modeling.

One good way to break down stereotypes and promote sex equity is to offer clear, consistent messages (prompts) when opportunities arise. Teachers do not have to wait for inappropriate situations to develop. They can take the initiative and make comments that are intentionally not sex stereotyping: "Ron, Glenda is the best set-up person on your team. You ought to try to pass the ball to her as often as possible."

A second strategy is to intervene to correct student interactions that are stereotyped or to reinforce student interactions that are not stereotyped. "Jake, don't say to Tom that he throws like a girl. Girls can learn to throw just as well as boys can." "Girls can do this every bit as well as boys can." "There is no reason why the girls won't be as capable of doing this as the boys will be." "I liked the way boys and girls worked together today. It shows that you understand that the girls can learn and play in the same way as the boys."

A third strategy is role modeling. The term **role modeling** refers to exhibiting behaviors specific to a role so that students can incorporate similar patterns into their own behavioral repertoire. The potential for sex-equitable role modeling is endless: a male who participates in folk dance and obviously enjoys it, a female who competes vigorously, a male teacher who lets students know that he likes to cook (or garden or collect antiques), a female teacher who rides motorcycles (or jogs or does carpentry). All these models break down stereotypes and in so doing tend to expand the potential for the next generation to have greater freedom. It must be emphasized, however, that role modeling must be truthful. You cannot model that which you are not. Attempts to deceive students will eventually prove disastrous to your credibility.

Many strategies complement direct role modeling. Pictures of female athletes can be used to demonstrate technique or to adorn a bulletin board. Posters and pictures showing men and women participating together are useful. The concepts of sport hero or heroine can be used effectively to heighten the effects of modeling. Male and female physical educators team teaching an activity can provide a direct and important message, especially if they participate together on equal terms. The combined effect of these strategies optimizes the possibilities that students will adopt and value the attitudes and behaviors in question.

Race Equity

Many of the examples and strategies cited in the previous section apply equally to racial equity. There is no need to describe or catalog the many problems our society has had during the past several decades in trying to come to grips with equal opportunity for minority groups. The prejudices and stereotypes in this area are old and deeply ingrained. They are not overcome easily, but each little step toward progress that can be made is an important one for the ultimate health of the society and the respect for the humanity of each student regardless of his or her racial or ethnic background.

Unfortunately, sport is an area where racial stereotyping has prevailed for far too long. For example, there are common notions about the ability of black students to play certain positions or to achieve in certain sport areas. The first goal for physical educators must be to combat such stereotypes directly, to attempt to abolish them, at least for the students with whom they work. This can be achieved directly if you teach in an integrated setting. It can be achieved indirectly if you teach in a segregated setting.

The direct approach would be through prompting, intervening on student interactions (correcting inappropriate interactions and reinforcing appropriate ones), and modeling whenever possible. Role modeling in which members of different races cooperate and work together toward a common goal can be very effective. Many students have never had the opportunity to work constructively with a member of a different racial background. If this kind of modeling cannot be brought directly into the teaching setting (by using expert demonstrators from nearby colleges or universities, for example), then it can be done indirectly by judiciously selecting visual materials for teaching skills and decorating bulletin boards.

Barnes (1977) has identified teacher behaviors that are counterproductive to the development of racial equity in educational settings. It should be noted that these kinds of behaviors often occur inadvertently—that is, the teacher does not intend them to be offensive. But they often *are* offensive. The intention is not nearly so powerful as the act itself. The following kinds of statements are counterproductive in reaching equity goals with minority students:

1. Labeling or referring to students as *disadvantaged, culturally deprived,* or *slow learners*
2. Global statements that stereotype a group, such as "you people" or "all of you"
3. Making statements that highlight differences in personal matters, such as clothing, physical appearance, or material possessions
4. Patronizing students, being overly "nice" or paternalistic or maternalistic, with a style of superiority
5. Telling racially oriented jokes or using racially oriented terms such as *Mex, Chink,* or *greaser*
6. Avoiding physical contact with minority students, keeping physical distance between you and them
7. Criticizing, judging, or in any way devaluing the culture from which minority students come
8. Stereotyping individual minority children on the basis of ethnic or racial stereotypes such as the notions that Japanese children are always good in science, Mexican American children are lazy, and black children are irresponsible.

Where racial equity is an important local issue due to school integration plans, it might be useful to consider special techniques to improve understanding and behavior among students. Teachers too can benefit greatly from strategies such as visiting the home of a minority student, visiting community play areas where minority students live, participating in community service projects that bring racial groups together, observing classes taught by teachers from the minority group(s), and generally educating yourself about the cultural background of the group with whom you have contact. Your own growing understanding will be reflected in your teaching behavior, and your teaching behavior will have an effect on your students.

Cultural Pluralism

One of the facts of contemporary American life is the diversity of cultures that contribute to our collective existence—cultures other than the traditional, white, middle-class, middle-American system of values and habits. Not only do diverse cultural systems within the United States contribute to our collective life, but so do cultures from other parts of the world. Increasingly, **global education** is becoming an important concept within educational theory and thought. Global education is cultural pluralism carried to an international level, the education of students to live and grow productively within a complex, multicultural, world society. Students cannot grow and

Humanism, the Individual, and the Group

When we think of humanistic education practices, a humanizing educational experience, or humanistic outcomes for education, do we usually think about the individual student or about groups? Many believe that during the past twenty years the delicate balance between an individual orientation and a group focus has shifted too far toward individual concerns. One such person is Ernest Boyer, a former U.S. Commissioner of Education. His concerns are for the *connectedness* among individuals:

> It is essential to put the concept of relatedness at the core of education if we are going to teach our young people to behave in a way that is responsible and civil in a world where resources are limited. And yet, the only things students seem to have in common are their differences.
>
> Today the commitment to individualism in education is stronger than the commitment to coherence. There is no agreement about what it means to be an educated person, and many teachers are more confident about the duration of an education than they are about its substance. Students are different from one another, of course, and they should be free to make some independent choices, but if we educate our students to respect only their differences without understanding what they share in common, we will have educated toward ignorance. . . . We cannot afford a generation that fails to see or care about connections. [Boyer 1981, p. 4]

thrive in a pluralistic society unless they acquire understandings, values, attitudes, and behavioral skills that show an appreciation for cultural diversity and that overcome the stereotypes acquired when one is raised in an area dominated by one culture, particularly if it is the dominant culture of the society.

To become more human as a person or for a society to become more humane involves many factors but certainly must include a tolerance for and appreciation of people from cultures other than your own. The human experience is extraordinarily diverse, and much is to be gained from a growing ability to appreciate and take part in cultural forms other than those with which one grew up. In addition to the interactional, intervention, and modeling skills mentioned earlier, global education can be enhanced through attention to the following issues (Wynn 1974, Kalectaca 1974):

1. Work toward overcoming cultural and racial stereotypes.
2. Understand the interdependence among cultures required for the development and maintenance of a safe, humane world.
3. Understand better the history of minority groups in the United States.
4. Make students aware of the impact of cultural prejudice.

5. Help students to better understand the perspectives of racial and ethnic groups other than their own.
6. Create situations in which students may grow in their abilities to communicate effectively with students from cultural backgrounds other than their own.
7. Help students to understand better how the dominant culture tends to penalize and hold down citizens from minority cultures.
8. Help students to understand and deal with their own feelings, attitudes, and behaviors relative to people from different cultural backgrounds.
9. Increase local resources that bring students into contact with diverse cultural traditions.

The world today is considerably smaller than was the world in which our parents grew up. The world in which you spend most of your adult life will grow even smaller. Nations will have to work together politically and economically to meet the important problems that lie before us. This will all be easier to the extent that students gain the proper attitudes and skills relative to living in a culturally pluralistic society and world.

Promoting Self-Growth in Physical Education

Physical educators have always suggested that personal development was a major outcome of participation in sport and physical education. Unfortunately, the performance of physical education has seldom matched their rhetoric. It is difficult to examine the descriptive research data reviewed in Chapter 4 and come to the conclusion that there is any widespread achievement of self-growth goals in physical education. That is a sad fact, but to try to color it any differently would be to disregard what evidence we have. Needless to say, that does not mean that students have not experienced self-growth through well-conceived, effectively taught physical education programs. It means only that those instances are too few and too far between. The purpose of this section is to identify specific self-growth tasks in which physical educators can help students to learn, to mature, and to grow.

Self-growth is an elusive concept. Educators differ widely in their definitions of self-growth. Diversity at the definitional level of course, leads to very different suggestions about how to best contribute to self-growth through instructional procedures. Self-growth cannot be viewed in isolation, because individuals do not exist alone. They exist as members of social groups—families, neighborhoods, peer groups, teams, co-workers, and other such affiliations. Thus, self-growth must not only enhance the individual but must also make the individual a more useful and successful member of the groups to which he or she belongs.

As with other concepts, I adopt the view that self-growth can be viewed, partially at least, as the acquisition and refinement of certain skills, some related to the individual and others related to how the individual interacts in a social group. These skills can be identified, practiced, mastered, and used. The result is a more mature, competent, independent individual and a more sensitive, responsible contributor to groups. The skills identified here as self-growth skills are (1) positive attitudes toward oneself, (2) positive attitudes toward others, (3) expressing feelings, (4) accepting consequences, (5) behaving responsibly, (6) helping others, (7) caring for the environment, and (8) behaving ethically.

Developing Positive Attitudes Toward the Self

Most psychologists and counselors are agreed that the foundation for self-growth and self-development is a positive attitude toward the self. Positive attitudes toward the self normally develop as students acquire skills and competencies and, thus, more and more identify themselves as people who can do things, accomplish tasks, and achieve valuable goals. Skill development and an ability to compete adequately in physical education are important contributors to this kind of self-growth.

More specifically, teachers can foster positive attitudes toward the self by helping students (1) to be willing to have their performances displayed, (2) to learn to make positive statements about themselves, (3) to learn to undertake new tasks with positive expectations for achievement, and (4) to take risks and become "doers."

Being willing to have one's performance viewed by others is a good behavioral indicator of how a student evaluates his or her skills. Students should not be asked to perform publicly when it is to their disadvantage. Public performance (as a demonstrator or in relation to providing group feedback to the class) should always take place in a positive context. Students should learn to value their skills and be willing to share them openly without fear of ridicule. This kind of openness and willingness to share is a strong indicator of a mature self.

Teachers can help students to learn how to make honest, positive statements about themselves. This behavior can be modeled by the teacher. The teacher can also reinforce it when students do it appropriately; that is, when they make honest, positive evaluations about themselves rather than "bragging." An even more direct approach would be to encourage certain students to do this more often, work with them to be sure they understand the dimensions of this behavior, and then reinforce their efforts when they try to do it.

It is well known that expectations can affect performance. Teachers who expect little, often get just that. However, realistic, yet high teacher expectations can be a powerful, positive influence on student achievement. Teachers can also help students to verbalize positive expectations about their own undertakings—they can gradually help a student to become the kind of person who thinks and says, "I can" more often than "I can't."

Finally, teachers can contribute to self-growth by helping students to learn how to take risks and to become "doers." Risk taking does not mean performing in unsafe situations. It means being willing to try new things, to be willing to be "out front." Risk taking should be learned gradually within a safe, psychologically supportive climate. If students are willing to do and try only what they know they can do quite well, then their horizons will be seriously limited. Safe, positive risk taking is an important ingredient in self-growth. Physical education experiences are often ideally suited to nurturing this important quality.

Developing Positive Attitudes Toward Others

Individuals do not grow and develop in isolation. They are always members of groups—families, neighborhoods, peers, classmates, teams, co-workers, and organizations. Our self-estimates of our own capabilities are conditioned primarily by how others react to us. When people react favorably to what we can do and how we do it, then we tend to view ourselves favorably too. Often, poor self-concepts grow when people do not get systematically favorable reactions from others. Thus, self-growth is largely a function of how the rest of the world reacts to us.

One important ingredient in helping those around us to react favorably to us is to show positive attitudes toward them. When you are nice to people, they in turn tend to be nice to you. Thus, one important skill in promoting self-growth is to learn how to react positively to others, in a systematic way. When students react positively to one another, the climate of the education setting becomes considerably more friendly and humane. Students supporting each other in their learning and performing is a strong and powerful self-growth factor as well as a major contributor to a warm educational climate, within which learning is more likely to occur.

Three major skills relevant to this self-growth area are (1) the ability to make positive statements about the accomplishments of other students, (2) complimenting, and (3) displaying tolerance for people whose characteristics differ from one's own (Stephens 1978).

Being nice to one another in an educational setting just doesn't happen by chance. But it can happen as a result of teacher planning and instruction. Students can be encouraged (prompted) to make positive, supportive statements about each other's performances and achievements. Teachers can also intervene when students complain about one another and can use the opportunity to provide corrective feedback about positive statements. Teachers can also model this skill by making a lot of positive statements themselves.

The same holds true for teaching students how to compliment one another. Prompting, corrective feedback, reinforcing appropriate instances of complimenting, and complimenting often oneself all can increase the rate at which students compliment each other. At first, students tend to feel a little awkward and uncomfortable "being nice" to one another. But this stage will pass quickly as they continue to practice being nice and as it begins to feel more comfortable to them (see Chapter 1). If teachers will take the time and effort to use these strategies and to keep students practicing until they move through and beyond the discomfort stage, then the educational climate will change quickly. Students will become more skilled, and "being nice" will catch on. Rolider (1979) and Westcott (1977) have both described important improvements in helping students to make positive comments toward one another in sport and physical education settings. Each of these studies found that direct teacher instruction produced the highest rate of positive student interactions, and that reinforcing appropriate instances and teacher modeling were also valuable. The combination of the three strategies should be even more valuable.

Displaying tolerance for people who have behavior and characteristics different from your own is also a powerful self-growth skill. Here too, the basic notion is that tolerance is more likely to lead to better knowledge of the person, better knowledge of the person's point of view is likely to lead to acceptance, and acceptance is more likely to lead to positive interactions. In turn, the person with whom you have been tolerant is more likely to be that way with you, which will, in the long run, contribute to self-growth. Often this skill begins with refraining from making derogatory comments or giving negative feedback. Using good listening skills and practicing empathy also is valuable in improving this skill (see Chapter 7). Another strategy that is particularly useful here is role playing, where students are asked to assume roles or identities different from their own so that they can learn from the other perspective. Again, teacher prompting ("Remember, if we want people to be tolerant of us, then we have to try to practice being tolerant when we are around them"), teacher reinforcement of appropriate instances ("Max, I really liked the way you showed patience while helping Erin"), and teacher modeling can all help to achieve improvement in this skill.

Promoting Responsible Behavior

No setting can be truly humanistic unless the people within it behave responsibly. Irresponsible behavior on the part of one person (in our case, one student) can "dehumanize" a class quite quickly. The full potential of each individual student cannot be achieved unless he or she is able to *depend* on those about him or her behaving responsibly. "Doing your own thing" is fine, except when in doing your own thing you prevent someone else from doing theirs! Human beings are social—they exist within groups. Individual development should never be viewed in isolation from groups. This does not mean that individuals always have to subordinate themselves to a group. But it does mean that people must learn how to behave responsibly if they are to be productive members of groups, and their growing humanity depends to a certain extent on their abilities to be productive members of groups.

Therefore, teachers who promote responsible behavior among individuals are contributing to their growth as people, especially when their rights as individuals are also protected and nurtured. Obviously, there needs to be a balance between "watching out for yourself" and "being a good team player." The skills included here as important to promoting responsible behavior are those of accepting consequences, behaving ethically, behaving consistently in routine chores, and cooperating within a group setting.

Accepting Consequences

Actions produce consequences. Sometimes those consequences are unpredictable. At other times they are fully predictable. Students who are to grow to responsible adulthood need to learn to accept consequences without excessive complaining or blaming others. This does not suggest that students should always accept consequences they consider to be unfair. What is involved here is teaching students to understand the differences between fair and unfair consequences, so that they accept the fair consequences maturely and have appropriate ways to react to and attempt to change the unfair consequences. Many specific skills can be taught and promoted to contribute to

Humanistic Teaching and the Notion of Control

Many people who are concerned with the humanistic development of the whole student have trouble with the concept of control as it is discussed in classroom management. They view coercive, punitive control as counterproductive, even immoral. But they also tend to be against any form of control, assuming that even positive control features are antihumanistic. The following summary excerpt from a study on first-year teachers in inner-city schools provides some insight into this difficult question.

> Many of those writing from a humanistic viewpoint have intimated that excessive concern with control is not good, but our results suggest that control is a vital problem. In fact, in the results reported here, the teachers who were most successful in establishing and maintaining control were also the most successful in providing a warm, understanding, supportive climate in which students felt comfortable and were able to work productively. The teachers who established control most effectively were the very ones whom students chose as their best teachers. [Hayman and Moskowitz 1975, p. 14]

Students need limits in order to learn to behave responsibly. Establishing limits and specifically teaching these limits so that they become internalized among the students is what effective, positive classroom management is all about. Not only is this kind of control not inhumane, but it may also be necessary in order to establish a truly humane educational setting.

this general skill of being able to accept fair consequences. Three are described here: (1) reporting one's own mishaps and accidents, (2) apologizing when one's actions have infringed on another student's rights, and (3) accepting, without complaint or blaming, the rightful consequences of rule infractions (Stephens 1978).

Mishaps and accidents often occur in physical education. Students break equipment. Students hurt one another inadvertently. Such accidents should be reported, for obvious reasons. Students who do report them show an admirable level of responsible behavior. Students who do not do so should learn that reporting is an appropriate behavior because it shows responsibility for one's own actions. Teachers can prompt this kind of responsible behavior by noting that accidents do happen and that the important thing is to report them promptly. Students who do report should be reinforced for doing so (and made into role models, when appropriate), and the teacher should also empathize with the student about the accident. Role playing can be useful with younger children for whom accidents seem to be a special problem.

Apologizing for infringing on others is an important skill. The first component of this skill is the ability to recognize when one has infringed. Taking a classmate's space, cutting in line, bumping into another student, and taking someone's equipment are all examples. Apologizing appropriately can usually be prompted frequently and then publicly reinforced when instances occur. Teachers can also model this skill simply because they too inadvertently infringe on students from time to time.

Accepting rightful consequences of rule infractions without blaming others or complaining is another step toward responsible behavior. This text has clearly advocated the establishment of class rules and contingencies that spell out the consequences for breaking rules. Students who break rules suffer the consequences. They should learn to do so without blaming other students and without complaining. This skill can be explained and verbally prompted by the teacher and instances of it can be reinforced—"Janie, when you were sent in from recess you did it right away without complaining, which shows that you acted very grown up." Inappropriate instances of blaming or complaining should be dealt with through corrective feedback and having the student practice the appropriate way to respond.

Behaving Ethically

Good sportsmanship has always been a goal in physical education. On an even broader scale, character development has often been attributed to participation in physical education and sport. For the most part, we probably have claimed far more than we have produced! Good sportsmanship is a kind of ethical behavior generic to sport settings. Ethical behavior in sport context means playing within the letter and spirit of the rules, not taking unfair advantage of an opponent, and respecting your teammates. These qualities are high-level skills that are built on a foundation of much more basic ethical skills. The responsible sportsperson will have acquired these more basic skills. Typical of them would be (1) the ability to distinguish truth from untruth, (2) the ability to monitor one's own behavior and report one's own infractions, and (3) the ability to not engage in an inappropriate behavior even when encouraged to do so by one's peers.

Young students (and even older ones, occasionally) often have to acquire the basic ethical skill of distinguishing truth from untruth, especially as it relates to their own behavior. Young students often create grandiose stories about their own behavior. Teachers should prompt "truth telling" as an important and appropriate behavior and should use every opportunity to point out the difference between truth and untruth. Students who tell the truth should be reinforced for doing so. Students who do not tell the truth should be asked, in a straightforward, nonthreatening way, whether the explanation they have just given is true or not true. A strongly reinforcing climate for truth telling must be created, because most students who lie are doing so in order to avoid punishment.

Physical education is a very good setting for children to learn to monitor their own behavior and report infractions they have committed. Students can score their own games and keep their own performance records. Instances of accurate monitoring can be rewarded. When students report that they have broken a rule, they should be reinforced and, when appropriate, used as models so that other children can see not only what self-reporting means but also that it is valued by the teacher. Eventually, older students should be able to play a very competitive game, striving hard to win, yet still being capable of calling their own violations.

A third example of an ethical behavior skill is the willingness to not do something that is inappropriate even though there may be encouragement to do so from peers. Teacher prompting can be very effective here, because students need to know that such a behavior is both expected and valued. Modeling of appropriate kinds of examples by the teacher is also useful. When a student is clearly resisting the pressure to misbehave, he or she should be reinforced strongly, although this no doubt should be done in a private way between the teacher and the student. Students should understand that resisting the pressure to misbehave shows maturity, responsibility, and an appropriate kind of independence.

Behaving Cooperatively

A humane educational setting is, among other things, a place where people cooperate. Cooperation is an important skill for students to learn, both for their own personal growth and in terms of their ability to function effectively as a member of a group. Far too often, humanistic education strategies have focused on individual development to the exclusion of group-oriented skills. Self-growth is important. But can any individual grow and develop humanely without being able to be a member of various groups? The position taken here is that group skills are important contributors to humanistic development of the well-rounded individual. Physical education is not taught as a tutorial. There are often large numbers of students, often in a limited space, and too often with limited equipment. For lessons to have their optimum impact on each student, there must be cooperation between teacher and students and among the students. Without cooperation, very little will take place in terms of learning and enjoyment, and without learning and enjoyment it would be difficult to describe a setting as humanistic.

Students learn many, many skills that might be appropriately labeled as cooperative behavior skills. Several are described here—you, no doubt, can think of several more. The cooperative skills reviewed here are (1) sharing equipment in the practice situation, (2) working cooperatively on a task with one or more partners, (3) playing a specified role as a member of a team, and (4) contributing to and accepting decisions made by the group.

Very few physical educators have all the equipment they want or need. Most often equipment has to be shared in order for a lesson to proceed smoothly. Sharing equipment is an essential cooperative skill for physical education. Teachers should prompt this skill often, reinforce it when they see appropriate instances of it among students, and use those instances for modeling purposes. Inappropriate instances should be corrected immediately, and the offending students should have to practice cooperatively as a consequence of their infraction. "Sharing and caring" should become one of the main *ethics* of the physical education program. If teachers emphasize, prompt, and reinforce, it will occur more frequently.

One style of teaching outlined in this text is referred to as **task teaching** (see Chapter 10). In this style, students work at carefully defined tasks, often in pairs and sometimes in small groups, depending on the nature of the tasks. Even in direct styles of teaching, students are often placed in drills and activities where they have to work with classmates to complete a task (for example, a circle drill in volleyball, where the task is to keep the ball up in the air using the set-up pass). In order to complete a task, students have to cooperate and help one another. A very good way to teach cooperative task behavior is to use cooperative games (Siedentop, Herkowitz, and Rink in press). In cooperative games, the score is achieved by working together toward a goal rather than working to defeat an opponent. For example, in cooperatively scored volleyball, two teams try to keep the rally going for as long as possible, perhaps competing against two other teams who are also cooperating to prolong a rally. Strategies for prompting, reinforcing, and correcting cooperative task behavior are similar to those just suggested for sharing equipment.

Team play is a very good setting within which to learn cooperative behavior of a very important kind—that of playing a specified role within a larger framework. In most team games, players contribute differently to the team performance. In basketball, for example, there are play-making guards, shooting forwards, rebounding forwards, and defensive players. This is not to suggest that all players do not have to perform all the skills, for teams to play well. That is not the point. The point is that successful *team* performance most often calls for *differentiated* roles. In volleyball, some players are best at setting up and others are better at spiking, while still others are best at defensive play. Learning to play a specific role that contributes to an overall group performance is an important form of cooperative behavior, and physical education is one of the best settings for students to learn this skill.

Finally, students should be encouraged to contribute to group decisions, to have their say, to present their ideas, and then to accept and implement the decisions of the group, even when group decisions differ from their own point of view. This is the essence of democracy, and situations in which students can learn this skill provide valuable lessons in democratic procedures and values. Again, the prompting, reinforcing, correcting, and modeling strategies are all applicable to this important set of skills, as they have been to each of the humanistic skills presented in this chapter.

CHAPTER 9

Long-Term Planning

Much that the teacher does before and after class must be considered if we are to obtain a complete description of his professional activity. The teacher in an empty classroom may not appear to be a likely object of study, but during these solitary moments he often performs tasks and makes decisions that are vital to his overall effectiveness.

Philip Jackson, *The Way Teaching Is* (1980)

CHAPTER OBJECTIVES

To describe factors that affect program-level planning

To discuss the strengths and weaknesses of traditional program goals

To describe the goals of physical education as play education

To define organizing centers and provide various examples of different ways in which they can be used in physical education

To show how to use appropriate guidelines in selecting activities to meet program goals

To explain the basic planning question and its role in instructional design

To explain and provide examples of terminal goals

To show how to conduct a procedural and hierarchical task analysis

To explain how to write acceptable behavioral objectives

Nowhere in education is there more smoke without fire than in planning for instruction. Virtually every school system has a curriculum guide detailing the goals, objectives, and activities to be pursued in school programs. Professional textbooks suggest activities and methods for instruction. National organizations prepare reports on "ideal" curricula. Professional journals are replete with suggestions and reports on how to plan for instruction. Unfortunately, physical education instruction often does not reflect the time, effort, and money spent on planning for instruction.

Larry Locke (1973) told a national conference on elementary physical education that the barrage of new methods, new curriculum ideas, and new instructional aids is an exercise in overkill. He related the story of a farm agent who attempted to revolutionize farming in his country by trying to persuade farmers to use new machinery, new fertilizers, and new farming methods. The farmers responded that they didn't need all that new stuff because they weren't now farming half as well as they knew how. The same might be said for teaching. Most teachers aren't teaching as well as they know how to right now.

The point is that planning for instruction cannot be viewed in isolation. Better planning is a waste of time unless it results in better teaching. The skills developed in this chapter have no meaning unless they are accompanied by skills developed in Chapters 10 and 11 (on daily planning and on implementing instruction) in the form of better teaching. Thus, this chapter on planning is intimately tied to Chapter 11, on the implementation of instruction. Teachers are not good because they develop good-looking units or nicely detailed lesson plans. They are good when those units and lesson plans pay off in better instruction. Planning should never be viewed as an end in itself, but rather as a means for achieving better instruction.

Planning for instruction is also related to concepts developed in Chapter 2, on the assessment of teaching and its outcomes. The notion of maximizing student learning time should be kept in mind at all times, both in long-term planning of programs and units and in short-term developing of daily lessons. The reduction of waiting time, managerial time, and transition time leaves more time for instruction and student practice, thus leading to more student learning time and greater achievement. Achieving these instructional goals on a daily basis is easier when they have been used as considerations in planning.

Factors Affecting Program-Level Planning

Too many programs are planned for an ideal set of circumstances, and few local situations are ideal. Good program planners are always conscious of practicing "the art of the possible." They are aware that programs need to achieve *real* results. Once a program is regularly achieving important results, it can then be expanded and become more daring, more ambitious. But, the first goal of initial program planning is to achieve limited yet important goals within the real constraints imposed on the program. The ideal program is seldom achieved in leaps and bounds. More often it is built gradually on a solid base of success. Programmers should first do what they can do well. They should gain support through solid accomplishments. Then they should move on to bigger and better things.

Realistic planning is an important first step. Several important factors should be taken into account when planning a physical education effort at the program level. These factors are (1) the nature of the community, (2) facilities, (3) personal and professional considerations, (4) current professional emphases, (5) educational programming within the school, and (6) the status of the learners.

Local school boards exert a great deal of control over what goes on in schools in their districts. So too does parent influence in neighborhoods surrounding the schools. This influence may be less direct in larger metropolitan areas than in smaller, rural areas. Nonetheless, the values of the local community should be considered when developing a total physical education program. Some local values may be reflected in prohibitions against certain kinds of activities, such as social dancing. Other values may be reflected in strong expectations that certain activities will be included, such as winter outdoor activities (in northern communities).

Communities also may have general views about the role of fitness, the proper emphasis on competition, and favored activities such as aquatics or gymnastics, or may have even more explicit views about program goals such as self-confidence, risk taking, and other such characteristics. To neglect such factors when planning a program is to ask for trouble. Over time, a physical educator can help to change the values and attitudes of a community, but to ignore those same values and attitudes in the first place is a serious error.

Facilities for physical education range from superb indoor and outdoor spaces complete with pools, a vita parcourse, wilderness areas, and camps, to no indoor facility and very limited outdoor spaces. Thus, facilities often are a major factor in determining the scope of the program and the activities included within it. To ignore facility constraints would be foolish. However, to use them as an excuse for developing a restricted program is equally foolish. The physical education literature is replete with evidence of how seemingly inadequate facilities have been modified and transformed to allow for activities that supposedly couldn't be done there. Likewise, activities can be adapted to fit facilities if need be.

Teachers doing long-range program planning should always capitalize on their own interests and skills. Unlike other subject matter areas, such as reading and mathematics, there are few national or state expectations for physical education curricula. Physical education programs can have almost totally different program emphases and still be equally good. Teachers are not equally interested in or prepared to teach a wide variety of activities. On the other hand, very few are hired to teach in specialized areas such as aquatics or racket sports. Each teacher should capitalize on his or her own interests and skills by emphasizing those in program planning. This makes sense simply because teachers tend to plan better, teach better, and be more interested in those activities for which they have a good background and a strong interest. One big mistake made by physical educators during the past several decades has been to assume that they must offer a tremendous variety of activities to have a good program. They end up having to teach activities for which they are ill prepared and which often contribute little to the program. Clearly, it is better to plan fewer activities but to make sure that each activity offered is one for which there will be adequate planning, good teaching, and a high level of interest.

Current professional interests in physical education represent yet another factor in program planning. During this century alone, at different times, physical education has placed major emphasis on fitness, lifetime sports, team sports, individual and dual sports, and recreational pursuits. Recently there have been trends toward the martial arts and wilderness sports, as well as movements such as the "new games" effort. Such trends often reflect the culture's interest in these activities. Therefore, they tend to represent the current interests of students, a factor that certainly warrants consideration in planning. Another reason for considering current programming trends in the profession is that the teacher is more likely to be able to get help in planning and implementing currently popular activities. Journal articles, clinics, and conventions often emphasize such activities, ways to develop equipment for them, ways to program them, ways to teach them, and helpful hints for making them successful.

In program planning, physical educators must also take into account the kind of school in which they operate. Is it an open classroom elementary school, an alternative high school, a flexibly scheduled middle school, or a traditionally organized junior high school? Does it have consistent time periods, or is there modular, flexible scheduling? To what extent is movement within the school possible, so that an "open gymnasium" or "practice period" might be useful? The answers to these questions are major factors in determining the *format* of the physical education program.

Just as scheduling features determine the format of the physical education program, the educational philosophy of the school affects the *content* of the physical education program. For example, some elementary schools emphasize individual student growth more strongly than academic achievement. Some high schools are organized more around vocational training than college preparation. Certain schools have definite goals about physical fitness. Others have a strong emphasis on moral education. The point is that any school with an explicit philosophy, like the ones just mentioned, will expect that philosophy to be carried out within the physical education program, too. If so, this expectation becomes a factor in program planning.

Finally, a program should always be planned with the status of the learners in mind. In most cases, physical educators can assume that they are serving a normal population of students. But careful planners must consider the possibility that the student population may have certain characteristics that need to be taken into account. For example, the student population may show poor cardiovascular fitness. The students may lack strength in the upper body. They may have a background in team sports with many outlets for team sports, but no prior training in or opportunity for recreational sports. Such factors deserve to be considered when planning the total program.

Careful, realistic planning helps avoid problems. Achieving obvious success in a limited program that represents careful planning helps win support from students, fellow teachers, administrators, and parents. This support becomes the foundation from which a program can expand and improve, improving its resource base as it accomplishes more and more. Few situations are more frustrating than to plan a program only to have to modify it immediately because no attention was paid to a constraining factor during the planning.

Selecting Program Goals

The appropriate way to plan a program is to first select program goals and then plan for ways to achieve those goals. But, although this strategy is obviously logical, it is seldom accomplished in practice. When asked about how a program is conceptualized, most people respond by listing the activities of the program rather than its goals. When thinking about program change, most people think about what new activities should be included. Most often activities are selected and arranged in a program. Then the overall goals that seem achievable through those activities are listed.

This common practice of selecting activities and then establishing goals based on the activities has been made very easy in physical education. The traditional four goals of physical development, skill development, mental development, and social development have been widely accepted in physical education since early in this century. This traditional set of goals is sufficiently broad that it can be espoused as a set of overall goals for almost any conceivable physical education program. My bet is that you can examine any school physical education curriculum guide from your local area in terms of the overall goals of the program and find that they fit fairly well the fourfold objectives of physical, skill, mental, and social development. Of course, the language used may differ. There may be talk about "fitness" rather than "physical development," "psychomotor development" rather than "skill acquisition," "cognitive development" rather than "mental development," or "attitudinal development" rather than "social development." But the meaning will be essentially the same.

The major weakness of the traditional goals is that they are so broad and so vague that they are not useful for program planning. The traditional goals are not hierarchically arranged; that is, they are assumed to be on the same level. Thus they give no guidance about what the program ought to accomplish first.

A number of different kinds of goals have been suggested in the physical education literature. For example, a program could have fitness as its main goal. Others have suggested skill development as the overall goal. Still others have suggested that qualities such as self-concept and personal growth are primary goals for the physical education program. The physical educator who sets out to plan a program will have no problem thinking about alternative main goals. Indeed, the problem will be to select some main goals from among the many attractive possibilities. But it is most important to remember that a program should accomplish something! It is much more appropriate to have a limited set of goals and to achieve them than to have many broad goals and achieve none of them to any great degree. Also, it is important to develop goals that relate to one another in some sensible way—goals that are hierarchical in the sense that achieving a subgoal contributes directly to achievement of the main goal because the subgoals and main goals are logically related to one another.

Goals of
Physical
Education
as Play
Education

151

Goals of Physical Education as Play Education

As an example of a hierarchically arranged set of goals for a physical education program, I offer a set of goals that I have advocated for some time (Siedentop 1980). These goals are derived from a definition of physical education as **play education**—as any activity that increases tendencies and abilities to play competitive and expressive motor activities. This definition suggests that the major effort in the teaching of physical education should be to increase the degree to which students like to do physically active motor play; that is, to teach them to love the subject matter and to want to engage in it more often. In the deepest sense, this is what I mean when I suggest that we have to develop *players*.

The major ways in which this is accomplished is to help students acquire skills, teach them what it means to be a player within the context of the activity, help them to prepare to do the activity in a meaningful way, teach them appropriate ways of behaving within the context of the activity, and to increase their knowledge of the activity and their own relationship to it as players. These objectives lead to the overall goal and are arranged hierarchically, as shown in Figure 9-1.

A major value of the play education goal system, and of others like it, is that the relationships among the subgoals are clearly demonstrated. Therefore, knowledge about an activity is never seen as an end in itself, but rather as a means to increasing the student's ability to participate in the activity as a full-fledged player. Increased skill is obviously important, but it is subordinate to helping students learn how to like the activities. This subordinate relationship puts constraints on teachers as to how they can develop skill; that is, skill development must be done in an atmosphere that is conducive to the development of positive attitudes.

Figure 9-1. *Hierarchy of Program Objectives for Physical Education as Play Education*

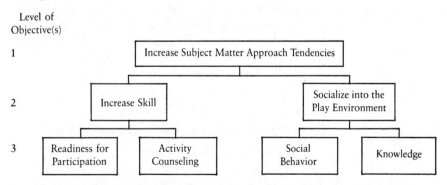

Source: Siedentop, D. *Physical Education: Introductory Analysis.* 3rd ed. Dubuque, Iowa: Brown, 1980, p. 267.

When developing a total program, it is important for planners to select main goals and then to determine which are the most important. Subgoals should contribute to the achievement of the main goals. It is more important for a program to accomplish limited goals well than to espouse many grand goals only to fail to achieve any of them very well.

Organizing Centers for a Program

Another major decision in program planning is how to define the organizing centers for the curriculum. An **organizing center** is a main theme around which learning experiences are arranged to achieve the overall goals of the program. Increasingly, there is evidence of physical education programs designed around nontraditional organizing centers. Traditionally, of course, the organizing centers for the program have been sport and dance activities. Units on football, volleyball, tennis, folk dance, and other such activities have made up the curriculum. Suggestions have been made for organizing the program around *movement themes* rather than sport and dance activities. Thus, the organizing centers would be movement concepts such as gathering or striking, and units would be built around these themes. Sometimes these newer efforts reflect different ways to reach fairly traditional goals. In other cases, the goals as well as the organizing centers are nontraditional.

It is conceivable that many different organizing centers could be used in physical education. Social development themes such as sportsmanship, self-concept, body image, and meaning in activity could be used as organizing centers. Some have suggested that the disciplinary knowledge of physical education could provide the themes for developing the kindergarten-through-high school (K–12) curriculum. Thus, the organizing centers might become exercise physiology, sport psychology, biomechanics, and sport sociology.

Although each of these approaches is possible, none is very probable. It seems most likely that physical educators will continue to use an eclectic approach in which sport activities are the dominant organizing centers. Yet, on a K–12 basis, eclectic approaches also emphasize movement organizing centers in the K–3 curriculum, and other more specialized organizing centers such as dance and gymnastics. This model offers great flexibility and has stood the test of time. Its major drawback, as with the traditional fourfold objectives, is that it sometimes tends to lessen program accountability because of its diverse, eclectic nature.

Selecting Activities to Meet Program Goals

Once goals are selected and organizing centers are arranged as main themes for the curriculum, the planner reaches the point where he or she must decide what to teach. Which activities from among the many available will be chosen for inclusion within the program? It is precisely at this point that program planning too often tends to break down. All the goal development and definition seems to be forgotten, and activities are chosen on the basis of factors that have little to do with the program goals. Planners should use the following major guidelines when selecting activities to meet program goals.

1. *Activities chosen should contribute directly to achieving the major goals of the program.* If cardiovascular fitness is the main goal, then every activity in the program should have a strong emphasis on cardiovascular training. Not all activities contribute equally to all goals. We know a great deal about which activities seem to best fit different goals. Thus, soccer is a good activity for cardiovascular training (as well as for other goals). Golf and tennis are good activities for a program emphasizing adult leisure skills. Rappelling and climbing are good activities for programs emphasizing risk taking and self-concept development. Team handball does not contribute much to a program goal based on carryover value. It is a fine activity contributing to many goals, but certainly has little carryover value in American society.

2. *A good activity is one that meets program goals.* The value of an activity, in terms of program planning, is strictly the degree to which it meets program goals. For planning purposes, *good* is a relative term. Of course, this says nothing about the value of any activity for other purposes. Just because an activity is not good for your program does not mean that it may not be the best activity for another program.

3. *A good program accomplishes goals.* If you are to err in planning, it is wise to err in the direction of trying to achieve too little rather than trying to achieve too much. Limited goals that are achieved are better than grandiose goals that are not achieved. Having many, many goals and a wide variety of activities sometimes looks good on paper, but seldom translates into program accomplishment.

4. *Know what you are doing.* A teacher must know an activity fairly well before being able to decide the degree to which that activity might contribute to program goals. Do students have the background to participate successfully? How much space does it take? Can equipment be made inexpensively? Are the basic skills simple enough to acquire in the time available? A teacher should know the answers to these questions before selecting a new activity for inclusion in the program.

5. *Accomplishment takes time.* It is difficult to imagine what level of accomplishment can be achieved in a program in which units are three weeks long, with three meetings per week. Nine meetings isn't enough to accomplish much beyond exposing students to an activity (the dangers of overexposure in physical education have already been mentioned). Planners should think carefully about how much time will be necessary to meet the goals they have established. If goals are limited

and teachers are instructing in activity areas for which they have expertise and interest, then there is no reason why units cannot be long enough to ensure real goal accomplishment. Boredom is not a factor in physical education as long as successful learning experiences are being arranged and clear progress is being made. Students tend to get bored by doing repetitive activities that require little skill or effort.

Program-Level Planning

The best physical education program is one that is conceptualized and planned on a K–12 basis. Of course, this requires that all physical educators in a school system work together to agree on overall K–12 goals and the means for reaching those goals. Because physical educators often disagree about goals and implementation, this level of programming planning is particularly difficult to achieve. The suggestions that follow could be used for K–12 planning, and they also form a useful framework for K–6, middle school, junior high school, or senior high school programming if they are done independently.

The first task is to set overall program goals, the second task is to agree on organizing centers for the program, and the third task is to choose activities that meet the goals. Once these *executive* decisions have been made, the real planning begins. It is not enough to select volleyball as an activity to meet program goals and then to arrange volleyball units at the seventh, ninth, and eleventh grades. Far too often planning is done only to this level and not beyond it, resulting in an experience for students that changes little from seventh through eleventh grades. The issue in planning is how the seventh-, ninth-, and eleventh-grade units should relate to each other and how each should contribute to the overall goals for volleyball. This requires a level of planning far more serious than merely sorting out activities to grade levels and assuming that progression, growth, and development will somehow magically occur when the units are taught!

Answer the Basic Planning Question: "What Do I Want Students to Be Able to Do?"

Once program goals have been chosen and a consensus has been achieved on the organizing centers for the program, the next step is to begin designing the actual educational experiences that will achieve the goals. The work of instructional design actually begins here. This is the point at which the real nature of the program begins to take shape. Therefore, it is important that this phase begin properly—by asking the right question at the very beginning. The first question the instructional designer must answer is "What do I want the students to be able to do after they have finished the instruction?" Notice that the focus is not on how to teach. Rather, the focus is on the performance capabilities of the students. The focus is on ends, not means; on product, not process.

Also, it is important to understand that this first and most important instructional design question must be answered in terms of performance, what the student should be able to do. This requires that the designer or planner focus specifically on outcomes rather than make general statements such as "play volleyball well." Unless statements of activity goals are specific, the statements will be of no use to the designer or planner. It is difficult to start with a final goal of "achieve cardiovascular fitness" and then to design instruction to reach that goal. It is far easier to start with a goal such as "run 4 miles in less than 28 minutes." Instructional experiences can easily be arranged to achieve the second goal, because the designer or planner knows exactly what is to be accomplished.

Clear statements of student performance goals have embedded within them the means for evaluation, both of students and of the instructional program. A statement of performance establishes a criterion. A **criterion** is a performance measure that can be used for student and program evaluation. Using performance criteria for evaluation purposes is referred to as criterion-referenced evaluation. In **criterion-referenced evaluation**, students are judged against a performance standard rather than against one another. The competition is against the standard rather than against one's classmates. (Judging performance on the basis of relative standing within a group is referred to as **norm-referenced evaluation**—what is traditionally called "grading on the curve.")

Thus, the designer or planner starts by defining outcomes in terms of student performance—what the students should be able to do after the instruction is completed. This is the first step in good instructional design. Without it, program planning is less meaningful, simply because nobody has bothered to consider exactly what the program is supposed to accomplish.

Develop Terminal Goals as Meaningful Units of Performance

The overall goals of any unit within a program are referred to as terminal goals. A **terminal goal** is a statement of student performance to be achieved as the end result of an instructional unit. It is important that terminal goals be defined as meaningful units of performance, ones that students could be expected to work toward and achieve. A **meaningful unit of performance** is one that has meaning in terms of a real-world outcome, an outcome that is recognizable and useful for settings other than the instructional setting.

For most physical education programs, at least those where sport activities are the organizing centers, the terminal goal must be defined in terms of the game setting or the parent activity setting. To define a terminal goal for tennis as performance on a wall volley test, for example, violates this principle. Terminal objectives for tennis should be defined in terms of playing the game of tennis, rather than in terms of the isolated skills of tennis, tested in nongame situations. This also means that "passing a test on tennis rules" is not a meaningful terminal goal simply because passing a test is not the relevant performance of tennis knowledge in the real world. Instead, a terminal goal such as "while playing, scores the game correctly and identifies rule violations correctly" would be more appropriate because it defines the final outcome of instruction as knowledge used correctly in the game setting.

Each unit within a program should lead to the acquisition of meaningful behavior that is useful to the student in settings other than the instructional setting. By specifying unit goals in terms of student performance and requiring that they be meaningful units of performance, the designer or planner takes the most important steps toward ensuring a relevant unit plan. These unit plans, taken together, constitute a relevant program. Here are some examples of terminal goals of meaningful student performance:

- Students dribble ball up court under defensive pressure without committing violations.
- Students rally with opponents from behind the baseline using forehand and backhand shots.
- During game conditions, students keep score accurately.
- During game conditions, students recognize violations and describe appropriate consequences.
- Using roll or flop techniques, students high jump a minimum height.
- While in the water, students clear breathing device.
- While in game setting, students keep proper defensive spacing and positioning relative to opponents.
- In game situation, students execute a three-lane fast break.
- In game situation, students execute double-play maneuvers.
- Students complete the vita parcourse, doing all designated exercises at each point on the parcourse, under a minimum time.
- In game setting, students use proper kicking technique according to situation.

Use Task Analysis to Develop Unit Content

How is the content of a unit actually developed? How does a designer or planner actually decide what is to be taught? The best way to accomplish this phase of instructional design is to complete a task analysis for each terminal goal that has been developed. A **task analysis** is a procedure whereby units of performance are identified that the student must learn in order to achieve the terminal goal. A task analysis starts with the terminal goal and works back toward that point where the essentials of the skill are identified. If a terminal goal is developed for a basketball unit such as "dribbles the ball up court under defensive pressure without committing violations," a task analysis would take that goal as a starting point and work back to see where one would have to begin to eventually reach that point.

Two kinds of task analysis are useful for designers and planners. The first, a **procedural task analysis**, is a description of a chain of events that together define a meaningful unit of performance. Activities such as bowling, shooting arrows in archery, vaulting in gymnastics, running a three-lane fast break in basketball, and the long jump in track and field are typical of those skills for which a procedural analysis is quite useful. A procedural task analysis would be diagrammed like this:

Instructional Goal = Complete Long Jump with Proper
Approach, Takeoff, and Landing

Running → Last Stride → Takeoff → Float → Landing
Approach   and Foot Plant   from Board

For skills in which a procedural task analysis is useful, the individual elements of the chain (the foot plant, the takeoff, and so on) can be learned somewhat independently and then put together to form the chain. Usually, the individual elements of the chain are fairly easy to learn. It is the "putting together" that represents the crucial aspects of the instruction. The final outcome requires that each element of the chain be performed smoothly and in an integrated fashion. A breakdown at any element tends to ruin the entire performance.

A procedural task analysis is useful for identifying the points at which instruction should be focused, both in identifying the elements of the chain and in pinpointing the crucial spots at which the elements have to be linked together smoothly for a skilled performance. The long jump represents a short, fairly simple chain; rebounding and initiating a fast break in basketball represents a considerably more complex set of elements. A procedural task analysis of a fast break is shown in Figure 9-2. Notice how the analysis allows the designer or planner to identify the important learning tasks (the elements of

Figure 9-2. *Some Possible Fast-Break Behavior Chains for a Basketball Player Rebounding*

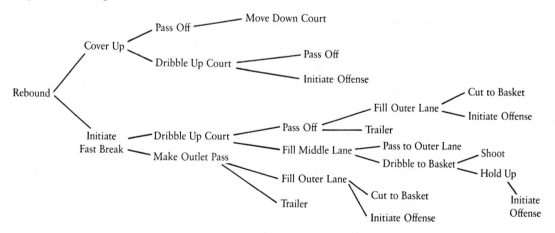

the chain) and also the points at which they need to be put together smoothly for a skilled performance.

The second type of analysis, a **hierarchical task analysis**, is a description of all of the subskills that must be learned in order to perform the terminal skill. In a hierarchical task analysis, there is a necessary relationship between the skills. One skill must be learned before the other can be learned (unlike the procedural task analysis, where elements can be learned independently). In a hierarchical analysis, the designer or planner starts with the terminal goal and asks the question "What will the student have to be able to do in order to accomplish this task?" This question is asked again and again until the basic entry skills for the task are reached. A hierarchical task analysis would be diagrammed as shown in Figures 9-3 and 9-4.

The hierarchical task analysis identifies only those skills *necessary* for accomplishing the higher-level skill. With practice, designers and planners become competent at identifying relevant subskills and adjusting the size of the subskill steps so that they are best suited to the needs of the learners. The size of steps from one subskill to another is crucial to the success of the design. If the steps are too large, students will experience failure too often and lose interest and enthusiasm. If the steps are too small, they might become bored. The designer or planner works to establish steps that are large enough to

Figure 9-3. *Hierarchical Task Analysis* (I)

Goal: The student will perform a swivel hips on the trampoline.

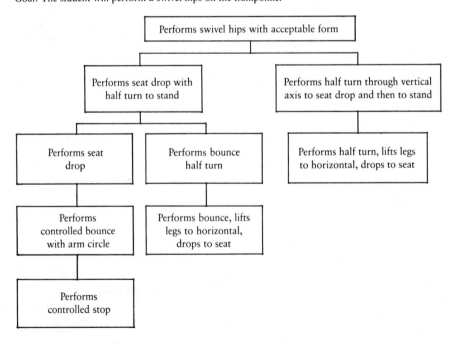

Goal: In a volleyball game, the student will successfully execute the overhead volley 80 percent of the opportunities afforded.

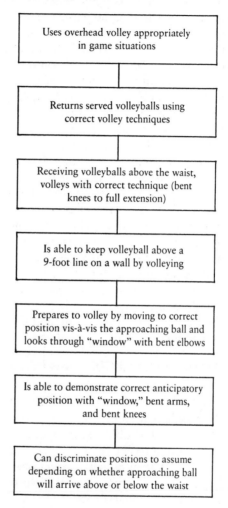

Figure 9-4. *Hierarchical Task Analysis* (II)

be continually challenging and small enough so that students have frequent success.

Once terminal goals for a unit have been identified in terms of meaningful units of student performance and then those meaningful units have been task analyzed, most of the unit's content is developed. The subskills and elements that have been analyzed become the stuff from which enabling objectives are developed. An **enabling objective** is a description of student performance that will contribute directly to the achievement of terminal goals. The list of subskills and elements identified through the task analysis step represents a content outline for a unit. Typically, the designer or planner will see immediately that there is more content than can be included in most units. This represents another benefit of conducting the task analysis. By having identified terminal objectives and having conducted the necessary task analysis, you will see immediately that what looked like a unit on a simple activity is, in fact, extraordinarily complex—that is, if you really want to achieve those terminal goals!

A common error made in planning for physical education activity is that of looking at the activity as a single entity rather than as a group of skills. Volleyball is an activity, not a skill. More precisely, volleyball is the name of a game. In planning a volleyball unit, you must plan your content in terms of the time it will take to master adequately some of the skills of volleyball; that is, set-up, chest passing, bump passing, various serves, spiking, rotating, receiving strategy, defensive maneuvers, offensive maneuvers, rules, and scoring. If you have classes on three days a week for five weeks, you should not assume that you can teach all there is to learn about these skills. The content outline will help you realize the complexity of learning these skills and will also help you exercise some restraint in planning. Plan a unit so that students accomplish something specific, even if it is of a limited nature. If you attempt to cover everything about volleyball, then you run the risk of creating a situation where students learn nothing that is of lasting importance. Many students reach college having had three or four units of volleyball throughout their elementary, junior high, and senior high school experience, yet are unable to serve overhand, bump pass, or execute a legitimate set-up pass.

Use Instructional Objectives to Identify Learning Tasks

An **instructional objective** makes clear to the teacher and learner what task is to be done, under what conditions it will be learned, and what standards will be used to judge completion of the task. The development and use of instructional objectives has been one of the most important advances in education in recent years.

Note that although instructional objectives make clear what is to be learned, this does not mean that the only thing learned is that which is stated in the instructional objective. The use of precise objectives is often criticized because it is thought to preclude the learning of other important educational outcomes. This criticism is invalid on several grounds.

First, if an educational outcome is of prime importance it ought to be stated as an instructional objective and become a primary objective of the instructional system. Second, if an educational outcome cannot be stated as an instructional objective, then it probably cannot be taught and no measure of whether it has been learned is possible. Third, the fact that certain outcomes are stated in terms of specific objectives does not mean that nothing else will be learned. Stating skill development in terms of instructional objectives in no way precludes the development of social and emotional outcomes. Aiming instruction directly at a social behavior outcome (stated as an instructional objective) does not mean that no skill will be developed.

The purpose of an instructional objective is to communicate an instructional intent by describing what will happen as the result of an instructional experience. In teaching volleyball, it is standard procedure to list on a lesson plan the objective of learning the overhead pass. The overhead pass is an observable task, but simply stating that the student will "learn" this skill is not sufficient. In writing an instructional objective for this task, the conditions under which it will be performed and the criteria by which it will be judged must be included. Where does the student stand? How does the ball come to him or her? How high does it have to be hit? Where does it have to go? How many attempts does he or she get? How many successful passes have to be completed? Consider the following two examples of instructional objectives (Rushall and Siedentop 1972):

> Standing in the back center of the court, the student will toss the ball to herself and execute four of five overhead passes that reach a minimum height of 10 feet and land in the front left section of the court.

> Standing behind a line drawn 12 feet from a wall, the student will make eight continuous overhead passes that hit the wall within a designated target area drawn at a height of 10 feet.

All the questions posed in the previous paragraph are answered in these two objectives. The learner knows the situation, the task, and the criteria by which the task will be judged. It is useful to construct objectives in terms of these three components. The second objective has the following components:

Situation	Task	Criteria
Standing behind a line drawn 12 feet from a wall	Eight continuous overhead passes	Hit the wall within a target area drawn at a height of 10 feet

It is important to make sure that an instructional objective excludes skills that the teacher does not want developed. To develop a task for serving in tennis that states only, "The learner will serve four of five legal serves" allows the student to complete the task by hitting a "bloop" serve, which no doubt is not the intent of the instructor. This can be avoided in at least two ways. First, the criteria could require that the serve must pass between the net and a string stretched parallel to and above the net at a height that would require the student to serve with sufficient velocity to make it a good serve. Second, the criteria could require that the serve must land beyond a certain line on the first bounce, thus guaranteeing a measure of velocity in the serve. The instructional intent is for the student to learn to serve accurately and with a certain velocity. This is achieved when the criteria are stated so that the only way the student can complete the task is by serving in a manner that is consistent with that intent.

There are two ways of making instructional objectives for any given task more or less difficult: (1) by manipulating the conditions under which the task is performed and (2) by manipulating the criteria by which the task will be judged. For example, a bump pass task could be made progressively more difficult by holding the criteria at a given level (reach a height of 10 feet and land within a designated target area) and manipulating the conditions in the following manner:

Condition 1: Bump pass by throwing ball to yourself.
Condition 2: Bump pass a ball lobbed to you by a partner standing 10 feet away.
Condition 3: Bump pass a ball thrown across the net.
Condition 4: Bump pass a ball served by an opponent.

The changes in conditions make the task gradually more difficult, even though the task is the same and the criteria for successful completion are the same.

The same purpose can be accomplished by holding the conditions constant and varying the criteria. If the task is the bump pass and the conditions are a "ball served by an opponent," the task can be sequenced by changing the criteria in the following manner:

Criterion 1: Reach a minimum height of 8 feet and land within bounds on your side of the court.
Criterion 2: Reach a minimum height of 10 feet and land within the front half of the court.
Criterion 3: Reach a minimum height of 15 feet and land within a specified target area in the front left or front right of your side of the court.

These criteria allow for a gradually higher and more accurate bump pass. Obviously, by combining changes in the conditions and criteria it is easy to sequence a series of instructional objectives to develop the instructional task of bump passing.

Objectives can also be sequenced by changing the performance requirements; the conditions and criteria might be held constant. Consider the following sequence of balance tasks:

Instructional Objective 1: Balance on one foot for 10 seconds with your arms in any position.
Instructional Objective 2: Balance on one foot for 10 seconds with your arms folded across your body and your knee held high.
Instructional Objective 3: Balance on one foot for 10 seconds with your eyes closed.
Instructional Objective 4: Balance on one foot for 10 seconds with your eyes closed and your arms folded.

In each of these objectives, the conditions are the same (standing on a line or standing on a beam) and the criterion remains constant (10 seconds). The performance becomes slightly more difficult in each objective. Thus, instructional objectives can be sequenced by changing conditions, altering the task itself, or changing the criteria by which the performance is judged. The combinations available with these three options allow for a wide variety of methods of sequencing objectives to achieve the completion of instructional tasks.

Instructional objectives can be written for skill, strategy, knowledge, and social outcomes. The value of analyzing a task in terms of instructional objectives is that it helps you and the learner understand precisely what is to be learned. Suppose you are teaching a basketball unit and you want your students to "understand" the 1–2–2 zone defense. The verb *to understand* is not acceptable in writing instructional objectives because it does not specify exactly what the task is. The following three objectives might reflect a certain level of "understanding":

> The student will diagram a 1–2–2 zone defense.
> On direction by the instructor, the student will take the correct position in a 1–2–2 zone defense.
> Given diagrams of zone defenses, the student will correctly identify the 1–2–2.

The first objective could be done from memory and is a memory-level task. The second objective refers not to a paper-and-pencil understanding of the defense, but to taking up a proper position (low left wing, upper right wing, point, or whatever) when instructed to do so. The third objective represents a higher order of understanding because the student must identify the 1–2–2 from among other zone defenses, which requires him or her to differentiate the 1–2–2 from the 2–3 or 1–3–1. When constructing objectives for knowledge and strategy outcomes, make sure that you are reaching the level of understanding that you desire.

Examples of behavioral objectives follow. Examine each objective and identify the component(s) missing from the component diagram immediately following the objective.

1. Dropping the ball from your hands, you will kick balls so that four of five go a minimum of 30 yards.

Situation	Task	Criterion
Dropping the ball from your hands	Kick	

2. While standing in water 4 feet deep, you will submerge and correctly count the number of fingers your partner extends.

Situation	Task	Criterion
	Submerge and count fingers	Correct count of fingers

3. Given a problem involving backward movement at a fast speed, you will solve the problem in at least three different ways.

Situation	Task	Criterion
A problem involving backward movement at a fast speed		Three solutions that are distinctly different

4. With a teammate standing 10 yards away, you will pass the ball in a diagonal direction so that the ball passes no more than 2 feet in front of the teammate.

Situation	Task	Criterion
	Pass the ball	

5. While running down court, you and your partner will pass the ball back and forth so that no violation is committed.

Situation	Task	Criterion

6. When in the pool area, you will always walk.

Situation	Task	Criterion
		Always

7. When the instructor is talking or demonstrating to the class, you will watch and not talk.

Situation	Task	Criterion
		Implied criterion of "always"

8. Given a diagram of a tennis court, you will identify and label all court markings.

Situation	Task	Criterion
		Implied criterion of 100% accuracy

9. Given a written description of a golf situation, you will correctly identify the rule involved and the penalty imposed.

Situation	Task	Criterion
Written description of a golf situation		

Instructional objectives should be evaluated on the basis of four qualities. First, the situation should be clearly specified so the student knows what will or will not be available to him or her. Second, the task should be stated so that it refers to an observable behavior. Verbs such as *identify, underline, label, dribble, pass, run, swim free style,* and *high jump* refer to tasks that will be recognizable to the student. Verbs such as *understand, appreciate, know, know how to do,* and *learn* do not refer to tasks that students can easily translate into action. The degree to which a task is properly stated is judged by the kind of verb used in the objective. Verbs that do not have behavioral referents will result in students coming to you seeking further information. If a verb is not sufficiently specific the solution is usually found in the criterion. The following objective uses a verb that is unclear and has no criterion:

The student will learn the overhand serve.

This confusion can be cleared up by stating a specific criterion such as the following:

The student will learn the overhand serve, as demonstrated by his or her ability to hit three of four legal overhand serves that pass between the net and a string stretched parallel to and 4 feet above the net and land within the court boundaries.

Any objective that uses an unclear verb usually has to have an "as demonstrated by" clause attached to it. It is even easier to remove the imprecise verb and state the objective directly:

> The student will serve three of four legal overhand serves that pass between the net and a string stretched parallel to and 4 feet above the net and land in bounds.

The criterion is judged by how clearly it expresses the standard by which the task will be judged. Often, as indicated in some of the objectives shown on previous pages, the criterion is an implied 100 percent. If students are supposed to walk on a pool deck, mount a trampoline only when four spotters are in place, watch demonstrations, or refrain from pushing ahead in lines, it is implicit that this behavior should occur all the time.

Objectives should not allow for performance that is not the intent of the instructor. Students should not be able to complete serve objectives by hitting "bloop" serves. Students should not be able to complete push-up objectives by doing incorrect push-ups. Students should not be able to complete analysis objectives simply by memorizing material. This problem is best avoided by stating the criterion in such a way that in order to complete the objective the student would have to perform somewhere within the boundaries of the instructional intent.

Many educators who attempt to write instructional objectives are concerned with the problem of form. Objectives should not include criteria based on the physical form of a performance unless physical form is the objective of the performance, as in gymnastics, diving, or dance. An objective that attempts to impose a particular form on a tennis serve is doomed to failure because the judgment about form is always subjective and students may hit really good serves that do not conform precisely to the form specifications. The best solution is to arrange the performance criteria so that in order to complete the objective the student would have to use a form that is within the general standards of acceptable form. For example, although very detailed criteria could be written for the form of a golf swing, it would be much better to write an objective such as "Standing 90 yards from the green, the student will hit four of five 9-iron shots that land on and remain on the green." The fact that the criterion states that the shot must "land on the green" ensures that this will be a genuine 9-iron shot with proper height and not a low run-up shot. The fact that the criterion states that the shot must "stay on the green" ensures that the shot will be hit properly so that the appropriate backspin is applied to the ball in order to have it stay on the green. Any form that could produce these results would have to be considered proper form. When the objective is stated in this manner, the goal is clear to the student and there is no room for arguing about whether or not "proper" form was used.

We started by selecting broad goals toward which the physical education program is to be directed. Now we have reached the stage of specifying individual instructional objectives that communicate clearly to the learner what is to be learned, under what conditions it is to be performed, and by what standard the performance will be judged as successful. Overall goals were first selected. Then organizing centers for the program were chosen. Then activities to meet the goals were identified. Then the actual process of instructional design began with the question "What do I want the learners to be able to do as a result of instruction?" Meaningful units of performance in the identified activities were developed as terminal goals for each unit. Task analyses were conducted so that relevant subskills and elements of the terminal goals could be identified. The task analysis resulted in a content outline from which actual learning experiences could be chosen and developed. The nature of the specific learning experiences was specified in the development of instructional objectives. Note that all this was done without regard to the style of teaching to be employed.

These program-planning procedures are necessary and useful regardless of what teaching methodology is employed in the actual instruction. When goals are held in common and specified clearly, there are many delightfully different ways to achieve them. When program and unit planning have been done well, the methodology used to implement them is not nearly as important as many believe—the major factor is not the methodology but the presence or absence of the prior planning. Good methodology cannot rescue bad planning. Without good planning, one could not possibly know exactly what to implement, regardless of the methodology chosen. Once planning at this level is done, it can be used in many different ways for many years and makes daily planning, to be discussed in the next chapter, quite easy.

CHAPTER 10

Planning the Daily Lesson

Most students (perhaps over 90 percent) can master what we have to teach them, and it is the task of instruction to find the means which will enable our students to master the subject under consideration. Our basic task is to determine what we mean by mastery of the subject and to search for the methods and materials which will enable the largest proportion of our students to attain such mastery.

Benjamin Bloom, *Learning for Mastery* (1980)

CHAPTER OBJECTIVES

To distinguish among direct instruction, task, and inquiry styles of teaching

To consider basic questions to be addressed when planning a lesson

To describe the role and provide examples of instructional aids and devices

To describe ways in which a motivational situation can be assessed

To show how a contingency management system is used

To suggest guidelines for planning lectures and demonstrations

To distinguish among informing, extending, refining, and applying tasks

To show how tasks are sequenced to form a coherent lesson

To describe options for monitoring the performance of students

To describe and provide examples of how planning principles can be used for game play

To characterize the lesson as a time script

If long-term planning has been done properly (see Chapter 9), the planning of individual lessons or groups of lessons is much easier. The content outline (see Chapter 9) reveals the skills to be taught and the order in which they may need to be introduced. Instructional objectives written for unit plans make the task of planning individual lessons even easier. Nonetheless, the daily lesson plan is important because here all the previous planning finally reaches the point at which it will actually be experienced by students. The choice of instructional methods now begins to interact with the content as defined in long-term planning.

The Relationship of Teaching Method to Planning

A variety of methods are available to the physical education teacher. All the many styles discussed in the physical education literature seem to be classifiable into three categories: (1) direct instruction, (2) task teaching, and (3) inquiry. Each method requires daily planning, and each can be done using the kind of long-term planning described in Chapter 9.

Chapter 3 described direct instruction as that style of teaching that has been most associated with effectiveness in classroom teaching. Direct instruction encompasses styles in which goals are clear to students, time allocated for practice is high, the performance of students is monitored carefully, and the lesson is controlled and paced by the teacher with high rates of academic feedback, and in a warm, nurturant classroom climate.

Task teaching has as its main feature the programming of learning tasks into the learning setting rather than being paced by the teacher through verbal instructions. When task descriptions are available, students can go at different paces rather than as an entire group moving from task to task at the control of the teacher. Task teaching is sometimes referred to as "station teaching," because often different tasks are set up at each station. Students move not only from task to task within stations, but from task to task between stations (dribbling tasks at one station, passing tasks at a second station, and so on). Contingency management teaching (Rushall and Siedentop 1972) is also a task style, with rewards tied to the completion of tasks in a system that produces strong motivation. Tasks can be done by individuals, by pairs (sometimes called "reciprocal teaching"), or by small groups.

The inquiry styles of teaching are most often referred to as "guided discovery" and "problem solving" (Mosston 1966). The major feature of these styles is that they are thought to contribute to important *process* goals. The term **guided discovery** refers to a teacher-controlled style in which a carefully arranged series of instructions gradually leads the student through a series of experiences in which a goal is finally reached. In **problem solving**, the initial task is posed by the teacher, but then students attempt to solve it in unique ways, with divergent responses being considered to be fully appropriate. The student explores alternative solutions to the problems posed and finds an acceptable solution. Some educators feel that the processes of guided discovery and problem solving provide valuable experience for the learner.

Many physical educators feel that the style of teaching should be chosen that is best suited to the activity and to the students being taught. Therefore, it is common to find inquiry styles used for movement lessons in the K–3 part of the program. Activities such as gymnastics, weight training, fitness activities, and aquatics are often taught using task styles. Most team sports such as volleyball and soccer are taught using direct instruction styles. This is not to suggest, of course, that an inquiry style could not be used to teach soccer. It could. So too could a task style be used to teach basketball. And movement lessons can be taught using direct instruction styles. The choice of style is often a personal one for the individual teacher; most teachers feel that they operate best within one particular style.

As I have consistently noted in this book, there is no evidence to suggest that one teaching style is any better than another. Direct instruction has been shown to be most effective in classroom teaching because it seems to be well suited to keeping students on task and engaged in the subject matter a high percentage of the time. But the ultimate lesson of teacher effectiveness research is clear: any style that produces high proportions of learning time for students can be effective! The proof lies not in the style itself but in the degree to which the style is used to produce high proportions of time in which students are engaged with their subject matter in a way that they can experience success.

Basic Questions to Consider When Planning the Lesson

Regardless of the style a teacher chooses, certain questions need to be answered when planning a lesson. These are the basic questions of instructional design, because answers to them go a long way to determine the quality of the learning experience from the learner's viewpoint. These basic instructional design questions are as follows:

1. How will students know what to do and when to do it?
2. How will students know how to do the task?
3. What opportunity will students have to practice the task?
4. How will students get feedback about how they are doing?
5. Why should students want to do the task?
6. How does one task relate to another to form a lesson?

Question 1 refers to instructions about how to organize, when to start, when to stop, when to change, and other such managerial information. Question 2 refers to information about how to do the task itself, what its main features are, what it looks like, what things to avoid, and how best to start practicing it. Question 3 refers to arrangements that maximize student learning time. Question 4 refers to what happens after a student actually practices the task: Does the student get accurate feedback? Does the student know what to look for in his or her own performance? Does the student know when the task has been completed? Question 5 is basically motivational. Many might argue that Question 5 should be answered first, and they may be right. Students will learn nothing unless they engage in practice, and they have to be motivated to do that. Each teacher has a different motivational level in his or her school and often motivational levels differ among classes within a school. Some answers to the motivational question will be found later in this chapter. Finally, Question 6, "How does one task relate to another?" focuses on the lesson as a coherent series of events leading to lesson goals.

Regardless of whether a teacher uses a direct instruction, a task, or an inquiry style, these six questions need to be attended to in planning the lesson. A task style may require different answers from a direct instruction style, but the *function* each question represents needs to be filled if learning is to occur.

A major learning problem in most educational settings is that each of these learning functions is filled by the teacher. If each teacher taught only one student, then the teacher could perform the functions easily and correlate them perfectly with the needs of that student. But few teachers have the luxury of giving only tutorials. Teachers must teach groups of individual students.

Notice that I did not say they teach groups of *students*—they teach groups of individuals. Each individual student may need information at a different moment, may need more or less practice time, may need different feedback, or may need to move on to another task. The major issue in teaching is "How can a teacher satisfy these learning functions for each individual at the moment that the individual needs it?" The clear answer is that the teacher can't do it! At least, not if the teacher performs all of the functions him- or herself as the lesson progresses. That's OK! This is not a call for individualized instruction. The fact of the matter is, as shown in Chapter 3, that research indicates clearly that direct instruction, where the teacher does indeed perform most of these functions, is currently the most effective way to teach in American schools. Individualized instruction, for the most part, has been shown to be less effective.

Do I Really Need a Learning System?

Situation. A teacher is using a movement education approach to teach beginning ball skills. The teacher uses this approach because he or she believes that the ball skills will be learned and also that the students will be more creative and self-reliant learners. The teacher does not use instructional objectives or monitor student performance because he or she feels that this makes things too rigid.

Results. The teacher never knows whether his or her goals are being achieved except through impressions, which no doubt are biased toward what he or she wants to see.

Analysis. No estimate of any teaching method can be made when the goals of the instruction are not made specific and when there is no attempt to ascertain the degree to which those goals are being achieved. If creativity and self-reliance in learning are considered important, then instructional objectives should be developed to attain those ends and student performance should be monitored to see whether students are becoming more creative and self-reliant.

Prescription. Objectives in terms of new forms created, problems solved, unique solutions, and the ability to work without direct supervision should be written out, and student performance in these areas should be monitored intermittently to ascertain whether the instructional system is meeting its goals.

This does not mean that individualized instruction is less useful. It means only that teachers who use individualized instruction do not always supervise and monitor their students carefully, and students then tend to get off task and are not engaged as much as they should be. Direct instruction allows teachers to keep students on task and in learning time as much as possible. That's why it shows up as an effective style. Although each student may not get exactly what he or she needs at the moment he or she needs it, and although the pace is that of the group rather than individuals, the style still produces enough learning time to be highly effective. Moreover, in direct instruction most of the learning functions described in the six questions are carried out clearly, quickly, and positively. Students do know what to do and when to do it. Instructions are clear and brief. Students have many opportunities to respond. Academic feedback rates are high. The teacher is businesslike and positive, thus creating a favorable motivational climate. Tasks tend to relate to one another in such a way that students continue to have success as they move from one task to another, all leading to a logical conclusion that reflects the lesson goals.

General Concerns in Lesson Planning

Physical educators need to consider several general concerns as they approach the task of planning daily lessons within a unit. The unit content outline, as discussed in the previous chapter, provides a solid foundation from which to begin planning. If behavioral objectives have also been developed as part of the unit planning (again, as discussed in the previous chapter), then the task of daily planning is that much easier. Still, certain concerns need to be attended to for specific situations. For example, a plan that might work nicely for one sixth-grade class or one ninth-grade class might not work quite so well for another, even though both classes may be in the same school. These general daily planning concerns involve providing instructional aids, assessing the motivational characteristics of classes, developing an extrinsic motivational system if necessary, and planning for any lecture or demonstration sequences used to give important information to students.

Identify Potential Instructional Aids and Devices

There is a distinction between instructional aids and instructional devices. An **instructional aid** is any implement, machine, or device used to clarify the presentation of material; for example, projectors, blackboards, magnetic play boards, stick figures, loop films, and written handouts. An **instructional device** is any implement or machine used in skill instruction to restrict the scope of the learner's response, to provide feedback, or to increase the number of attempts a learner has per unit of time. It is important to make an inventory of the instructional aids and devices available in your teaching situation. This inventory can be used to select aids and devices to use in your daily instruction, and to determine what aids and devices may have to be obtained from other sources in order to implement your instructional plan.

The purpose of an instructional device is to improve the learning environment so that the student can learn more easily and efficiently. An instructional device can be as simple as taping an extra line on a badminton court to provide a target for practicing the long serve. It remains for you to develop those devices that will best enhance your instructional system. Although it is true that a ball boy machine is a useful instructional device to increase the amount of practice per unit of time, you will probably not have such commercially manufactured devices available. Thus, it is up to you to develop "homemade" devices that will contribute to better learning.

Instructional devices are useful in any of the teaching methods described in this text. Instructional devices have three primary functions in an instructional system.

1. *Instructional devices can restrict the scope of the learner's response.* If you hang a tennis ball from a bamboo pole or a shuttlecock from a rafter and have students practice overhand shots, you are limiting the response of the student by how and where you hang the object to be struck. When you put a string or a hurdle in a long jump pit and have students jump over it to achieve height in the long jump, you are using that device to restrict the kind of response made. When you mark an X on a wall and have children watch the X as they walk a balance beam, you are again imposing restrictions on the response.

2. *Instructional devices can be used to provide feedback.* Precise feedback usually means quicker, better learning. Teachers can provide only a limited amount of feedback, and this is why instructional devices are important. For example, providing a target area for serving allows the student to judge each serve in terms of its proximity to the target. Providing mirrors for a dancer allows the student to see him- or herself performing the movements. Telling students to set a volleyball "high" is not sufficient unless they get precise feedback on their efforts. Having things arranged so that each set goes over a 12-foot-high rope lets them know immediately whether their set was sufficiently high.

3. *Instructional devices can be used to increase the amount of practice per unit of time.* Tennis students get more chances to hit when they have a machine throwing balls to them or when they hit against a wall. A shuttlecock hung from a rafter not only restricts the overhead stroke of the badminton players but also allows them to have a maximum number of swings per unit of time. Time is a valuable commodity in teaching and should be used to its utmost. Chasing balls, retrieving shuttlecocks, and not receiving a proper ball to hit are misuses of time.

Instructional devices for feedback are of sufficient importance to merit your special consideration. The term **artificial feedback** refers to feedback that is not part of a task the way it is normally performed; it is used for purposes of instruction. Obviously, a student can learn to shoot baskets merely by getting feedback about whether the previous shot went in and whether it was short, long, or off to one side of the hoop. This kind of feedback is intrinsic to basketball playing. In most sports, intrinsic feedback is very strong and is usually sufficient to develop skill. Many of us have learned to play certain sports quite well without having had any formal instruction that involved artificial feedback. But there are many aspects of skill training that can be enhanced by judicious use of artificial feedback devices. For example, how does a young jump shooter in basketball learn to jump straight up on his or her jump shot instead of wandering to one side or the other? The intrinsic feedback for this aspect of jump shooting is very weak. It helps to mark an X on the floor and then put strips of tape every 4 inches on each side of the X. Players dribble up to the X and shoot their jump shots, and when they come down from the shot, they can see precisely how far off the mark they have wandered. Both the X and the tape strips provide artificial feedback to improve the skill of jumping straight up on the jump shot.

Assess the Motivational Situation

A highly motivated student will learn a great deal regardless of the teaching method used. A sport skill can be learned to a high degree of proficiency without a trace of formal instruction. Perhaps you also have personal knowledge of the opposite situation—students may not seem to learn much even though the instruction is well planned and well implemented.

An analysis of the motivational situation in which you teach is perhaps the single most valuable piece of information you can have in planning for instruction. This is true because motivation is a crucial variable in the learning process. To spend a great deal of time planning for instruction without taking into account the level of motivation that you are likely to encounter during teaching will be frustrating when you attempt to execute your instructional plan—only to find out that the students do not react to it in the manner in which you thought they would. The following are some methods by which you can analyze the motivational needs of your teaching situation.

1. *Consult your cooperating teacher.* It is important that you find out what your cooperating teacher (the teacher to whom you as an intern are responsible) has had to do to motivate students. You can learn about this through discussion with him or her, and also by observation if you have the opportunity to observe his or her teaching. To what extent does the classroom management seem to be a problem?

2. *Consult other teachers in the school.* Other teachers can provide valuable information about how well students like physical education. The physical education teacher is not a good source of such information, because a teacher is usually the last to find out how students feel about his or her classes. Other teachers can tell you how students seem to react to physical education. This should not be seen as "telling tales," but

rather as a sincere effort to help you learn about the situation you are entering.

3. *Watch the students.* Some simple data collection and a perusal of certain school records provides important information. Do students get to physical education on time, or do they straggle in? When they enter, do they appear to be eager and happy, or subdued and uninterested? Is there a high absence rate or cutting rate in physical education? Do students appear to be glad or disappointed when the class ends? Do physical education skills seem to be valued within the peer culture of the school?

4. *Assess general and specific attitudes toward achievement.* Many schools are located in neighborhoods where children are taught at home that achievement in school is important. This helps motivate students in all phases of school life. In other situations academic achievement may not be strongly rewarded at home, but achievement in physical skills is highly valued. In still other situations students come to school not having learned that achievement is important, and they come from a peer culture that values fighting and other physical skills much more highly than sport skill. Each of these situations presents a remarkably different motivational problem.

5. *Directly assess the attitudes of students.* It is quite possible to use an attitude instrument or rating scale to assess directly student attitudes toward physical education. Through use of a rating instrument, you can find out students' attitudes toward their previous physical education experience, the importance of sport skill in their priorities, and how well they like being in physical education now.

Using some or all of these methods will provide the information necessary to plan for optimal motivation in your instructional system. A good instructional system enhances whatever motivational level exists within the class. The other elements of planning for instruction also have motivational implications. For example, well-written objectives, properly sequenced activities, and a quickly paced time plan all contribute to a more positive motivational response from students.

Motivation for learning, like classroom management, can have a negative or a positive orientation. In many educational situations, students are motivated to learn because they are threatened with punishment if they do not learn. A positive motivational climate, however, not only helps students learn more quickly but also sends them messages about school, learning, and teachers that will help them develop a lasting positive approach to learning sport skills.

Arrange an Extrinsic Motivation System If Necessary

If your motivation analysis indicates that students are normally motivated (which means that they have learned that achievement in school is important and their behavior in physical education class shows a desire to achieve), then effective use of verbal and nonverbal interactions will help set a motivational climate for the instructional system to be effective. Positive interactions based on appropriate learning behavior and skill development will set a general classroom climate conducive to achievement (see Chapters 5 and 7).

The components of an instructional system can increase the students' motivational level. When students have clear goals and know what criteria exist for measuring achievement toward those goals, they can monitor their own progress and this itself improves motivation. Sequencing objectives properly so that students are challenged but experience success regularly also increases motivational level. The motivational implications of the instructional system, combined with verbal and nonverbal interactions, are the elements of a strong motivational system.

The potential motivational power of the instructional objectives cannot be overemphasized. By stating each objective clearly and by providing evaluation criteria, you really make a game out of each objective. To hit four successful serves out of five attempts, to successfully make three out of five bump passes to a specific target, to dribble a ball through an obstacle course below a set time, and to kick a certain number of balls against a target area—each provides a game element as students compete against the standard to reach the objective and compete informally among themselves to see who can do best. This cannot happen if the objective is not clear and the criteria are not sufficiently specific.

If students lack motivation in physical education, then an extrinsic system of motivation may be necessary. Do not hesitate to use an extrinsic motivational system if your analysis indicates a strong need for motivation. This is particularly true if the students' previous experience in physical education has been negative and if they now view physical education as a class to avoid if possible. It is also true if your analysis indicates a general lack of achievement orientation toward the learning of physical education skills. If either situation exists, your use of verbal and nonverbal interactions may not be sufficiently effective to overcome their previous experience. That is, if achievement is not important to them, then praise from the person most directly associated with the achievement environment will not be important either.

Contingency management may be used as an extrinsic motivation system. A **contingency** is a statement of relationship between the completion of an instructional task and a system of rewards. The management of a reward system to motivate students toward desired educational outcomes is the management of contingencies; hence the term *contingency management*. The use of an instructional system means that you already have half of a contingency management system completed, as you will notice when you inspect the four main steps in developing a contingency management system.

1. Specify primary instructional tasks in behavioral terms.

2. Sequence instructional objectives to develop instructional tasks.

3. Select rewards that are appropriate to your situation and not generally available outside the situation.

4. Specify precise relationships (contingencies) between task completion and rewards earned.

As the first two of these steps have been discussed at length in this section, the focus here is on selecting rewards and arranging contingencies. Rewards may range from contrived reinforcers to naturally occurring reinforcers. At higher levels of education, grades are often used as a reward system, and this is certainly a possibility for contingency management. The key to using grades is being reasonably sure that they have sufficient strength to act as rewards for the majority of the students. Other rewards that have been shown to be quite effective with younger children are badges, stars, membership in a special club, and membership in advancing skill groups (such as moving from tadpole to dolphin in a swimming program).

A very profitable way of establishing a reward system is to use the naturally occurring rewards available in the school. The best way to find out what these rewards are is to examine the activities that students like to do. Their favorite activities can be used as rewards. This technique allows them to engage in a favorite activity to motivate them to learn another activity. This technique is widely known as the Premack principle, because it was developed from the work of psychologist David Premack (1964). The **Premack principle** states that a favored activity can be used to motivate learning in a less favored activity.

The favorite activities can be confined to physical education or they can be schoolwide activities, the choice being dictated by the extent to which you can control access to schoolwide activities. Some physical education activities that are usually valuable as reward activities are swimming, pick-up basketball, rope jumping, trampolining, and using scooters. It should be emphasized that the proper way to establish the Premack principle technique is to see what is favored by your students. Schoolwide activities that have been shown to be successful as rewards include going to the library, reading comic books, watching television, playing cards, working in an auto shop or biology lab, and gaining access to a student union.

Specifying the contingencies for a motivational system usually involves the use of points. Each task is given a certain point value. Each reward is given a point value. The student earns points by completing tasks and then is free to trade in those points for a reward of his or her choice. It is important to emphasize that a contingency management system must have a variety of rewards available. This is one reason why grades are not necessarily the best reward system. Ideally, the variety of rewards should be sufficient to have each student optimally motivated and should allow students to shift back and forth among the rewards in order to maintain the highest motivation possible.

Another variation that has proven successful is to exchange points for

Points	Reward Activity
5	Use of jump ropes for 5 minutes
5	Use of tumbling tubes for 5 minutes
5	Use of minitramp for 5 minutes
5	Shooting baskets for 5 minutes
5	Entry into one dodgeball game
25	One extra physical education period
15	Choose and lead one group activity during class
50	Serve as teacher's aide for younger group for 2 weeks

Figure 10-1. *Reward Menu for an Elementary Physical Education Program*

Exchange System: 1 point = 10 minutes of free time
Free-Time Activities
Basketball
Swimming (minimum of 4 points)
Reading or talking in bleachers
Gymnastics
Individual lesson
Fencing

Figure 10-2. *Reward System for a Junior or Senior High School Physical Education Program*

minutes of free time. During free time, students can engage in certain activities designated as free-time activities. The most beneficial aspect of this variation is that it simplifies the exchange system. Students earn a certain amount of free time and spend it as they wish (within the constraints previously agreed to by the teacher and the class). Two examples of reward systems are shown in Figures 10-1 and 10-2. To develop a complete contingency management system, you would only have to assign each instructional task a point value.

Notice that in each system points can be accumulated in order to earn larger rewards. Notice that the elementary system is more ordered, while the system for older students is more flexible and easier to administer.

If students at the high school level are considered normally motivated, and if you choose an individualized instruction methodology, a contingency management system using grades can be a very effective way to present your instructional system. Figure 10-3 shows a contingency management plan using grades as rewards (Siedentop and Rife 1974). This plan is appropriate for senior high students. It does not use points but instead divides the instructional tasks into levels that correspond to the grades to be earned. This kind of system is appropriate for any activity in which the major focus is on the development of individual skills (swimming, basketball, soccer, tennis, and so on).

Notice that there is an overhead clear objective for each of the three grade levels. This instructional task was considered to be of sufficient difficulty that

Level C Tasks

Short Serve: Hit three of five birds that pass between the net and a line stretched parallel to and 18 inches above the net so that the bird lands within an 18-inch area behind the opponent's short service line.

Long Serve: Hit three of five birds that reach a minimum height of 9 feet and land in play within 3 feet of the opponent's back boundary line.

Underhand Clear: Receiving birds hit to you below wrist level, return three of five that reach a minimum height of 9 feet and land in the opponent's back court.

Overhead Drop Shot: Receiving a high shot in your backcourt, drop three of five that pass between the net and a line stretched parallel to and 18 inches above the net and land in the opponent's forecourt.

Overhead Clear: Receiving a high shot in the back 6 feet of your court, hit three of five clears that reach a minimum height of 9 feet and land in play within 6 feet of your opponent's back boundary line.

Rallying: Rally 10 consecutive shots with the instructor.

Matches: Participate in six matches (singles, doubles, or mixed doubles). Record and report scores and participants.

Knowledge: Make 90 percent or better on a written test covering rules and strategy.

Level B Tasks

Overhead Clear: Receiving a high shot in the back 4 feet of your court, hit three of five birds that reach a minimum height of 9 feet and land in play within 4 feet of your opponent's back boundary line.

High Doubles Serve: Serve three of five that pass over opponent's outstretched racket and land in play within 2 feet of the long doubles service line.

Smash: Receiving a high shot at your midcourt, smash three of five to your opponent's midcourt.

Underhand Drop Shot: Receiving a bird below the waist at your midcourt, return three of five that pass between the net and a line stretched parallel to and 18 inches above the net and land in your opponent's forecourt.

Backhand Clear: Receiving a bird in your backcourt, clear three of five that reach a minimum height of 9 feet and land in play within 4 feet of your opponent's back boundary line.

Net Shot: Standing in front of the short service line, rally five consecutive times with a partner so that each shot passes between the net and a line stretched parallel to and 18 inches above the net.

Level A Tasks

Overhead Clear: Receiving a high shot in the back 2 feet of your court, hit three of five that reach a minimum height of 9 feet and land in play within 2 feet of your opponent's back boundary line.

Backhand Clear: Receiving a bird in your back court, clear three of five that reach a minimum height of 9 feet and land in play within 2 feet of your opponent's back boundary line.

Push Shot: Receiving a bird at midcourt, push three of five that pass between the net and a string stretched parallel to and 18 inches above the net and land in play beyond the opponent's short service line.

Drive Serve: Hit three of five drive serves that land in the appropriate service areas.

Figure 10-3. *Badminton Contingency Management Plan*

it was sequenced into three progressive objectives in which the situation and criteria were made slightly more difficult.

Contingency management is a useful motivational technique that can take advantage of the naturally occurring rewards existing in the educational environment. Using contingency management should not eliminate emphasis on teacher-initiated motivation through verbal and nonverbal interactions. Indeed, the use of verbal and nonverbal positive interactions can be strengthened when they are combined with the rewards in a contingency management system. It should be hoped that over a period of time students will come to know the thrill and enjoyment of gaining skill in physical activity. This will create intrinsic motivation for achievement in physical education, and the contingency management system will no longer be needed.

Plan Lectures and Demonstrations Carefully

Physical educators tend to plan carefully for drills and games, but to do lectures or demonstrations "off the cuff." A lecture or demonstration can be used to introduce a new activity, to show various strategies in an activity, to teach higher level skills, or for motivational purposes. I feel that lectures and demonstrations should be kept to a minimum. Physical education should be primarily activity time. Students should spend a high percentage of time in active learning, which does not include sitting down listening to a teacher talk. Any material that can be presented in written form should be duplicated and handed out to students to study and learn outside of class. In this way activity time is not decreased any more than is necessary to clarify the material. Sometimes, however, a lecture or demonstration is useful, and it should be planned carefully. The following guidelines are suggested for planning lectures and demonstrations (Powell 1969).

1. A 50-minute lecture is approximately 5,000 words at a pace of 110 words per minute.
2. Lectures should be accompanied by a lecture outline that emphasizes the important points.
3. The vocabulary of the lecture should not be above the level of the students.
4. Visual aids should be used to enhance interest, focus attention, and clarify points that are difficult to transmit with words alone.
5. Visual and verbal explanations should reach students at the same time.
6. Provision should be made for feedback from students about the success of the lecture.

A well-planned lecture or demonstration can be enormously effective. Overhead transparencies can be used simultaneously with explanations of zone defenses in basketball. Loop films can be used simultaneously with explanations of gymnastics skills. Magnetic boards can be used to emphasize offensive maneuvers in soccer. Pictures and/or drawings can be used to emphasize key elements in the golf swing.

The language of the verbal presentation is important. The language must be appropriate not only for the age level of the students but also for their skill development level. Every sport and movement activity has a technical skill language of its own, and it is highly inappropriate to assume that students know that language as well as you do.

Physical preparations for a lecture or demonstration should be completed before the students enter the gymnasium. This again relates to the proper use of time. Students should never have to sit around waiting for you to get a projector out or put up charts on a wall. This should be done before class. The wasted time is valuable in terms of potential learning and creates situations in which behavior problems are much more likely to occur.

Planning the Lesson

Many school systems require teachers to prepare daily lesson plans and to have the next day's lesson plan on their desks when they leave school in the evening. Even where lesson plans are not required, they should be considered essential. If done well, reflecting appropriate long-term planning, they can serve several essential purposes. First, they remind teachers of *precisely* what is to be accomplished in each lesson. Second, they provide a *script* for showing how the major objectives are to be reached. Third, they can and should be used when judging the results of the lesson. Fourth, together with the other daily plans for any particular unit they are the best way to review and improve unit plans and instruction. Fifth, if you must be absent for some reason, a good lesson plan allows the substitute teacher to continue the unit without disrupting the flow of learning activities for the students.

A good lesson plan ought first of all to describe clearly the major goals for the day's activities. Well-written objectives (see Chapter 9) are probably the best way to describe the overall goals for a lesson. The good lesson plan ought also to show clearly how the activities are to be developed so that they reach the intended goals and so that the interrelationships among the activities are evident. A good lesson plan will also provide a clear "script" of the time to be devoted to each phase of the lesson. Finally, the good lesson plan ought to indicate any organizational and managerial factors that must be handled in order to allow the sequence of activities to flow smoothly and to maximize the time learners spend actually engaged in the tasks.

The Function of Tasks in a Complete Lesson

Any physical education lesson can be viewed as a series of tasks that are sequenced in order to achieve the overall goals of the lesson. Rink (1979) categorizes the kinds of tasks that are useful for building good progressions leading to goal achievement as (1) informing, (2) refining, (3) extending, or (4) applying tasks.

Informing tasks communicate a "Do this" message to the student. They provide new information to students and new directions to begin a new activity sequence. They are the first step in a new progression. Examples of informing tasks are teacher messages such as "Now let's work on dribbling with the other hand," "Next we will begin to practice the bump pass," "Today we will start with the zone defense," and "Everybody find his or her own space."

Refining tasks are designed to improve the qualitative aspects of performance by guiding the student to better or different ways to do the task. Examples are teacher messages such as "Let's try it again and roll the ball more slowly this time," "Now, let's see if we can get that set-up pass a little higher," and "This time let's see if we can get more trunk rotation into the putt." Refining tasks are building blocks in progressions.

Extending tasks are designed to quantitatively expand the content of the task by adding parts of a skill, changing the focus for the skill, adding a different dimension, seeking a variety of solutions, or combining separate skills into meaningful chains. Examples are moving from hitting the ball off a tee to hitting a pitched ball, teaching the ball toss in tennis first and then adding the serving motion, and teaching the screen in basketball and then adding a roll to create the screen and roll movement.

Applying tasks are designed to move the focus of the student outside the skill itself to a consequence of the skill so that the student has a standard of performance against which to test his or her growing abilities. Examples are teacher messages such as "Now, let's try to keep it in the air for ten consecutive hits," "Everybody shoot 20 free throws and keep a record of how many you make," and "Now, let's concentrate on how many throws hit the target." So too are putting students into modified game or game settings or scrimmages that are simulations of game settings.

In physical education teaching, two patterns of task development are often seen. They can be graphically displayed as in Figure 10-4. The graph represents a progression of tasks. Each task is represented by a dot. The dots are connected in the sequence in which they were presented.

In Example 1, the lesson is a series of informing tasks. No task is refined or extended. There is no application of any of the tasks learned. Example 2 specifies one or more informing tasks and then application tasks. There is no refinement of the task and no extension of the task prior to applying it. It is difficult to build useful progressions under either of these formats. In Example 1, students learn a series of new, isolated tasks and never get beyond that introductory stage. In Example 2, the student is usually thrust into an applying task before he or she is ready for it, not having had any opportunity to

Figure 10-4. *Patterns of Task Development: Examples 1 and 2*

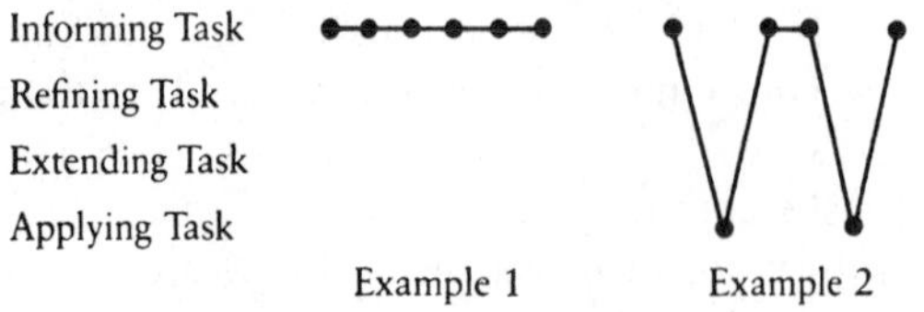

Informing Task
Refining Task
Extending Task
Applying Task

Example 1   Example 2

Informing Task
Refining Task
Extending Task
Applying Task

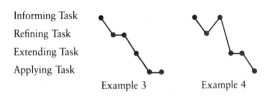

Example 3   Example 4

Figure 10-5. *Patterns of Task Development: Examples 3 and 4*

refine or extend the task before it is presented in the more complex application task.

A far more useful approach to planning lessons is to consider a more limited number of tasks and then to refine and extend them, finally achieving some natural conclusion to the progression in an application task. Such lessons are shown schematically in Figure 10-5.

In Example 3, an informing task introduced the lesson. It was followed by two refining tasks, which were then followed by an extending task. The lesson was concluded by two applying tasks. In Example 4, an informing task was followed by a refining task. A second informing task was introduced and followed by two extending tasks, concluding with an application task. These progressions stand a much better chance of achieving lesson goals than the progressions shown in the first two examples.

Use Task Objectives

For each task within a lesson, a teacher can prepare specific instructional objectives (see Chapter 9). Once such objectives are written, they can be used in several important ways. First, the teacher can use them to communicate to students precisely what is expected of them in each task. Second, objectives can be used to communicate the same message to students in written or graphic form in a task-teaching style (on task cards for individual students, on task posters on walls, or on a task plan). Third, the objectives also provide a means for students and teachers alike to know when a task has been completed. Fourth, the teacher can formally or informally monitor the amount of time (or number of trials) it takes students to complete a given task. Tasks should be easy enough to ensure success—they should not take 20 to 30 chances to achieve the goal. They should also be challenging enough to maintain interest—they should probably not be achievable on the first try every time. The following three objectives represent refining, extending, and applying tasks for a volleyball lesson.

Refining Task: Standing behind a line drawn 8 feet from the wall, initiate this task by tossing the ball above your head and hit a legal set against the wall trying to achieve good height. Do this for 10 trials.

Extending Task: Standing behind the line, initiate this task by tossing the ball above your head and hit a legal set so that it hits the wall above the 12-foot line. Do this 10 times.

Applying Task: Standing behind the line, initiate this task by tossing the ball above your head and then see how many consecutive legal set passes you can make that hit the wall above the 12-foot line.

These objectives could be directed to students verbally, or they could be presented ahead of time on task cards or other such devices. Regardless of how they are presented, if they appear on the lesson plan in a manner similar to the way in which they have just been stated, they leave no doubt as to what will be done next in the lesson.

Instructional objectives can be sequenced by arranging a series of tasks in order to ensure a logical or developmental progression that leads to an ability. The following sequence contains samples of a progression designed to develop laterality. These are samples from a larger sequence that breaks the components down into a series of refining tasks.

Following verbal instructions, the child is able to touch his or her left leg with his or her left hand (laterality of the body).

Following verbal instructions, the child is able to place his or her left foot on a 4-foot-high box situated directly in front of the chair on which he or she is sitting (laterality in relation to objects).

The child is able to identify when a box has been placed on his or her right or left side (static objectives related to laterality).

While standing or sitting still, the child is able to identify positions with regard to him- or herself as the instructor moves around him or her (laterality in relation to moving objects).

The child is able to move around two stationary chairs, identifying his or her position in relation to the chairs as he or she moves (moving body's laterality in relation to objects).

Although each of these refining tasks is different, they all add up to a terminal ability; that is, demonstration of adequate development in the perceptual-motor concept of laterality. Again, the objectives could be within any instructional style. Whichever system is used, the child would understand what is expected, and the instructor would have clear criteria by which to judge the student's performance.

Develop a System for Monitoring Performance

No system is complete without a component that monitors the system's output to ensure that the system is meeting its objectives. Without a monitoring component, an instructional method is not an instructional system; it cannot be held accountable nor can it be modified to improve its performance. The importance of the monitoring feature in an instructional system cannot be overemphasized. Its absence has prevented much of physical education instruction from achieving a respected status within education. The argument is straightforward: how can you know how well you are teaching unless you have some systematic way of determining how much your students are learning?

Several steps must be taken before a monitoring system can be imple-

What If the Student Can't Do the First Task?

Situation. A gymnastics class is being conducted using an individualized instruction approach, with five apparatus stations in the gym. At each station a task card is posted with a sequence of instructional objectives. Students attempt one objective, and if they are successful they move on to the next when they get another turn. A girl attempts the first objective on a high bar and cannot lift herself up because of lack of arm strength.

Results. The girl drops from the bar shaking her head and unable to do the first objective.

Analysis. The first instructional objective is too difficult. A needs inventory would determine whether students have sufficient arm strength to do high bar tasks.

Prescription. A remedial loop should be developed with the instructional goal of having students jump up, catch hold of the high bar, and lift themselves up to balance on top of the bar. The first sequence of objectives should be to hang from the bar (support his or her own weight) for progressively longer times. The next objectives should deal with lifting up halfway, three-quarters of the way, and all the way. The final objective in the loop is to pull up and balance on the bar. When this sequence is completed, the student should be able to do the first instructional objective.

mented. First, the criteria for performance must be specified and made public to the students. This was explained in the instructional objectives section (see Chapter 9). Second, the criteria must reflect the goals of the unit. Instructional objectives are judged on the degree to which they accurately reflect the intent of the instruction. The systematic use of instructional objectives ensures that the criteria necessary for a monitoring system will be available. Without objectives, it is unlikely that the criteria will be made public to students. Without publicly specified criteria, evaluation may fluctuate greatly from day to day and from class to class.

Once criteria are developed, it remains to implement a system for monitoring student performance. The monitoring system chosen will be determined primarily by the kind of teaching system; that is, a teacher-directed system will require a different monitoring system than an individualized instruction system.

With a teacher-directed system, students will be working in squads or as a class on the same objectives. Two methods for monitoring performance lend themselves well to this situation. First, students can self-monitor their performance. Just before they change stations or move on to another objective, the instructor can ask for a show of hands on how many achieved the objective. The instructor has two roles here: (1) he or she is the record keeper; (2) he or she should intermittently estimate individual student performance to ensure that the self-monitoring is reliable. Record keeping of this kind is best done by a checklist. The resulting data show the percentage of students passing the objective, give some estimate of the difficulty of the objective in terms of the time allotted to it, and provide individual records for each student. A second method would be for the instructor to check students off individually on a checklist. This is a more reliable method of monitoring performance, but it is time consuming and prevents the instructor from focusing on feedback and instruction.

With individualized instruction, a monitoring system is built into the system of instruction itself. Because progress through an individualized system depends on task completion, the monitoring of task completion becomes part of the system. The key here is the teacher's role in the monitoring system. One obvious role is for the teacher to assess each student and check off the task completion. This requires an enormous investment of instructor time and tends to prevent the teacher giving individual help. This is especially true if students attempt to get checked off before they are really ready to pass an objective. A modification of this approach is to insert the intermediate requirement that each student must be checked off by another student before being checked off by the teacher. This minimizes the teacher's monitoring time yet retains a high degree of reliability. A further modification would have students responsible for checking off other students, with the teacher moving around providing intermittent reliability checks.

It should be noted that, regardless of the instructional system used, monitoring student performance is much easier if the instructor has student aides or gym helpers. Student aides can run the entire monitoring system, thus freeing the teacher for other interpersonal and instructional work.

A problem-solving approach is best monitored by use of a teacher-controlled checklist system. Often, if individual checkoff is not feasible in terms of time, an estimate of group performance can be made. In this manner, a teacher may move on to another objective when 80 percent of the class appears to have mastered the previous objective.

A monitoring system should produce some permanent record of student performance. Daily monitoring records can be later transferred to permanent individual and class records. This is another task that can be done by student aides, and is another good reason for developing a student aide program in physical education. Periodically, the records should be scrutinized closely to determine the degree to which program objectives are being met.

Remember Instructional Principles During Games

How often have you seen students participate in bump pass, setting, and serving drills, only to observe no evidence of those skills once a volleyball game begins? How often have you taken time to teach skills only to see students revert to bad habits once a game is started? Who is to blame? The students? They want to have fun, and often they are given no instructions other than to play the game. The fault lies in the instructional system. Games can be directed toward the achievement of specific objectives and still be fun. Indeed, a strong case can be made for the proposition that students will gradually learn to have more and more fun in game play once they begin to use newly acquired skills in the game situation.

No one would argue that constructing instructional objectives for game situations is more difficult than for drill purposes. The fact that this is a difficult task should not deter you from making the effort. The effort will be rewarded in a manner equal to its difficulty. Objectives for game play call the students' attention to important instructional goals. This tends to make the game play considerably more educational, and in the long run more fun. What follows are some examples of instructional objectives that could be used for game play. These, of course, are examples of applying tasks. Remember that applying tasks are often done in scrimmage and game play. In many activities, scrimmage and game play represent the really important application, the one from which the students will derive most satisfaction.

> Seventy percent of all basketball shots will come from a maneuver directly related to the offensive pattern. (Instructional intent is to have players use the offensive patterns they have practiced.)
>
> Eighty percent of all long serves will fall within 3 feet of the opponent's baseline. (Instructional intent is to have students use long serve in badminton games.)
>
> Eighty percent of all offensive plays will be preceded by a bump pass and set up or two set up passes. (Instructional intent is to have volleyball players use two preliminary passes to set up for a spike.)
>
> Seventy-five percent of all backhand and forehand shots attempted from the baseline area will have sufficient power to reach the power line on the first bounce. (Instructional intent is to have tennis players attempt to stroke the ball firmly instead of "dinking" it. Power line is an extra line drawn behind the baseline, and balls that bounce to the line are shown to have sufficient velocity.)

Just like any instructional objective, these examples require some kind of monitoring to provide feedback to the learners and to show that the objective is being met. In game play, this can best be accomplished by having a student act as a monitor. Periodically the instructor can ensure that reliable judgments are being made by the student monitors. It should be understood that this use of student monitors is different from the use of student aide monitors referred to earlier. The contention here is that it is an educationally valuable experience for a student to monitor the game play of his or her classmates. This allows the monitor to focus on the skills and see how his or her classmates are performing them. There is much evidence to suggest that this is a useful form of learning, and the number of monitors needed at any time is sufficiently small to ensure that no one student would spend too much time in this capacity.

Build the Lesson as a Time Script

My last suggestion for lesson planning is to build the actual plan around a time script. A time script is simply a graphic method of showing how much time each of the phases of a lesson is intended to take. After several attempts at planning a lesson, you will be able to judge quite accurately the length of time a particular task might take. Forcing yourself to develop your lesson along a time script will keep you aware of how much you might reasonably expect to accomplish in a lesson. Naturally, it is good practice to have each lesson end at some logical conclusion, a point of closure that brings things together for the students. This point is often an applying task of some kind. You are more likely to reach this point in the lesson with enough time left to complete the last task if you have thought carefully about the time dimensions of the lesson as you have planned it.

Conclusion

This chapter has dealt with factors that need to be considered when planning lessons; teaching style, basic questions that need to be answered for each plan, availability of instructional aids and devices, motivational considerations, and lecture or demonstration sequences. The chapter has also introduced you to the model of lesson development based on informing, refining, extending, and applying tasks. Arranging tasks in progressions to reach goals is a key element in good lesson planning. Furthermore, the chapter has encouraged you to think about using instructional objectives in your lesson planning, to sequence those objectives (each representing a task in the progression) carefully, to develop a system for monitoring the performance of students, and to remember the use of application tasks stated as instructional objectives for scrimmage and game play.

You probably have already noted that to develop a plan as described here would take some time. On the other hand, throwing out a few balls and letting the students go at it doesn't require much planning time at all! Certainly, planning does take time. But, once done, a good lesson plan can serve you well for years to come. And good lesson plans are seldom well developed the first time around. The goal should be to make a good start at a series of lesson plans for a unit. This will provide a foundation from which the plans can be developed when the unit is taught again. Once a unit is taught several times, the lesson plans become well developed and can be used for years to come.

CHAPTER 11

Implementing Instruction

The teacher's job involves many roles besides that of instructing students. At times the teacher will serve as a parent surrogate, an entertainer, an authority figure, a psychotherapist, and a record keeper, among other things. All of these are necessary aspects of the teacher's role. However, they are subordinate to and in support of the major role of teaching. Important as they are, they must not be allowed to overshadow the teacher's basic instructional role.

Jere Brophy and Thomas Good, *Teacher-Student Relationships: Causes and Consequences* (1974)

CHAPTER OBJECTIVES

To explain the rationale for student-centered assessment

To describe instructional strategies relative to ensuring learner safety

To suggest strategies for teacher communications to students

To describe strategies for demonstrations

To outline strategies for active supervision

To explain and provide examples of appropriate forms of instructional feedback

To suggest strategies for effective use of questions

To show how students can be used as teaching agents

To describe and provide examples of systems for monitoring student performance

To explain techniques for maintaining the momentum of a lesson

This text does not aim to develop teachers who fit some preconceived model of an ideal or effective teacher. Some suggestions have been made about the need to create a positive learning environment, and to that extent there are boundaries of student-teacher interaction that should be observed. Other suggestions dealing with enthusiasm, use of feedback, questioning skills, and modeling are made not for the purpose of suggesting that there is one best way for doing these things, but to show that such factors have been identified as important variables in educational environments and that attention to them as teaching skills is justified and necessary. The fact is that no model of an ideal or effective teacher has yet been developed, except in the very general terms suggested here.

This chapter focuses on instruction, on the act of teaching itself. It might seem that this important chapter would focus on the performance of the teacher, because instruction is assumed to mean the teacher's performance in the gymnasium or on the playing field. It cannot be emphasized too strongly that this is not the case. Although many suggestions for teacher performance are made here, the main emphasis of this chapter is not on how a teacher performs, but rather on what happens to students as a result of instruction. This important distinction can easily be seen by having you respond to a crucial question: What is the best way to judge the effectiveness of the teaching act? Please record your immediate reaction to this question.

_____

_____

_____

_____

Was your answer phrased in terms of things that teachers do? Did you record something like "presents material clearly" or "motivates students" or "provides necessary feedback"? If you answered the question in such terms, then you focused on teacher performance as the best means for judging instructional effectiveness. If you answered, "the number of skills students acquire," or "how well students like the activity," or "how well students learn to play the game," then you focused on the results of the instruction. I contend that the latter is the better criterion by which to judge instruction.

This view is merely a restatement of comments made earlier on the nature of teaching (see Chapter 1). The general thrust of those comments is worth repeating: a definition of teaching that makes no reference to student learning is devoid of meaning. A teacher's effectiveness must be judged by the degree to which students achieve the goals that the teacher set out to have them achieve. This is consistent with the model advocated throughout this text. The only way to judge the effectiveness of an instructional approach is to compare the results of the system with the goals it was designed to achieve.

In the absence of valid student achievement data, this text has advocated using student learning time for estimating the relative effectiveness of a teaching strategy. The strategy that produces the higher learning time for students is more likely to result in achievement and, if done in a positive climate, will also result in good attitude development and self-growth among students. This **student-centered assessment approach** should be kept in mind as you read this chapter. When reading, thinking about, and practicing feedback skills, questioning skills, or other instructional skills, remember that they are good to the extent that they affect student learning positively and that the best way to do that is to maximize student learning time.

It is in the implementation of instruction—the actual teaching lesson—where all the skills described and discussed in this text come together. This chapter, therefore, cannot be considered in isolation but must instead be viewed along with the strategies discussed in other chapters, particularly Chapters 5 and 10. Preventive classroom management (Chapter 5) and lesson planning (Chapter 10) are integral to the successful implementation of instruction. The fact is that you will teach more effectively if you have planned adequately and if you have acquired the skills of preventive classroom management. This chapter focuses on teacher skills used in implementing a lesson:

1. Ensuring the safety of learners
2. Improving task presentations
3. Actively supervising student practice
4. Improving feedback skills
5. Using questions properly
6. Using students as teachers
7. Monitoring students' performance
8. Maintaining the momentum of the lesson

Ensuring the Safety of Learners

A major responsibility of every physical education teacher is to provide a safe learning environment for students. Safety should be considered when planning, but it is in the implementation of a lesson that safety must be foremost. Whenever a potentially hazardous activity is being undertaken, the teacher should emphasize clearly the *rules* that have been established with regards to the hazard. These rules should be described, prompted often, and students should be held accountable for obeying them. To do less is to risk both student injury and a lawsuit.

This is not to suggest that activities involving risk should not be used in the physical education program. Quite the contrary, one goal of the program should be to help students learn to take some risks and want to participate in activities. Many sport activities have the potential for injury. What needs to be emphasized are the rules regarding safety in terms of the specific activity and the space within which it is practiced and played.

Psychological safety is also important for a good learning environment. Students not only need to *behave* safely but they also need to *feel* safe about what they are doing. This means quite simply that they should feel comfortable about their participation, should be willing to participate fully. They will have psychological safety to the degree that their efforts are supported and are not met with ridicule and negative comment.

Students will also feel comfortable, and tend to behave safely too, if they have experienced an appropriate progression to shape their skills and if they have a background of related successes. If they have experienced the proper progressions, they will be challenged by current tasks and feel able and willing to do them safely.

Finally, the teacher must be constantly alert to unsafe student behavior. Students are not mature adults. Often, in the excitement of an activity, they do not behave in fully mature ways. Teachers need to be aware of student behavior that jeopardizes the students' own safety or the safety of others. Unsafe behavior should be desisted immediately, and specific feedback should be given as to why the behavior is unsafe. Active supervision (discussed later in this chapter) is the best strategy to help teachers keep in close contact with what their students are doing.

Communicating Information Without Consuming Class Time

Learning time is a precious commodity and should be used judiciously. Much of the information communicated from teacher to student during class time could be communicated just as effectively in another manner without using class time. Mimeographed handouts are inexpensive, provide the learner with a permanent record of instructional intent, and reduce the possibility of students misunderstanding a verbal presentation. Instructional objectives, rules, diagrams of playing fields, diagrams of defensive and offensive maneuvers, and other matters can be communicated to students through handouts. Of course, it is useless to provide handouts for students if there is no mechanism in your instructional system to ensure that they use the handouts. An informal method of ensuring this is to intermittently ask students questions that pertain directly to the handouts. If you provide a handout listing instructional objectives at the end of Monday's class, at the start of the next class you might ask several students what the criteria for certain objectives are. If you hand out a diagram of a badminton court, you can ask a student to show the back boundary line for the doubles serve. Students' understanding of the material should be formally assessed only if the handout is of sufficient importance to warrant taking time for this. Thus, you might administer a short rules test before beginning actual game competition in a new activity. If students have a handout on the rules and if they must pass a short quiz in order to gain access to the game, then chances are they will learn the material. Thus the game can proceed at a much higher level, because the situations in which rules will need to be clarified will be minimal.

Decreasing Time Spent in Class Presentations

The most important factor in decreasing time and increasing clarity is careful planning. (For planning principles, see Chapter 10.) Only the most relevant information should be conveyed in a presentation. Students should not be expected to remember highly detailed explanations. The following suggestions can help improve presentation skills.

1. *Plan carefully.* If information can be presented in some manner ahead of time, make sure you present it that way.
2. *Limit the information.* Students can benefit from only a limited amount of information at a time. Explanation of the details of a skill or strategy should be limited.
3. *Use language the students can understand.* Use language appropriate to their age level and also appropriate to their skill level.
4. *Talk slowly.* Always remember that you know the material better than students do. Clear communication will be aided if you present information at a speed that allows the students to process the material.

Most physical educators talk a great deal more than is necessary. The danger in providing too much information is that students will not sort out the most important and relevant aspects of the presentation. Experts in the area of motor learning are nearly unanimous in agreeing that students learn most effectively when they have a general idea of what is to be accomplished and are aware of the major technical aspects but not the details.

Presentations are very important when used to introduce new material, a new unit, or a new strategy. They most often occur at the start of class and should follow the guidelines already discussed in terms of economical use of time and general method of presentation. Beyond that, these initial presentations should go according to the following principles:

Introducing a Lesson

1. Instructional tasks should be clearly identified.
2. Importance of tasks should be clearly established.
3. Students should understand specifically what they are to achieve.
4. New material should be related to previous experience.
5. Students should have an opportunity to seek clarification.
6. Criteria for evaluation should be specified.
7. Instructional aids should be ready ahead of time and used simultaneously with verbal presentations.

Instructional aids can clarify complex material. Have you ever attempted to explain a tennis serve to someone verbally without showing them how or using aids? Not only is it a difficult task, but it takes a great deal of time and usually raises more questions than it answers. How much easier it is to communicate such information with the help of a demonstration, a sequence of photographs, a film loop, or even a still photograph! The lesson is that complex motor behaviors are better communicated via the visual system than the auditory system.

Any method of visual presentation will likely result in clearer communication in less time. Most of what a learner needs to know about the beginning stages of a skill sequence can best be communicated through a demonstration or some visual aids. The instructional aid should be presented simultaneously with a limited verbal explanation. The verbal explanation should serve to point up the major features of the visual display; that is, it should direct the attention of the student to the most relevant aspects of the display. Instructional aids that are lively and attractive are likely to have a stronger motivational impact.

It has been said that one picture is worth a thousand words. That adage can be taken seriously in teaching physical education. Visual displays do convey information about motor skills better than verbalization. But repeated displays of the same skill are unnecessary (remember, the adage says "*one picture . . .*"). Unless the students' attention is directed at different aspects of a display, one presentation will provide them with all they need.

Instructional aids should be set up before the class begins. An instructional aid that takes class time to set up is not worthwhile. If a film loop or motion picture takes too much class time, it defeats its instructional purpose; a set of stick figures or live demonstrations would be more useful.

Task presentations should be organized so that they are most effective when done. To accomplish this, the students should be placed so that they can see the main elements clearly and hear the instructor clearly. Students should also be in an organizational set-up that allows the teacher to see them both for purposes of supervision and for establishing eye contact in the task presentation itself. The presentation should be made in the setting in which it will be used. A task presentation about goal keeping in soccer should be made near the goal. A task presentation about volleying skills at the net in tennis should be made at the net. Setting up task presentations carefully will help to keep student attention and contribute to task understanding—as well as helping to keep the time spent down to a minimum necessary to accomplish the goal.

Planning Demonstrations Carefully

The live demonstration is still the best means for modeling a skill so that students can get an idea of what it is they should be doing. Because live demonstrations are important in teaching, physical education teachers should develop a broad base of sport skills. Demonstrations should not be done "off-the-cuff" any more than any other aspect of teaching. The good demonstration is planned and goes smoothly. It takes the least amount of time possible to convey a limited amount of information relative to specific aspects of a skill. The following guidelines are suggested for demonstrations:

1. The demonstrator should be a good model; that is, he or she should be able to do the skill well. If the teacher cannot do it well, he or she should plan ahead of time to have a student available who can do it well.
2. All materials necessary for the demonstration should be set up and

How Much Time? How Much Information?

Situation. A junior high instructor is introducing some advanced tumbling skills (handsprings). As the class begins, the instructor asks a student to bring over a projector and then threads a film loop. The students are shown an assisted handspring while the instructor explains and discusses the skill. Then the students are shown two other film loops on other handspring skills. During each showing, the instructor details the execution of the skill.

Results. The students are given far too much information, and far too much time is spent in the presentation.

Analysis. The equipment is not ready. The repeated showing of film loops is questionable. The verbal explanation is probably far too detailed for an introduction. No live demonstration is given. Students have to sit for a long time. The question is "When they finally get up to try the skill for the first time, will their attempts be much better because of the detailed presentation?" The answer is probably no!

Prescription. The students need to have an overall visual impression of what the handspring looks like, with their attention drawn to the two or three crucial aspects of execution. Then they need specific beginning objectives to get them started practicing the skill and specific feedback about their performance. The presentation gives the illusion of high-level teaching, but is actually contrary to principles of effective instruction.

ready to go. For example, if a tumbling skill is to be demonstrated, the mats should be ready *before* the class begins.

3. The demonstration should be directed at the students visually and conceptually. It should be performed for them in a manner they can understand.
4. Each important feature should be identified, explained, and performed in sequence. The number of features in any one demonstration should be limited.
5. Instructional aids should be used *if* they serve to emphasize or clarify difficult material and do not take too much extra time.
6. Safety points should be emphasized if relevant.
7. The demonstration should be performed in conditions that are as close as possible to those under which the skill will be performed by students.

8. Feedback should be obtained from students to see if they understand the relevant features. This is usually best done by intermittently asking a student to identify a feature.

A well-done demonstration is one in which the basic structural elements of a skill are presented to students in a clear and unequivocal manner. In giving a demonstration the key is to have command of how the skill looks, in a most basic sense, when done properly. Elegance or high-level performance is not essential, and too much attention to detail is probably distracting. For example, if you can do a high jump over a 3-foot, 6-inch standard and execute all the key movements correctly, you should not feel inadequate as a demonstrator. If you decline to demonstrate because you fear that you may be inadequate, you are sending out a clear message that it is not OK to be less than an expert. Certainly, if you have not mastered the basic elements of a skill, then you should get someone else to do the demonstration. But if you can give a decent general idea of how the skill should look, then you should go ahead and do it. Students will get the message that less than expert performance is not only tolerated, but understood.

The live demonstration is important in learning, but it also is significant in another way. I have already emphasized the importance of the physical educator as a model of an active, skilled person. Demonstrations present a golden opportunity to show students that you are an active, skilled person. It will enhance your status in their eyes, and will make your feedback and other interactions more effective.

Actively Supervising Students' Practice

Classroom research shows that effective teachers supervise student seatwork more actively than ineffective teachers. The same strategy is also important for physical educators. Students often are dispersed to practice tasks, sometimes alone, sometimes with partners, and sometimes in small groups. These tasks may take the form of drills, individual tasks, or even miniscrimmages. Students usually spread out to use all the available space. In such student practice settings, teachers must work hard to ensure that students stay on task and get as much good feedback as possible. One way to ensure the best use of practice time is to supervise it actively, to move around the space, to find ways through prompting and feedback to let students know that they are being supervised and are being held accountable for engaging in the task.

Active supervision is important for several reasons. First, it is the best way to keep students on task. The teacher who stands in one corner of the gym or at the edge of the field simply loses touch with students who are far away. Active supervision can also keep the teacher close to potential safety problems or to potential misinterpretations of the task. When a teacher is actively supervising practice, he or she tends to know what is going on—and it is vitally important that the students know that you know! Active supervision also helps a teacher to distribute feedback fairly to all of the students.

The best way to supervise actively is to position yourself in such a manner that as many students as possible are kept within view. This means that moving around the perimeter of the space is the best strategy, especially at the outset of a lesson, when you are trying to establish an on task focus. It is also useful to avoid becoming too predictable in your movement patterns. Simply moving around the perimeter in a clockwise direction also alerts the students as to when you are likely to be in their area. Unpredictable supervision helps students to stay on task. Active supervision can also be done across some distance; that is, you don't have to be physically near a student to provide some supervisory kind of behavior that helps the student. Prompts and feedback can be offered to students who might happen to be 50 feet away from where you are standing. These strategies not only help to keep the students on task but they also help the teacher to get as much feedback as possible to as many students as possible.

Increasing Positive Feedback

There is a strong tendency in physical education instruction to rely exclusively on corrective feedback; that is, to provide information correcting student performance errors. Evidence indicates clearly that student teachers in physical education use limited rates of corrective feedback, but almost never react to skills that are done right or done well (Hughley 1973, Darst 1974, Hamilton 1974). Negative feedback for skill attempts is hardly ever found; that is, one almost never encounters a response such as "That was a lousy headstand." Corrective feedback is not necessarily negative, and it can be delivered in a positive manner. Nonetheless, if over a period of time a teacher reacts exclusively to errors in student performance, an error-centered climate is created. Changing to a positive feedback focus is another aspect of shifting from a negative to a positive style of teaching. The shift in style here differs from the shift in style for positive and negative reactions to student behavior suggested in Chapter 5. In that chapter it was proposed that negative interactions be minimized. Here, I am recommending a balance between positive and corrective feedback.

The general strategy of a positive feedback approach is to build on the strengths of a student performance by providing feedback on those aspects of the performance that were done well or correctly. This not only serves to strengthen those aspects of the performance but also is another positive interaction that contributes to a generally healthy learning climate. If you are emitting feedback at a ratio of four positive to every one corrective comment, then the climate will be very positive and the corrective feedback will aid student learning without diminishing the generally positive relationship.

There is a great deal of intrinsic feedback in sport. If a student hits a volleyball serve that goes out of bounds, he or she knows it immediately because the lines on the court provide feedback. It would be pointless to say to that student, "Your serve went out of bounds." But if a serve stays in bounds and you say "That was a nice serve," the feedback is not redundant because you are making an appreciative comment not merely on the fact that the ball stayed in bounds but on the general performance of the serve. Even though such feedback has no precise information content, it nonetheless may have a powerful effect on certain students.

As you attempt to increase your rate of feedback, you should avoid redundancy. In most skill situations, a rate of 4.0 feedbacks per minute is easily attainable. A ratio of four positive to every one corrective feedback creates a favorable atmosphere for learning physical education skills.

Improving Feedback Statements

The best way to avoid redundancy and enhance the power of the feedback statements is to increase the percentage of feedback statements that contain specific information or have a value content. This approach to improving interactions was suggested in Chapter 5. The discussion there centered on interactions based on student behavior other than skill attempts; here the discussion is limited to skill feedback. Examples of feedback interactions follow. They are divided into general feedback, nonverbal feedback, feedback with specific information content, and feedback with value content. The interactions are for a variety of age levels. Obviously, if the interaction is to be perceived as sincere and significant, it must be worded and delivered in a manner consistent with the age and developmental level of the student.

General Positive Feedback Interactions

Nice shot.	That's the right idea, Mary.
Good effort.	You made a heck of a serve.
Good move.	Squad 1 did the job.
Tough defense, Jim.	You're ready for the NBA, Al.
That's better, Jill.	That's an interesting interpretation, Barb.
A-1 job, Roberto.	You did that really well.
Very good, Jeanne.	That was a tremendous pass, Bob.

Nonverbal Positive Feedback Interactions

Smiling (approving facial expressions)	Making an "OK" sign
	Patting on the back
Nodding	Touching a child and smiling
Clapping hands (shaking hands)	Clenching fists in approval
	Winking
Applauding	Punching the air
Thumbs up	Scruffing the hair of a student

Positive Feedback Interactions with Specific Information Content

Good move, John. You shot from right behind the screen.

That was nice. Your circle was different from everybody else's.

That's better. Your arms pronated much more than before.

Beautiful! You really had your knees tucked up that time.

Great placement, Ray. You must have seen him cheating to his forehand.

That's the way to keep those arms straight.

Way to keep your back straight, Betty.

Everybody in this circle made the switch to the step-hop on exactly the right beat.

Positive Feedback Interactions with Value Content

Nice shot. When you shoot from that close in, your percentage will really be high.

Way to help out on defense, Pat. When you cover like that, we can take some chances.

That's the way to bend. When you do that, you can turn quickly.

Great jump! You can go that far because of the way you bend your knees before you take off.

That's good! When you keep your head up, you can see what your teammates are doing.

There is ample evidence that specific information content in a feedback statement can aid learning. The more highly skilled a student becomes, the more he or she can benefit from highly precise and technical information in the feedback statement. As a general rule, from 50 to 70 percent of your feedbacks should contain specific information.

The value content of a feedback statement tells the student why it is important to do the particular aspect of the skill in the manner in which it was done. It lets the student know why a performance is considered to be good. This not only strengthens that aspect of the performance but also teaches the student how to verbalize about the particular skill so that he or she can explain to someone else why a skill should be performed in a certain way.

A combination of all these feedback sophistications will help you maintain a varied and strong feedback component in your teaching. The direct effects of teacher feedback are significant in helping students learn, and the indirect effects are also of substantial importance. The indirect effects are carried in the hidden messages conveyed from teacher to student through a feedback interaction. When a student does a tripod (or a jump shot, or a *schottische* step) and you touch the student on the shoulder, smile, and deliver a verbal feedback statement with information content, you are not only helping improve that skill but you are also telling the student that he or she is someone worthwhile who demonstrates worthwhile skills in a very acceptable manner. In other words, you are telling the student that he or she is worthy and acceptable and that you enjoy working with him or her. Over a period of time, such interaction helps students build healthy, positive self-images.

Directing Feedback to the Target of Instruction

A common error is to provide feedback that relates to aspects of the performance other than the one that is the direct focus of the learning. For example, if you are focusing on accuracy in the volleyball serve, it is incorrect to provide feedback on the velocity of the serve. If you are focusing on having golfers keep their elbows close to the body in the backswing, it is counterproductive to provide feedback about the action of the front leg in the downswing. To be most effective, feedback must be related to the instructional intent that is in operation at the moment the feedback is given.

This principle is also highly applicable in any teaching situation where the problem-solving method is being used, especially if the goal of the instruction is to have learners discover new ways to solve the problems. For example, suppose that in a movement education lesson a child solves a problem by using his or her stomach as a base of support. Perhaps you say to the child, "Robert, that was a good way to do that, you used your stomach." The problem here is twofold. First, the feedback focused on how the problem was solved rather than the fact that the solution was new or different. Theoretically, such feedback strengthens the use of the stomach as a base of support but does not necessarily strengthen creativity. Second, you can never assume that any feedback is solely individual unless it is delivered in private. This feedback was delivered to an individual, but other children were no doubt close enough to see and hear that Robert was receiving approval from the teacher. The result may be that many other children will begin to use their stomachs as a base of support for solving a problem because they too want approval. This is a simple modeling effect, but it is very likely and powerful in a teaching situation. If the intent of the instruction is to foster creative movement behavior, then the feedback must be consistently related to new and different things and not to descriptions of the performances themselves. If you consistently say "That's different," or "You found a new way to do that," then students will understand that approval is contingent on doing something different from what other children are doing.

Staying with One Student Long Enough to Make Feedback Effective

Feedback delivered by a teacher should provide extra information that is not available from intrinsic sources. Often, teacher feedback is directed at some aspect of form or some other technicality about which the student cannot get information just from seeing the results of a performance. A student knows when he or she has sliced a drive in golf, but often comments from an observer are needed to produce a swing that will allow the student to hit the ball straight.

A major question in teaching is how to distribute feedback interactions among students. If you have 30 students and can provide feedback for only one at a time, then you must decide how you are going to do this. A common method is to walk about the gym or playing space and watch one trial by a student, provide a feedback comment, and move on to the next student. Another method is to station yourself in a central location and watch one student at a time, providing comments from a distance. The first method tends to move you about the class in a regular, predictable pattern. The second method allows you to be less bound by the physical layout of the class organization. But neither of these methods is as appropriate as a third alternative. I believe that the best way to distribute feedback comments is to stay with one student for enough trials to get a good idea of the performance and then to provide a sequence of feedback interactions that will help the student progress. This means that you may not see the student more than once during each class, but at least the time spent with the student will be useful.

The random, intermittent feedback delivered in the one-at-a-time method may help a student, but the teacher never gets a thorough knowledge of the performance by viewing one trial, and the student certainly can get more constructive feedback through a series of interactions that focus on some aspect of the performance. Theoretically, it is a question of being able to deliver five feedbacks per student for each class (based on a class of 30 students meeting for 30 minutes with feedback being delivered at a rate of 5.0 per minute) and deciding whether more learning will occur if the feedbacks are delivered sequentially or intermittently throughout the class time. Theoretically, each student gets the same number of feedbacks, but the distribution is different.

This discussion of distribution of feedback interactions should reinforce your awareness of the limits of a teacher's ability to guide learning through use of feedback. Obviously, the more that artificial feedback can be programmed into the learning environment, the better will be the instructional system.

Using Group-Directed Feedback and Modeling

Feedback for skill attempts is most often directed at an individual who has just made an attempt. Although it is obvious that the individual can most profit from the feedback, it should also be obvious that there are times when feedback related to the performance of an individual could be helpful for a group. Relating feedback about an individual's performance to the larger group is referred to as **group-directed feedback**. Evidence indicates that this kind of feedback is hardly ever used by physical education student teachers (Darst 1974, Boehm 1974).

Group-directed feedback is another aspect of modeling. **Modeling** refers to using the behavior of one individual as an example for others to imitate. In this case, the reverse might also be true; that is, a performance error of one individual might be used to help others avoid the same kind of error. Modeling and group-directed feedback are powerful tools for teaching and learning. This is largely true because in modeling very complex behaviors can be easily understood through the combination of seeing the performance and hearing feedback about one or more aspects of the performance. If you have a student perform a headstand and you call the group's attention to the push-off and full extension of the legs, you can, in a short period of time, emphasize several crucial aspects of a skill and show students how to do it correctly. Modeling a well-performed skill is usually highly rewarding to an individual.

Modeling and group-directed feedback should not be used too often because it does take the attention of the group away from their own skill practice. To use group-directed feedback at a rate of one per minute would be overdoing it, but it is such a good method for teaching complex aspects of

---

Does Your Feedback Accomplish What You Intend?

Situation. A teacher is conducting a movement exploration lesson. Questions are posed in such a manner (divergent-broad) that many student responses are elicited. The teacher points out that a particular student has solved the problem by moving in a backward direction while all other students have used only a forward or sideward direction.

Results. More students begin to use a backward direction.

Analysis. The feedback results in an effective modeling situation, as other students imitate the student who received the positive interaction. This is good if the teacher's goal is to alert students to the possibility of using different directions in solving movement problems. The technique is not appropriate if the goal is to have students become creative. The teacher has (purposely or inadvertently) strengthened the children's tendency to imitate certain students, and imitation is probably counterproductive to creativity.

Prescription. Feedback and modeling must be highly specific to the instructional goals. In this case, the problem can be remedied by continually making it clear that differences are what is most highly prized and that imitation is not an appropriate method for solving problems. The feedback must be precisely related to the goals of the lesson. *Be specific!*

**Encouraging
Questions,
Comments,
and
the Expression
of Ideas**

203

skill in a short period of time that it should be used on key occasions. While you are focusing on practicing this particular skill, do not worry if you overdo it.

Some principles for using group-directed feedback and modeling follow.

1. Group-directed feedback works much better if the class has been taught a predetermined signal for attention so that the least amount of time is wasted getting the group's attention to begin the feedback.

2. Explain quickly and directly the aspect of performance on which the feedback is based. For example, in teaching basketball defense you may want to call attention to the angle of pursuit in a defensive move to cut off an offensive player driving for the basket, so the attention of the class should be drawn to the angle of pursuit as the key element.

3. Provide the feedback quickly and emphatically, making sure that it has an information content and a value content. Group-directed feedback should almost always have ample information and value content so that students understand what the feedback means and why the performance aspect was emphasized.

4. Bring the modeling session to an end quickly and enthusiastically so students can get back to their own tasks.

Encouraging Questions, Comments, and the Expression of Ideas

Although physical education should be an activity experience rather than an intellectual discussion experience, every teacher should encourage discussion related to the development of skill and playing of games. Students may ask why one technique is better than another. This allows you not only to give feedback with an information and value content, but also to interact strictly on the basis of the question asked (that is, you can provide the proper feedback and then compliment the asking of the question). Students may comment about previous experiences or they may want to express ideas about how to play a defense, how to solve a problem, how to develop arm strength, or how to measure the beat of a musical selection. You should not only answer their questions, but you should also find ways to let them know that you value questioning, commenting, and the expression of ideas. This is one of those "hidden messages" that the learning environment sends out to students.

Questioning and commenting should generally be encouraged, but you must be careful with younger students not to encourage this kind of behavior strictly for the attention the student gets for it. I am not suggesting that you cut a student off immediately if you feel that he or she is just asking or commenting in order to get attention. This is a natural thing for younger students to do, and it will diminish if you have some patience and use your interactions carefully. Students must learn how to distinguish between those situations in which questions are relevant and comments are called for and those situations in which they are not. You can easily teach them this by reacting in a positive manner to appropriate questioning and commenting, and usually ignoring what you consider to be attention-getting questioning and commenting. This is another situation where the information and value content of the feedback can be very helpful. For example, instead of just saying, "That was a good question, Jack," you might say, "That was a good question because it brings up a confusing rule, and by answering it we can help others avoid violating the rule in the future." The information and value content not only strengthens the general predisposition of students to question and comment, but also teaches them what an appropriate question is and why it was important to ask it and have it answered.

Using Questioning as a Teaching Method

Questioning is one of the most important of a teacher's verbal methods. Questioning is at the heart of any problem-solving or inquiry method of teaching and should also be used in teacher-directed and individualized instruction methods. Using questions as an intentional part of an instructional method is really best understood as an aspect of an instructional objective. As you recall, an instructional objective consists of a statement of conditions under which a task is to be performed, the task itself, and the criteria by which completion of the task will be judged. A question is a way of stating the task and setting the conditions under which it will be performed. Some questions imply the criteria by which the task will be judged, while others purposely leave the criteria open. Like any instructional objective, questions must be clear and precise.

Questions can be categorized into four types according to the cognitive activity involved (Baird and others 1972). Questions from each category are used for different purposes, and it is important that the question be consistent with the purpose for which it is used.

Categories of Questioning

1. *Recall questions* require a memory-level answer. Most questions that can be answered yes or no are in this category.
2. *Convergent questions* call for analysis and integration of previously encountered material. Problem solving and reasoning are often required to answer these questions because they call for applying two or more recall items in an appropriate manner. Convergent questions almost always have a range of answers that are considered right or wrong.
3. *Divergent questions* call for solutions to previously unencountered material. Answers are considered to be creative and not necessarily empirically provable. Many different answers may be correct, because by its nature divergent questioning produces divergent answers from students. This question type requires the highest level of problem solving and reasoning.

**Using
Questioning
as a
Teaching
Method**

205

4. *Value questions* call for expressions of choice, attitude, and opinion. Answers are not judged as right or wrong.

Questioning for Basketball

Recall Questions

Should your eyes be on the ball when you dribble?
How many seconds can you stand in the lane?
Which hand should be up on defense against a right-handed player?
Where does the point player play on a 1–3–1 zone defense?

Convergent Questions

How are the 1–2–2 and 1–3–1 defenses similar?
Why should you stay between your opponent and the basket?
What are your responsibilities if your opponent shoots and moves to the right to rebound the shot?
What should you do if you are dribbling and you see a teammate open ahead of you?

Divergent Questions

How would you rebound against someone who was taller but not as quick as you?
What different ways could you pass the ball on a fast break?
What kinds of offensive moves would be good against a defensive opponent who was quicker, but not as tall or strong as you?
What kind of offensive strategy would you use if you had a 3-point lead with 3 minutes left in a game?

Value Questions

How do you feel about using your hands to keep in contact with your opponent on defense?
What would you do if the only way you could get the ball back at the close of a game would be to intentionally foul an opponent?
How do you react when you get fouled but the referee doesn't blow the whistle?
If you had to choose between scoring a lot and having your team win, which would you choose and why?

Obviously these questions are used for different purposes. For example, creativity is not going to be developed by using recall or convergent questions. This is not to suggest that recall and convergent questioning has no place. Recall and convergent questioning are useful and necessary to make sure students understand materials presented in or outside of class. If you hand out an assignment to prepare students for the next class, the best way to hold them accountable is to throw out a few recall and convergent questions at the start of class. The usefulness of value questioning is well documented in

Chapter 7 where it is emphasized that students need to learn how to express feelings and emotions.

Questions can also be framed in a broad or a narrow context (Baird and others 1972). A broad question does not restrict the student's answer unnecessarily, even though the question may be a recall question. A narrow question includes in the task specification a statement of criteria that restricts the answer. The difference can be seen by the following questions:

Broad: What are the main principles of defensive play in basketball?
Narrow: What are the five main principles in individual defensive play in basketball?

Sometimes, the restrictions of a narrow question are important. For example, you might ask, "How many spotters must be in place before you can mount the trampoline?" The question is narrowly restrictive but purposely so because it relates to an important safety principle. More often than not, however, it is better to frame questions in a broad rather than a narrow context.

The following guidelines are suggested for the important skill of questioning:

1. *Questions should be clear and precise.* Just as in an instructional objective, a student must understand what is being asked in order to have a fair chance of constructing an answer.
2. *Questions should elicit single answers.* One question can be answered with one response. Multiple questions framed in a single context confuse the student because he or she does not know which question to respond to.
3. *Questions should be presented in a meaningful order.* The instructional intent of a system is made clear through a coherent progression of questions.
4. *Ask questions before naming students.* If you say, "James, what is . . . ?" you are likely to get James's attention but lose the rest of the group. It is far better to say "What is . . . , James?"
5. *Don't repeat student answers.* Nothing is more boring than to have a teacher repeat a student answer. Repeating an answer also tends to send the "hidden message" that only certain answers are acceptable and this quickly frightens other potential contributors.
6. *Allow students time to respond.* Don't expect quick responses. If you are trying to promote thoughtful, creative responses, then you must allow students the time to prepare such responses. If the question requires recall, then perhaps a time limit is part of the appropriateness of the answer.
7. *Don't reword questions.* If you have planned adequately, your questions will be clear and phrased in language appropriate to the level of the students. Rewording questions that are unclear tends to lose the students quickly. It is better to go on to another question.

8. *Make sure the interaction is consistent with the level of the question.* A positive interaction for a recall question should be directed to a correct answer. A positive interaction for a divergent-level question should be directed to the fact that a different solution was produced, not to the solution itself.

9. *Redirect questions to involve more students.* A good way to spread the effect of questioning techniques is to redirect questions. Redirecting means asking the same question of another student. If redirection is used, then feedback, confirmation, and positive or corrective interaction on the first response should be delayed until all responses are completed. The following pattern is suggested:

Question 1
Response 1
Redirect
Response 2
Redirect
Response 3
Feedback for Responses 1, 2, and 3

10. *Too many questions show too much domination by teacher.* The suggestions made here allow time for student responses and emphasize divergency and redirection. This approach, combined with encouragement of student questioning and commenting, should create a classroom climate where questioning techniques may be used without having the teacher dominate the session.

Using Students as Teaching Agents

The teacher need not be the sole visible agent of learning in an instructional system. Students may use programmed materials, task cards, or receive instruction and feedback from other sources that are programmed into the environment by the teacher but are not directly teacher controlled during the actual learning time. Another important way of diffusing the teaching, and therefore increasing its impact, is to have students act as teaching agents. It should be pointed out that this does not mean turning the responsibility for instruction over to students. That is why the term *agent* is used—it connotes a situation in which someone or something represents the teacher but does not take over his or her function completely. The teacher is responsible for planning a learning environment within which the goals of the instructional system can be achieved efficiently and in a manner that is conducive to student growth and strong interpersonal relations. But this does not mean that the teacher him- or herself has to be the sole agent of instruction, demonstration, or feedback.

Students can do an excellent job as teaching agents. They often provide superb demonstrations that are good models for students because the teaching student is closer in age and developmental level to the learning students than is the teacher. A teaching student can often provide feedback and relate in a personal way that is not possible for a teacher due to the differences in age, language, and outlook.

There are two basic methods by which you might use students as teachers. First, you can develop a physical education teacher aide club. This can be implemented anywhere within the context of a K–12 program. Second-graders can act as effective teaching students for first-graders. Seniors can act as effective teaching students for freshmen. The value of having teaching students who are older than the class being taught is that there is some separation in terms of age and therefore the teaching student's responsibilities can be carried out more effectively. With a regular program of teaching students, you can develop a core of trained aides who can be used in a variety of situations over a long period of time. This allows them to develop their teaching skills and contribute to and be familiar with the planning and teaching methodology of the instructional system.

A second method is to use students within a class to teach other students in the same class. With this method the students do not receive permanent assignments as teaching students, but instead all students at one time or another act as teaching agents. This method is analogous to what Mosston (1966) has described as **reciprocal teaching**. The most comprehensive use of this method would be to pair students and have each student act as a teaching student for the other member of the pair. In this role their primary function is to provide feedback. Although this method does not develop a trained core of teaching students, it does spread the effect of the teaching agent among all students, and it allows each student to learn what there is to learn from playing this role. Another useful feature of this method is that providing feedback for another student forces the teaching student to focus on aspects of the performance that he or she might otherwise ignore, thus creating an analytical appreciation of the skill or game in question. In both of these teaching student methods, you should not ignore the potentially substantial benefit of the satisfaction derived from acting in a helping role.

The concept of teaching student is sound, but should not be employed haphazardly. If you are willing to delegate part of your teaching role to representative agents (students), then it is your responsibility to see that your agents carry out their tasks in a manner consistent with the instructional system. This means that teaching students must understand clearly the basic principles of positive interaction, positive feedback, corrective feedback, modeling, and presenting only limited amounts of information at a time. They must understand the basic design of the instructional system, the sequencing of the instructional tasks, and the criteria by which the tasks will be judged. You, as teacher, should intermittently assess the performance of teaching students to see that they are indeed behaving in a manner that is consistent with your instructional system. It is of no value for you to be consistently positive if you are going to delegate a portion of your teaching to a student who will bully and coerce other students.

The criteria by which teaching students are chosen is largely up to you. It may be that you want to pick the most highly skilled students, the most positive interactors, or the students who seem to enjoy physical education the most. Each of these presents a different model for other students, and some combination might prove to be most desirable. Another method, already mentioned, is to have students earn the right to be a teaching student by saving up points in a contingency management system. This ensures that your teaching students are those who greatly value the chance to act in that role.

Monitoring Students' Performance

When you examine the components of an instructional system, you will notice that consistent knowledge of student performance provides information that will let you know if the system is functioning effectively. If some problem exists, the performance information will help you determine which component is not working.

It must be emphasized that monitoring student performance does not mean testing students regularly. Traditionally, students have been tested at the end of a unit in order to assess their progress and assign them grades. An instructional system does not use this approach. When instructional tasks are defined and instructional objectives sequenced so that students can accomplish those tasks, then testing in the traditional sense becomes irrelevant, either for assessment of student growth or for grading. Student growth is better measured by the number of tasks they have completed, and grades can be assigned far more reliably in this manner than by administering skill tests or fitness tests.

Your monitoring system will use some kind of checklist format. The big question is "Under whose control will the checklist be completed?" Several alternatives are listed:

1. *Student-controlled checklist:* Students check themselves off and the teacher's role is to do enough monitoring to ensure that students are reliably assessing themselves.
2. *Partner-controlled checklist:* Students check partners and teacher occupies a reliability role function.
3. *Student- or partner-controlled with teacher control at task level:* Students or partners check completion of instructional objectives while teachers check the terminal performance of the instructional task. The assumption here is that checking the instructional task provides assurance that the instructional objectives have been accomplished.
4. *Task-level monitoring controlled by teacher:* The teacher can monitor task performance and formal evaluation of instructional objectives can

be abandoned. This saves time but does not provide much information relative to the functioning of the instructional system at the instructional objective level. In other words, it won't tell you if tasks are sequenced properly and if remedial loops are needed at certain points.

5. *Teacher-controlled checklists:* The teacher does all the assessment at the instructional objective level. This method is probably the most reliable, but it requires an enormous investment of time from the teacher and may not be justified in light of some other important teacher functions.

6. *Teacher aide–controlled checklists:* A teaching student performs the assessment function and the teacher provides periodic reliability checks. This is probably the best system, especially if a program of teaching aides has been developed so that the teacher has had a chance to train the teaching student to function effectively in an assessment role.

The differences in these checklist monitoring systems are in (1) who does the monitoring and (2) at what level performance is monitored.

Who Does the Monitoring?

Teacher
Teaching student
Partner
Student

What Level Is Monitored?

Instructional task completion
Instructional objective completion
Number of trials for each objective

The format of the checklist will be determined primarily by the choices made about these two factors. A checklist that is completed by students and is detailed to the point of recording the number of trials needed to pass each objective really becomes a diary of the students' activity in physical education. This kind of detailed information can provide the teacher with abundant data from which to make changes in the instructional system. A checklist that assesses only the completion of instructional tasks and is monitored by the teacher is very reliable and takes the least amount of assessment time, but is not a rich source of information for improving the instructional system. Obviously, a trade-off will be made according to the purposes for which you want to use a monitoring system.

The importance of monitoring student performance must be weighed against the time it takes. A teacher who spends most of his or her time assessing student completion of objectives limits the instruction, feedback, and interpersonal relations functions that also merit attention. This is why a monitoring system is so important. As with feedback, the more that monitoring is built into the learning environment and freed from direct teacher control, the better the entire system will function.

A monitoring checklist can take almost any format, and you should use the format that is best suited to the specifics of your situation. A monitoring checklist should allow for recording the most information possible with the least effort. The range of information recorded can be as little as checking completion of instructional tasks to as much as checking the number of trials needed to complete each instructional objective. Students have to understand that the checklist is a form of assessment designed to help them learn. If they perceive it to be strictly a test, then they are likely to engage in all the test behaviors that they have learned in school, and this will usually spell trouble for you and yield less than reliable information.

Four checklists are shown in Figures 11-1, 11-2, 11-3, and 11-4. The form of the checklist in Figure 11-1 corresponds to the badminton contingency management plan shown in Figure 10-3. This checklist can be completed by a teacher, a teaching student, a partner, or a student him- or herself. It is designed to assess performance at the instructional objective level.

The checklist shown in Figure 11-2 is for an advanced badminton system that is also monitored at the instructional objectives level. Here, however, the assessment is to be completed by another member of the class. Each member of the class has his or her own checklist and secures the cooperation of a classmate to fill it out. Class records are later made up by collecting information from the individual checklists. This kind of partner assessment works well with older students who have learned to function in an individual assessment climate. The fact that this checklist calls for individualized assessment does not necessarily imply that the class is being taught by an individualized instruction method. This kind of monitoring system is effective in a teacher-directed class. Students might practice skills in squads or groups, or all might work on a specific skill at the same time and only the assessment component might be individualized.

The checklist shown in Figure 11-3 is for a monitoring system that operates at the instructional task level rather than at the instructional objective level. This list can be completed by a teacher, a teaching student, a partner, or a student. The assumption here is that completion of an instructional task (which is a terminal skill that has been developed through a sequence of objectives) gives evidence of all the intermediate abilities. The tasks defined on this checklist would be stated elsewhere in terms of the conditions and criteria that define completion of the task. The checklist need not contain this information.

The checklist shown in Figure 11-4 is designed for use with a beginning gymnastics instructional system. It details performance to the point of recording the number of attempts a student takes to meet the criteria for each objective. The content of this checklist corresponds to skills suggested by Baley (1965). Assessment for this kind of monitoring system would have to be done by the individual student, a classmate or partner, or a teaching student. For a teacher to take time to monitor performance at this detailed level would not be feasible. This system calls for individual records rather than a group checklist, as shown in the beginning badminton and basketball examples. The individual records would later be transferred to a class record for purposes of permanent record keeping. This kind of monitoring system would provide permanent records for use with individual students and also for future planning.

Checklists can be used to develop a monitoring system and a permanent

Students	Level C Objectives								Level B Objectives						Level A Objectives			
	Short Serve	Long Serve	Underhand Clear	Overhead Drop Shot	Overhead Clear	Rallying	Matches	Knowledge	Overhead Clear	High Doubles Serve	Smash	Underhand Drop Shot	Backhand Clear	Net Shot	Overhead Clear	Backhand Clear	Push Shot	Drive Serve

Figure 11-1. *Checklist for Completion of Instructional Objectives (Badminton)*

Student Record: _____

Skill	Date Passed	Checker
1. Short serve		
2. Short serve to backhand serving right to left		
3. Short serve to backhand serving left to right		
4. Flick serve		
5. Long serve		
6. Long serve to backhand serving right to left		
7. Long serve to backhand serving left to right		
8. Drive serve		
9. Doubles serve		
10. Underhand defensive clear		
11. Underhand attacking clear		
12. Overhand defensive clear (5 to 5)		
13. Overhand defensive clear (2 to 3)		
14. Overhand defensive crosscourt clear		
15. Overhand defensive clear to backhand		
16. Overhand defensive clear with movement		
17. Round the head defensive clear		
18. Overhand attacking clear		
19. Backhand defensive clear (5 to 4)		
20. Backhand defensive clear (3 to 2)		
21. Overhand drop		
22. Overhand drop to backhand		
23. Round the head drop		
24. Overhand drop with movement		
25. Straight smash		
26. Smash for accuracy		
27. Smash for reaction to opponent's movement		
28. Passing smash		
29. Crosscourt smash		
30. Underhand net rally		
31. Sidearm forehand net rally		
32. Sidearm backhand net rally		
33. Combination net rally		
34. Push shot		

Figure 11-2. *Checklist for Completion of Instructional Objectives (Advanced Badminton)*

record system. The information from individual student checklists can be transferred to permanent record cards kept in the physical education office in the school. A permanent record card would provide every teacher with a specific record of what each student has accomplished in physical education. It would also be a continuous source of information for a needs inventory. Such monitoring would tend to make grading obsolete. Summaries of individual student records could be sent home to provide parents with a detailed report of what their sons and daughters have learned in physical education. This creates a built-in public relations system that would help develop community support for a physical education program.

At the risk of being repetitious, I must emphasize that the brief titles of tasks on a checklist refer to fully developed instructional objectives that specify a task, the conditions under which the task will be performed, and the criteria by which it will be judged to be completed. Any record of student performance must reliably indicate whether the criteria for the objective have been met. If the criteria are not rigidly adhered to in the assessment process, then the checklist is of little value because it is not a reliable record of what a student has learned. Consistency in applying the criteria to each student is the fundamental principle of an effective monitoring system.

Figure 11-3. *Checklist for Completion of Tasks (Basketball)*

Tasks	Students and Date Completed
Dribbling obstacle course	
Jump shooting	
Free throw shooting	
Driving lay-ups	
Defensive movement	
Passing	
Rebounding	
Strategy	
Game play	

I can do	It took me _____ times	I can do	It took me _____ times
V-sit		Assisted handspring	
Bridge		from mat	
Arching		Handspring	
Jump and tuck		walkout	
Jump and turn		Roundoff	
Russian dance		Forward walk	
Leg circles		Backward walk	
Front scale		Hops	
Side scale		Side cross step	
Blind balance		Turn	
Crab walk		jump	
Donkey kick		one leg	
Front roll		cat walk	
Forward roll		Knee scale	
Dive roll		Front scale	
Backward roll		Side scale	
straddle		V-sit	
jackknife		Backward roll	
extension		Straddle stand	
Cartwheel		Split	
Neckspring		Needle scale	
Headspring		One-leg balance	
straight leg		Front walkover	
from walk		Squat balance	
to seat		Head balance	

Figure 11-4. *Student Checklist (Gymnastics)*

Maintaining the Momentum of the Lesson

Some of the most important skills of preventive classroom management involve maintaining the pace of a lesson. These skills were described in detail in Chapter 5 and are only briefly referred to here. They are cited again simply because they are so important.

Pacing a lesson can mean many things. Certainly it should mean a proper balance between vigorous and less vigorous activities. Pacing also can be thought of in terms of a variety of activities leading to a culminating activity. Some activities introduce tasks, some refine tasks, some extend tasks, and others apply tasks. The activities are well paced when they lead logically to one another and finally to a culminating activity in which the various tasks are brought together and applied.

But, as we saw in Chapter 5, pacing can also refer to how the flow of activities is managed by the teacher and to what intrudes on that flow of activities. Chapter 5 introduced the notions of smoothness and momentum. The term *smoothness* refers to the absence of stops or breaks in the flow of activities. The term *momentum* refers to the rate of movement within and between activities and the absence of events that slow down the movement. It was suggested that teachers develop the skill of overlapping—being able to deal with more than one event at a time. It was also suggested that teachers refrain from bursting in on an ongoing activity—called a *thrust*.

Another serious break in momentum can occur if a teacher becomes magnetized—captured by an irrelevant event so that too much time and attention is devoted to that event. Dangles and flip-flops also involve activity interruptions that destroy momentum.

The point is that momentum is important to the success of a lesson, and it is in the best interests of the teacher to behave in such a way as to maintain and protect momentum that has been established through careful planning and effective teaching. Don't do the job of planning and get a lesson going well only to have it turn out poorly due to events that break the momentum of the lesson.

CHAPTER 12

Learning About Schools

We need have no fear that good teachers will be driven off by close examination of the teaching role. The attractions are genuine and powerful. So long as they have not been promised a rose garden, most people can be happy with a plot of wild pasture—just so long as the annual crop of roses outnumbers the annual crop of brambles, even by only one.

Larry Locke, *The Ecology of the Gymnasium: What the Tourist Never Sees* (1975)

CHAPTER OBJECTIVES

To differentiate between formal and informal organizations

To explain how schools differ from other organizations

To describe the pressures that affect first-year teachers

To identify and explain the major themes of studies that examine how schools affect teachers

To explain and provide examples of major issues concerning school rules

To make and discuss suggestions for how to survive in schools as a new teacher

To explain and provide examples for current applications of law to the teacher's daily job

Teachers live a large part of their lives in schools. They live among students. They exist in a bureaucratic structure. It is not surprising that the organizational characteristics of schools and the nature of the minute-by-minute life within them dramatically affects the kind of person a teacher becomes over the years. Most teacher educators recognize that what they do on campus is of less importance than what happens to interns during student teaching, and even less important than what happens to a first-year teacher. This is not to suggest that teacher education experiences, even those on campus, are unimportant—only that they typically do not have the same power to influence the prospective teacher as does the experience in school.

It is important that prospective teachers learn about schools *before* they begin to teach full time. This is true for two important reasons. First, if you know a lot about schools, the manner in which they operate and the power of influences they have over teachers, then you can adapt more readily to them and your initial teaching experiences will be less frustrating and more successful. Second, if you should choose to try to effect some change in schools, then a knowledge of how schools work is essential to the success of your change effort. Thus, whether you want to be an "adapter" or a "change agent" or some combination of the two, it will be to your advantage to learn about schools.

Schools are organizations. As such they tend to be unavoidably bureaucratic. There are policies, forms to fill out, and reports to be made. Small elementary schools in small systems can sometimes avoid this feeling of bureaucracy. Large schools in large systems too often are dominated by the feeling.

The formal organization of schools is hierarchical. Principals report to a superintendent; teachers report to principals. The lines of authority are clear and often rigid. As systems grow larger, the number of administrators increases and the hierarchical nature of the formal organization is emphasized.

Schools respond to many divergent interests, so there are many divergent interest groups within schools. Schools respond to parents, school boards, state departments of education, to teachers' organizations, professional organizations, and students. The formal organization takes all these interests into account, but not always to an equal degree. Because of the need to respond to different interest groups, it is unlikely that all members of a school organization will agree about the major goals of the school. They are unlikely to be "pushing in the same direction" at all times. This can frustrate and complicate life for the naive teacher who enters a school assuming that all policies and all decisions are based on "what's best for the students." Life in schools is not quite that simple.

Schools also have **informal organizations**, which are patterns of influence that exist outside, and sometimes in conflict with, the formal, hierarchical structure of school administration. Informal organizations develop in different ways and are seldom the same from school to school. You won't read about them in the school district's official description of the system. You are more likely to learn about them in the teachers' lounge. Some things in schools get done through the formal organization. Other things get done through the informal organization. Teachers can suffer, at least potentially, until they learn which organization is best for getting certain kinds of tasks done.

Although schools are like other organizations in many respects, they differ in certain important ways (Tumin 1977). Schools are most often public institutions financed through public funding. They are controlled by school boards, elected by local citizens. Maintaining **local control** of schools is a cherished American tradition, even though it means very different things in small rural districts and in large urban districts. Some states have hundreds of districts and therefore have hundreds of local school boards. Hawaii has only one school district—the whole state. Therefore, it has only one school board. Thus, local control means something very different in each state and often within states, depending on the size of the school district.

The fact that schools are often so thoroughly public means that their actions are highly visible—what they do is often in the public eye. Parents, politicians, and local media people feel quite at home in scrutinizing what goes on in schools and sharing their feelings in public. In that sense, at least, the organization of the school is highly accountable to a number of public interests.

A second way in which schools tend to differ from many other organizations is that their success as an organization is very hard to define. People disagree, often vigorously, about what should happen in schools. If people disagree as to what the goals of schools should be, then it is clear that they will also disagree on what criteria should be used to judge schools. Some believe that schools exist to teach basic tool skills such as language, mathematics, and knowledge of democracy. Others see schools as vocational training. Still others believe that self-growth and self-actualization are the most important goals. The differences are sometimes so great that to achieve one set of goals almost prohibits reaching another set of goals—such schools are in a "no-win" position.

The New Teacher

Teachers come in all sizes and shapes. They differ in many respects. Yet they enter teaching with many of the same characteristics, expectations, and problems. Most often, the new teacher is also a new adult, in the sense that he or she is entering a professional career for the first time (career shifts among adults are no longer uncommon, but the feeling of first entry still holds for a majority of first-year teachers). This means that a new phase of life is beginning as well as a new career.

New teachers often have to relocate. For some, it means leaving home for the first time—perhaps even making that final move of independence that establishes a person as an adult in our society. The relocation often means new friends, a new place to live, and new responsibilities. Thus, the adjustments of the first year of teaching are made even more difficult by the accompanying transition away from university life and into adulthood.

New apartments and new friends may represent one kind of transition, but the first-year teacher encounters a far more profound transition in the school in which he or she is employed. Schools have different value structures from university and college teacher education programs. Universities tend to be places where idealistic values are supported, often preached in teacher education programs. Schools tend to be more conservative, most often reflecting the values of the community in which they are located. In addition, public schools are not typically tolerant of people who question the values implicit in school policies and procedures, especially when the questioners are first-year teachers fresh from the university. The result is often conflict—and, conflict appears to be something with which first-year teachers live on a daily basis.

The first year of teaching is often complex and even bewildering. There is

Diary of a Beginning Teacher

September 1, 1966

Am I tired!!! Everyone told me I would be, but I didn't really believe it. Things went better today than I had expected, although I did mess up my attendance. The classes went pretty well except for the last period. All the other classes were only 30 minutes long but sixth period was 55. I hadn't realized this and didn't really have enough to fill up the extra time—I guess I'm not practiced at the gentle art of stalling. I've got so many things running around in my head that I have to remember, especially paperwork, that I'm sure I'll never remember it all.

The secretary in the office must shudder every time she sees me coming. I have so many problems with all of the records.

I feel guilty because I haven't got any long-range plans for my class, but I'm still too confused.

Postscript, May 10, 1968

Although my official record says that I have now had two years of teaching experience, it might be more accurate to say that I have had one year of experience and one year of teaching. My first year of employment seems to fit much better under the category of pure experience. My second year has been nothing like the first. For every one problem I have had this year, I had 15 or 20 last year. My first year, more often than not, was defeating, depressing, and exhausting. All this, however, was for a purpose: the second year and the years to come. From the first it was obvious that I was learning a great deal more than I was teaching. I would not give up a moment of my experiences last year (well, maybe one or two moments) because every mistake, every crisis, made this year easier.

As I reread the diary which I wrote last year, many half-forgotten events came back and many unforgettable ones were relived. I was amazed by some of the things which I didn't know or thought I did. Yet, it is not really amazing at all. Last year was for me a year of learning. The cliché says that experience is the best teacher. Well, experience *makes* the best teacher too, and last year was an experience.

Source: Morris, J. Diary of a beginning teacher, *Bulletin of the National Association of Secondary School Principals*, October 1968, 6–22.

never enough time to prepare. What you thought was adequate preparation turns out seldom to be exactly that. Students sometimes test new teachers, and if the test reveals weaknesses, the students are sometimes not above trying to probe those perceived weaknesses even further.

Discipline often becomes the major focus of the first-year teacher's effort. Although the preparation program might have taught good teaching techniques and even good planning strategies, there is typically less done to teach good discipline techniques. True, you might know about some discipline skills, such as those described in this text, but you probably have had little opportunity to actually try them out. This is true quite simply because preparation programs cannot, in fairness to students, set up problem situations for trainee teachers in order for them to get practice at discipline skills.

The new teacher is also socialized rather quickly into the teaching profession. Often there is a decision to be made about whether to join a teachers' union (sometimes called a professional organization, but functioning as a union). In this case, too, there probably has been little that preparation programs have done to help a trainee teacher to be ready to handle the decisions required by professional socialization during the entry year of teaching.

One of the more difficult aspects of first-year teaching is getting accustomed to the school routines and the extra duties they require of teachers, many of which are part of the organizational bureaucracy referred to earlier. Teachers take attendance and report it to a central office, they pass on school notices, they collect money, they send home for permissions, they do hall duty, they do lunchroom duty, and they become involved in a host of other quasi-administrative chores—chores that tend to take time away from their planning and preparation for teaching.

None of this is to suggest that first-year teaching is always a horror story and that the new teacher is inevitably headed for disappointment. One must always remember that new teachers also have their own classes for the first time—really their own! They can teach in their own style without having to please a college instructor or a school cooperating teacher. They have time to get to know students with the knowledge that the relationship may extend over years. They also encounter the joys of actually helping students to achieve and grow.

The degree to which the first year of teaching is viewed from a primarily positive or negative perspective depends on the balance that is achieved by all the forces described in this section. The outcome is hard to predict. Many, many teachers leave the profession after just one year—leave it of their own accord, feeling that they simply cannot or do not want to deal with the many problems encountered. Others have their aspirations reaffirmed and become even more committed to a career in teaching. What is absolutely clear is that the first year would be considerably easier if teacher education programs would better prepare their students for the realities of school organizations and life in schools. That, in effect, is the purpose of this chapter and the next.

Much of the blame for the difficulties encountered in first-year teaching must be placed on the teacher education programs from which the teachers graduated. I have tried to identify the major skills for effective teaching and explain them clearly, suggested strongly that they need to be practiced often, and provided observational suggestions through which feedback can be provided to the teacher education student. The skills emphasized in this book are precisely those most needed by new teachers—they are first-year survival skills in that sense! The following summary comment from a study of first-year teachers in inner-city schools (Hayman and Moskowitz 1975) points to skills that have been emphasized in this text:

> Confirmed strongly in the present study was the finding that the struggle for effective instruction (and learning) in the inner-city junior high school is effectively won or lost at the very beginning of the school year. The first meeting with the class, in fact, appears to be crucial in this regard. Successful teachers establish a productive climate at the very start, and they do it with specific types of orienting and expectation-setting behaviors. Few new teachers have the knowledge or the skills needed to effectively take control at the very beginning, and they suffer frustration as a result. . . . Successful teachers were also much more adept at engaging in reinforcing, motivating behaviors than were new teachers, and their superiority persisted throughout the school year. [p. 14]

On the other hand, it is not possible to create experiences for trainee teachers that are exactly like those they will face as first-year teachers. Thus, survival skills are "bets" in the sense that they are the best way to prepare trainees to "win" the first-year experiences.

Teachers' Views of Life in Classrooms

Several important studies have attempted to obtain information about the perceptions teachers have about what they do each day in schools. The two most notable of these studies have been reported in Lortie's *Schoolteacher* (1975) and Jackson's *Life in Classrooms* (1968). Through interviews and questionnaires, an immense amount of data were gathered and then analyzed. There were five major recurring themes in the views of the teachers. The views of teachers about what they do are an important source of information to consider when trying to learn more about schools.

A major recurring theme in the data from these two important works was the here-and-now urgency of teaching, the immediacy of events in the daily life of the teacher. A teacher who has to deal with a number of classes, each of which contains a large number of students, has little time for reflection and contemplation. Attention is riveted on the here and now—at least it had better be, if success is to be achieved. Eventually, this "present-ism" changes teachers. If you are required to always attend to immediate events, you are less likely to be contemplative and reflective. You become a somewhat different person. This is clearly a major effect of living in schools as a teacher.

A second theme was that of informality. Rather than define specific styles of teaching, teachers tend to narrow that issue down to formal versus informal teaching. The distinction usually rests on the manner in which the teacher chooses to use his or her authority, his or her managerial style. A strong desire for informality was apparent, yet it clearly meant less formal rather than *not* formal—a difference in degree rather than in kind. Informality often is related to "being accepted by the students" or "getting along with the kids." It seems clear that this influences teachers to understand and adapt to current language and dress styles among students.

A third recurring theme was the concern expressed about threats to professional autonomy. This general concern was expressed in many ways, such as having to implement an inflexible curriculum, being required to plan too far in advance, and being observed too often by supervisors and administrators. The investigators felt strongly that concerns for autonomy did not reflect a desire for total independence or a desire to be "left alone." Teachers feel strongly about the collective nature of school life. The concerns about autonomy evidently reflect the desire to be free from inspection while performing major instructional duties. Teachers want help. They most often like the idea of working together with specialists from other areas. On the other hand, they also want to feel in control of their own classroom.

A fourth theme emerging from the data was that of individuality. Criteria for success in teaching are terribly vague. Teachers, therefore, tend to use individual judgment to develop success criteria for themselves. These success criteria are much more often focused on what individual students do rather than what happens to the group. The individualization of success criteria also tends to make teachers resistant to outside accountability and to suggestions for change.

The final theme extracted from the studies is that of conservatism, not necessarily the political kind of conservatism but rather a "maintenance of status quo" kind of attitude. Most teachers seem to believe that limitations on their success are due mostly to institutional constraints and to lack of support. They view improvement as the removal of constraints and the addition of support. They are skeptical about new methods simply because they believe that they are well equipped to do the job if proper support were forthcoming. Individualism also contributes to this conservative ethic, because so many judgments about success are reduced to individual judgment. The very nature of life in schools, therefore, tends to promote and strengthen this conservative view, which is very often difficult to deal with when attempting to effect change in schools.

The point to be made from this brief review is that these forces in schools will affect you too. Regardless of the attitudes you have when you enter teaching, the nature of life in schools will tend to push you in the direction of the attitudes and values just described. To the extent that you understand these attitudes, you have a chance to protect yourself against them if you should so desire.

School Rules and Policies

Schools are organizations. Organizations have rules. Typically, teachers tend to support the need for rules and typically, many of the rules are created and enforced for the benefit of the teachers. Because rules are so important to the daily lives of teachers, it is appropriate to examine some issues related to them, as well as to encourage you to get experience in learning about the rules and policies of schools in your local area.

Every teacher is responsible for carrying out schoolwide policies designed for the educational and personal welfare of the student. Not all teachers agree with all the policies of a school, and there are no doubt mechanisms for having teachers contribute to policy decisions. But until a policy changes it is a teacher's responsibility to see that the policy is carried out. For example, you may not agree that students should have to wear a special uniform in physical education, but if this is a departmental or school policy then you should carry it out. Lack of consistency in carrying out school policies sends a message to students that policies need not be followed by all and that if a policy is disagreed with it is simply ignored. If a policy exists that you, in all good conscience, cannot abide by then you can seek a special dispensation from school authorities. If this is granted, then you can disregard the policy knowing that you have gone through the appropriate channels of appeal. If, however, the permission is not granted then you have to decide whether to conform to the policy or to leave that teaching position.

A **rule** can be defined as a formal statement of expected behavior for which consequences exist if the expectations are not met (Duke 1978). Schools often have long lists of rules for student behavior. And teachers often develop extra rules specific to their own instructional setting. I have strongly urged you to consider the establishment and teaching of rules as an important form of preventive classroom management (see Chapter 5). Rules define limits, and it is only within defined limits that people can grow and develop. The complete absence of rules would lead to chaos and anarchy. Few would argue that chaos and anarchy are characteristics of growth-enhancing environments.

On the other hand, it is clear that students can be unduly coerced and restricted by rules that go well beyond that which is necessary to produce and protect a safe, nurturant learning environment. The fact that I advocate the development of rules does not mean that I endorse without question all rules! There are good rules and bad rules. There are often too many rules. Students often react vigorously against rules they consider to be unnecessary and/or unfair—bad rules or inappropriately conceived rules are potential sources of problems for teachers—often creating more problems than the offenses they seek to control. The following questions are worth asking, both about school rules in general and about rules you might develop for physical education (Duke 1978):

1. How are school rules decided and by whom?
2. How are rules communicated to students and their parents?
3. How are rules enforced and by whom?
4. To what extent are rules enforced consistently?
5. What are the consequences for disobeying rules and how are they determined?
6. Are the consequences applied uniformly to all students?
7. What kinds of records are kept on violations? How are they used?
8. What rules are disobeyed most often?
9. If a student is accused of breaking a rule, what recourse does he or she have?
10. Which rules require the most time to enforce? Which require the least time?
11. Are there provisions for reassessing rules periodically?

Clearly, the answers to these questions can tell you a great deal about the nature of a school and the relationships within it. The questions ought also to serve as clues to you as you think about the kinds of rules you might establish for your own classes or for the total physical education program.

Several concerns about rules need to be examined very carefully. These concerns all relate to the basic question "Why are the rules established?" Common sense might lead you to answer that question quickly, with something like "They are established so that students can learn and grow." But life in schools isn't that simple! Other strong motives affect school rules besides the desire to produce and maintain a good learning environment.

One major concern about rules is that they are not often communicated effectively to students and parents. Seldom are the consequences for violations specified in advance. This failure leads to an unfortunate lack of consistency in dealing with rule violations. Lack of consistency in treatment is something against which students react most dramatically. It offends their sense of fairness.

There are often too many rules. Many rules are perceived by students to be unrelated to school functions. These rules are hard to enforce and are often most frequently violated by students.

The rules that tend to be enforced most actively are often those designed for the protection of teachers and administrators. It is a fact of organizational life that many rules are designed to protect the organization rather than the clients served by the organization.

Students seldom have a voice in determining rules or the consequences for violating rules. Therefore, the group to whom the rules are directed are effectively left out of the process by which the rules are developed and maintained. This hardly represents an exercise in democratic educational practice—but it is a fact of life in most schools.

You will have to decide the manner in which you will develop your own rules. I certainly encourage you to gradually allow students more and more input into rule development and rule maintenance. But you will not be able to escape developing a relationship to the school rules. Your behavior as a teacher will implicitly establish your attitudes toward those rules and communicate that attitude to students.

Surviving in the Organization

To grow and prosper in schools, first you have to survive. You have to earn tenure. You have to learn how to handle the workload—and enjoy it, too. There is no one set way to survive in schools. The first level of survival is wanting to stay in the profession. From 20 to 25 percent of the teachers who enter schools each year leave after their first year! For whatever reasons—often very complex and sometimes having little to do with the teaching experience itself—they do not survive. They choose to leave.

A second survival point is tenure. Granting tenure is usually a decision made by school administrators after the third year of teaching. At that point your fate is in the hands of a principal or some other administrator.

No single set of suggestions should be taken as complete when discussing how to survive in the organization of the school. Tumin (1977) has suggested some "rules" for surviving in schools. They are included here because they are realistic in terms of what is known about life in schools and because they are practical.

1. Don't make big fights over little matters. You cannot exert real influence until you have credibility. You will not achieve credibility if you challenge every point made by a colleague. Don't be afraid to challenge—just make sure it is an issue for which it is worth putting yourself on the line.

2. Until you are tenured, let more experienced teachers take the lead in matters that are viewed as adversarial by administrators. Schools are conservative organizations. Administrators do not take kindly to people they view as "trouble-makers." You can help. You can express yourself. But try to do so in a way that allows others to assume the major leadership roles—at least until you have tenure. Then you can become more assertive and active.

3. Administrators tend to judge you in terms of your loyalty to them and the manner in which you contribute to goals they see as vital to *their* success. It would be nice if all administrators were first of all concerned with how well you are teaching. Some are. Many are concerned, but not as much as they should be.

4. Do not burden administrators with unnecessary problems. They have enough problems dealing with budget, school boards, and parents. If

you are always transmitting your problems to your administrator, you will probably be viewed as someone who can't handle the job.

5. Conduct an orderly class. Administrators often have difficulty distinguishing creativity from chaos. Far too often they see orderliness and assume that a great deal of learning is going on. As you know, both perceptions can be inaccurate because they confuse classroom or gymnasium climate, management of student behavior, and management of learning tasks. It helps here to know your administrator—or at least the degree to which he or she tends to confuse those elements of classroom life.

6. If colleagues and administrators are going to form negative judgments about you, make sure it's over something important. Teachers are no different from other people. They gossip. They make value judgments on trivial matters. They attribute major personality and character defects to people who dress or talk differently from the way they do. Every local school exists in a community that has norms and standards of behavior that are considered to be acceptable. You will survive more easily to the extent that you can accommodate those local norms. Of course, if the norms violate a principle that you feel is really important, then of course you should hold your ground and be willing to take the consequences.

7. Don't make snap judgments about your colleagues, and try not to deal in stereotypes. Older teachers are not always conservative. People who dress differently than you do are not always "out of it." Administrators are not always people who have no real interest in students. If you do not want colleagues to stereotype you, then don't do it to them.

8. Don't expect all teachers to share your views on the right way to do things. You have just come from a preparation program where you have, hopefully, learned the latest approaches to teaching and to curriculum in physical education. Some of your colleagues will have been prepared in a different program, one in which perspectives on teaching and curriculum might have been very different. You will need their help and support. You cannot hope to get it by unduly criticizing their approaches or by implying that they are "out of touch" and that you have the real truth.

9. Try not to learn from teachers who have retired on the job. You will soon encounter teachers who do very little—or at least as little as possible. They may have burned out—only to retire on the job. They may be victims of role conflict and may have chosen coaching as their major priority. They may be disillusioned. You will no doubt wonder how they continue on in the organization, but every organization has them and an organization with a guarantee like tenure probably has more than most. Do not imitate them!

10. Do not develop patterns of teaching primarily to "get in" with students. Every suggestion in this text can lead you to more productive, positive, humane interaction patterns with students. But such interactions are done to promote learning and student growth, not to gain acceptance in the student culture. Friendly, surely. Warm, of course. But do it as an adult.

11. Try to avoid taking on roles for which you have no expertise. You are unlikely to be an expert in all things. This is especially true for roles as counselor and analyst. Students go through developmental stages that can be fraught with problems. If students have real problems, they should be referred to the appropriate person who can provide the relevant help. Learn to distinguish between those problems for which you can provide legitimate help and those where your involvement might be counterproductive, both to the student and to yourself.

12. Be very careful when you attempt to be a change agent. It is to be hoped that every new teacher will try to bring some change to the school in which he or she first works. This has always been one of the most important sources for continuous change and updating in schools, the infusion of new ideas and strategies that accompany new teachers. But be careful about how you do it. Make sure that the change is in the best interests of the students and not just your own personal trip. Realize that schools are highly resistant to change and particularly so to new educational fads. Innovations have come and gone from schools with great rapidity over the past 20 years—and schools have stayed remarkably the same. To be a change agent, you have to have credibility and support. Change is seldom brought through adversarial strategies. Every change tends to imply that the status quo is not good enough. Someone will have some of him- or herself invested in the status quo you will be trying to change. Be careful!

If all these suggestions tend to rub you the wrong way or tend to offend your sense of "being yourself," then you had best look carefully at the kind of school you want to become involved with for your first job. You can be yourself in every truly important way if you survive! You can effect change if you do it through the organization. But you cannot impose change on unwilling colleagues. That just isn't the way schools work.

Teachers and the Courts

It is a fact of life in our society that the judicial system has played an increasingly important role in national, state, and local affairs over the past several decades. The courts seem to decide everything from the busing of school children to whether the Raiders can move from Oakland to Los Angeles. One term that has become commonplace in the past few years is *malpractice*. The schools have not escaped this phenomenon. A recent article in *Phi Delta Kappan* was entitled "Professional Malpractice: Small Cloud, But Growing Bigger" (Patterson 1980). We have all heard of medical malpractice and legal malpractice. Now it appears that we are in the beginning stages of a number of suits in which teachers are being sued for educational malpractice.

Physical educators have always been conscious of legal liability because they work in settings in which there are potential safety hazards. Trampolines, ropes, obstacle courses, bats, shots, arrows, and other pieces of equipment can be hazardous unless used and supervised properly. Teachers have always been cautioned to establish safety rules, to instruct students carefully in the proper use of potentially dangerous equipment, and to use good safety techniques such as spotting properly in gymnastics.

What is new is a tendency to sue not only because of specific safety consid- erations but also because students were not provided with proper prior in- struction—thus the educational malpractice. Spotting improperly is one thing. But not providing the necessary progressions for a student to safely take part in an activity is an entirely different matter. It opens up to judicial scrutiny the planning and teaching efforts of teachers. You should take this very seriously. Being sued for $1 million is no joke. It has happened with in- creasing frequency during the past few years, and there appears to be no rea- son to suspect that the trend will not continue.

Parents and students are increasingly willing to use the courts to redress their grievances against schools and teachers. Teachers cannot afford to be ignorant of the basic principles over which schools and teachers are sued. That you "did not know" is no defense!

McDaniel (1979) has recently reviewed the school law principles that ap- pear to have the widest applicability in schools today. Here is a brief explana- tion of them.

1. *Worshipping in educational settings:* Prayer, worship services, or Bible reading intended to promote a religious belief are prohibited. Any act by a teacher intended to promote a religion is probably a violation of the neutrality principle that has guided most court decisions.
2. *Academic freedom:* Democracies try to protect freedom of expression, and both teachers and students have been afforded protection in this area. When reasonable judgment has been used, teachers can take on controversial issues. Allowing all sides to be heard seems to be an im- portant consideration in this legal area. Increasingly, courts are pro- tecting free expression in terms of hair length, beards, and symbolic demonstrations such as the wearing of badges, buttons, and armbands. Controversial literature can be used if teachers can show that they have

exercised good judgment and that it is relevant to the topic under study. A typical test is to judge the appropriateness of the literature to the age and maturity of the students.

3. *Engaging in private activities:* Teachers can engage in private activities to the extent that they do not impair teaching effectiveness and they are not illegal. Teachers can write public letters of criticism, engage in public debate, belong to unpopular organizations, and have private lives—all without having it held against them by the school.

4. *Due process:* Teachers are entitled to due process. So too are students. Teachers who deny students due process may be liable to lawsuits. Increasingly, courts are willing to look at issues of unfair punishment for student violations of school rules. Specific guidelines now exist for things such as expulsion from school.

5. *Punishing by using academic penalties:* Schools may discipline students. Academic penalties can be given—but they must be for academic violations, clearly related to the offense. Academic penalties cannot be used for violations of school rules that are nonacademic in nature. Students cannot be kept from graduating or have their grades reduced because they have violated school rules. Grades related partially or solely to attendance are questionable. Academic evaluations should be based only on academic performance.

6. *Corporal punishment:* Some states prohibit corporal punishment entirely. Even in states where it is permitted, local school districts often decide to bar it completely. Where it is used, it must be used according to clear guidelines. The punishment must never lead to permanent injury. The punishment must be fair in terms of the offense and must not be an act of revenge. Schools that want to use corporal punishment should have clear procedural guidelines that protect both the students and the teachers.

7. *Neglecting safety concerns:* Rules for safety should be established and enforced consistently. Teachers are responsible for monitoring student activity so that safety is maintained. Violations of safety rules need to be acted on immediately. Above all, be where you are assigned to be! You cannot supervise adequately if you are not even at the site.

8. *Slandering or libeling students:* Students have rights. Teachers cannot treat students any way they want to and be free from lawsuits. Derogatory terms, ridicule, maintaining the confidence of students, refusing to make subjective judgments of character, and violating student privacy through searches are all areas in which teachers need to be very careful.

9. *Knowing the law:* Again, ignorance is not a permissible defense. Teachers should ask their administrators to make clear what policies and procedures have been developed for the school. The better informed a teacher becomes, the more likely he or she is to avoid situations in which problems might arise. Some of the laws referred to here are for the protection of teachers. Some are for the protection of students.

The courts are not "out to get" teachers. In fact, many current judgments have been made for teachers. Recently, the *NEA Reporter* (1980) announced the following judgments, in which teachers were supported by NEA (National Education Association) legal resources:

A home economics teacher in Texas was awarded $71,000 for back pay, emotional stress, and injury to reputation. The jury decided that her rights had been violated when her school board had dismissed her for circulating an Ann Landers questionnaire.

A Denver teacher was granted $11,000 by a jury which decided that his activities as an NEA association member had been taken into account as part of his school's decision not to renew his contract.

A Columbus teacher won a court decision which required that a letter be removed from his permanent file. A principal had written the letter criticizing him for his activities on behalf of a teacher's organization.

The Montana Education Association won a class action suit against the Montana School Boards Association. The suit required that school boards throughout the state put an end to dismissal of nontenured teachers for vague reasons.

The point is that the courts and the judicial system are not "out to get" anybody—except those who by their actions violate the Constitution. Most educational organizations and teacher's organizations have strong liability protection programs. In some cases, teachers receive liability protection by belonging to their teachers' organization or the local or state educational organization. Liability insurance can also be purchased independently, often as an addition to homeowners' insurance. To be without it today is a big mistake.

CHAPTER 13

Becoming a Professional Teacher

Our schools can and should be better. But educators must take the lead, together, to make them so. Large numbers of parents and students are ready to join us, I believe, in making our schools, one by one, better places in which to live and work. The slogans for improvement are, for the most part, meaningless rhetoric. Our schools must be reconstructed, one by one, by citizens and educators working together. Nothing less will suffice.

John Goodlad, *Can Our Schools Get Better?* (1979)

CHAPTER OBJECTIVES

To show and illustrate how teachers can maintain their own accountability systems

To examine the basic kinds of role conflict experienced by teacher coaches

To explain and discuss the implications of the role conflict evidence for a career in physical education and coaching

To explain and provide examples of ways in which an individual can continue to develop as a professional teacher

It has been my aim to present important teaching skills in a realistic manner. The topic of professional role development tests that aim, because it is very easy to slip into quite unrealistic discussions of the professional development of the "perfect" teacher. Too many texts present an idealized portrait of a selfless person dedicated totally to the development of each student, not caring unduly about the financial implications of his or her professional role, willing always to go the extra step with students and colleagues, forever attempting to upgrade his or her knowledge of subject matter, possessing a highly developed service motive to school and community, and embodying the finest qualities of the ideal American citizen. Historically, the teacher has been considered a paragon of virtue in the community, and, from time to time, when people have discovered that teachers are ordinary human beings, the result has often been cruel treatment and dismissal. Fortunately, the past several decades have seen a shift to a far more realistic view of what a teacher is and should be. Indeed, with the rash of teacher strikes that seem to accompany the opening of school each fall, it is common to hear people describe teachers as noncaring, totally mercenary, cynical, and un-American.

As a teacher in training, you know that neither the idealized version nor the totally critical version of your motives is correct. The purpose of this chapter is to help you examine some of the forces that have influenced and will continue to affect your development as a professional teacher, thereby helping you arrive at some realistic assessment of what your professional role is or may become, and what kinds of factors will affect that role as you begin your teaching career.

In teaching more than any other occupation, the trainee preparing for a career suffers from what Ryan and Cooper call "overfamiliarity." The teacher trainee has spent the better part of his or her life in a school. The trainee has known literally hundreds of teachers of all shapes, sizes, and personalities, and has seen dozens of different teaching styles. The problem is that the trainee too often assumes that this wealth of experience has taught him or her all that there is to know about what it means to be a teacher. The fact that he or she does not know all there is to know about teaching may come as a jolt!

> Most of the 200,000 or so new teachers who enter American schools each year receive a rude awakening. Although the routines—homeroom, clubs, bells, books, and ball games—are all familiar to the new teacher, there is much about life in school he doesn't fully appreciate. Most new teachers, for example, have had relatively pleasant experiences as students. If they had not succeeded in school, they probably would not be in a position to become teachers. As a result, new teachers are frequently astounded by how difficult learning is for some children and how unhappy many children are in school. Many students are difficult to reach and apparently unconcerned about learning. Beginning teachers are surprised at the amount of administrative and clerical work that goes with the job. Nor did they realize that good teaching takes so much time-consuming preparation. Another shock for many is the amount of energy, both physical and emotional, teaching requires. Somehow these facets of teaching rarely get communicated to the audience of students. [Ryan and Cooper 1972, p. 136]

The problems to which Ryan and Cooper refer, as well as other aspects of professional role development, will begin to confront you daily. Listen to the professional matters you hear discussed in the teacher's lounge, at lunch, or during a departmental or faculty meeting. If things follow their natural course, these are the matters that you will become concerned about as you grow into a professional teacher.

This chapter has two themes. The first is the examination and identification of ways in which a teacher can control his or her own performance in the gymnasium and playing field. This theme deals with the continued development and maintenance of good teaching. The second theme deals with exploration of the realities of the professional teaching role. The first theme can be approached directly, and suggestions are made as to how to achieve control over your own teaching performance. The subject is one in which answers can be found and definite statements made. The second theme is quite different. In this text it is approached in an exploratory fashion, without attempts to moralize or otherwise impose on you any preconceived notions of the ideal professional role.

Self-Accountability

The professional teacher is specifically and overtly accountable to him- or herself for good teaching. Self-accountability is the essence of professionalism. It may be, however, that in the near future teachers will be held accountable to outside agencies for what transpires in their classrooms and gymnasiums. This kind of accountability may take diverse forms and may run the gamut from very general observations of teaching to specific measures of student performance. The teacher may be judged by peers (members of a teaching union or organization), administrators, or representatives of a school board. The teacher who takes steps to maintain good teaching will be far ahead when this day arrives (if indeed it ever does arrive).

The reference to self-accountability here is not a pie-in-the-sky notion of making sure that you try hard to do a good job of teaching; it goes far beyond a periodic summing up of your efforts in the gymnasium. Many teaching skills have been suggested in this text, and specific methods for assessing those skills are also described. The concept of a learning system in which monitoring of student performance is a crucial element has been fully explored in several chapters. All this was presented in a "learning format" in which feedback necessary for you to develop those teaching skills would be provided. This kind of feedback is necessary for learning, and the help of systematic observation is indispensable to your development as a teacher. But you will not be able to take a supervisory team with you on your first teaching job. The skills you developed during internships will not automatically transfer to a new teaching situation, nor will they automatically maintain themselves over a period of time. If you want to continue to develop teaching skills and, most importantly, if you want those skills you have developed to continue to be a part of your teaching performance, then you will need to take specific steps to ensure this.

For example, the chapter on implementation of instruction (Chapter 11) focused in part on the importance of instructional teacher feedback, rates of positive and corrective feedback, ratio of positive to corrective, and the information and value content of feedback statements. If you achieve the goals you set in this skill area, will you automatically behave that way for the remainder of your teaching career? Every bit of evidence that can be mustered would tend to say no—unless you take steps to see that your feedback rates, ratios, and percentages are maintained at the level you think is important for good teaching. It is in the taking of these specific steps that a teacher becomes accountable to him- or herself and can at any given time be confident that he or she is performing capably as a professional.

One of the best ways to ensure that you continue to teach in a manner consistent with your beliefs is to *intentionally* set up some accountability measures for yourself. That's right—voluntarily set up your own accountability system. Enlist the aid of a physical education supervisor, a colleague teacher, or the principal. Set some "job targets" for yourself and ask them to help you to be accountable for those goals. Perhaps you want to have a measure of learning time taken periodically by a colleague. Perhaps you want regularly to get feedback from your own students about their views of how the classes are going. Perhaps you might go as far as to develop your own observation system and invite someone several times each month to code your teaching. In this way, you can develop a regular source of data from which you can judge the degree to which your actual performance as a teacher matches your desires about the kind of teacher you want to be. Self-accountability does not necessarily mean that you do not create overt accountability mechanisms for yourself. You expect your students to keep on task, and you provide some accountability mechanisms for them. Perhaps you ought to consider a few for yourself!

Identifying Specific Goals

It is difficult to hold yourself accountable for good teaching without defining carefully the elements that comprise "good teaching." The various chapters in this text have suggested numerous elements of teaching that you might consider, and it is expected that you have your own feelings about what constitutes good teaching. The point is that these elements must be specified in order to develop a self-accountability system, and they must be specified in a sufficiently clear manner that you or any other observer could make reliable judgments about the degree to which the elements are being achieved.

Are your students learning? Are your students learning to like the activities as they learn them? Does the manner in which you teach create a positive classroom climate? Do your students perceive you as a supportive, positive, sincere interactor? Are your students well behaved? Is their good behavior prompted by a negative or a positive atmosphere? Do students spend most of their time in active learning, or is there too much time spent in management or instruction? The chapters in this text have spoken to these elements of teaching and have suggested ways in which they could be measured so that feedback could be generated in order for you to develop your teaching skills. A self-accountability system can be developed by specifying the elements you consider to be most important to your definition of good teaching and setting goals for yourself in these areas.

Maintaining Your Performance

Once you have developed a teaching skill, there is no need to monitor it as carefully and frequently as was done during the skill development stage. Once a skill is developed, your goal is to maintain it at a level that you feel is representative of good teaching. You might consider a 90 percent appropriate behavior rate, a 3.5 rate of feedback per minute, a ratio of four positive behavior interactions to every one desisting interaction, a 70 percent active learning rate, and a certain number of skill objectives passed per unit as sufficient evidence of good teaching. These elements focus on your behavior and that of your students and may represent the level of professional self-accountability that you want to maintain. Once goals such as these are set they can be measured periodically to ensure that they are being met. Data such as these can be periodically collected in several ways:

1. A teaching student can use behavior-rating techniques similar to those your supervisory team used during the skill development stage. This should be done infrequently (once every two weeks is probably sufficient unless there is evidence that the goals are not being maintained). It should be done as much as possible without your knowledge; that is, you should have one or more students do this periodically and not instruct them as to exactly when it should be done. The danger in knowing when the assessment is being done is that you will teach one way during the assessment period and another way when you know you are not being assessed.

2. A fellow teacher can do the rating. One of the best ways to maintain your teaching behavior is to use a team approach, in which you trade assessments with a colleague.

3. Any teaching skills that involve your verbal behavior can be recorded on a portable tape recorder and coded by you later. An easy way to maintain feedback and behavior interaction rates and ratios is to tape record 30 minutes of teaching per week, then take the tape and code it yourself.

4. Use visitors to record. Some schools that regularly have visitors use them to make recordings as they observe the school in operation. A visitor to your gym class might be handed a sheet that points out many aspects of the curriculum and teaching method and also asks the visitor to record certain things (for example, "Now watch the teacher for 4 minutes and mark down the number of positive and corrective feedback statements the teacher makes to students concerning their skill attempts"). When the visitor leaves, he or she turns in the observation form and you have some data.

Almost all the teaching skills mentioned in this text are assessed by having one human observe the behavior of another human. The development of a self-accountability system to maintain your own teaching performance is predicated on your being able to have someone observe your teaching behavior (or observing it yourself via videotape or audiotape). Once you have a system for generating these data, you can hold yourself accountable. This kind of self-accountability can be the source for a strong, personal confidence in your status as a professional teacher. It also can help you provide quick, defensible, and definitive answers to anyone who asks or implies the question "How well are you teaching?" You don't have to convince anybody through argument or make any kind of sworn testimonial to your teaching ability. You merely have to show them the data. You can "put your data where your mouth is." There is no way that they can argue with your data. They may say it is not relevant to good teaching, but you should be able to counter that argument easily. They may say it is not reliable, but you can counter that argument by asking them if they would like to do some recordings.

Poor Teachers Are Made, Not Born!

American teachers have often been criticized for their lack of initiative and their seeming willingness to "give in" in the face of pressure. In 1904 John Dewey criticized what he saw as teachers' "tendency to intellectual subserviency." In 1936, in the book *Are American Teachers Free?* Howard Beale charged that American teachers are "dominated by cowardice and hypocrisy." In 1970 Charles Silberman, in his influential book *Crisis in the Classroom*, said that "what is mostly wrong with the public schools is not due to venality or indifference or stupidity but to mindlessness."

Recently, Vincent Crockenberg (1975) has argued that critics have misunderstood the nature of the problem in schools—that the focus should not be on the teachers as people but rather on the organizational characteristics of schools, the conditions under which teachers work. He suggested that "teachers are denied the conditions necessary for the development of mind because of the way in which schools are organized and controlled" (p. 189). Crockenberg argued that teachers will continue to "give in," to act mindlessly, until they gain significant control over the determination of school practices and school policies. He concluded his argument with the following analysis:

> If teachers are to overcome mindlessness, if they are to teach purposefully and intelligently, they must be allowed to work in a context where they do not simply act on the purposes and decisions of others (often unseen others). They must be allowed to formulate their own purposes, initiate their own actions to further those purposes, and then modify their purposes and their practices in the light of the consequences. [p. 196]

To be a professional is to be in control. Physical educators have the opportunity to make these kinds of decisions—if they want to badly enough! Teachers are not inept—but the context within which they work often tends to produce mental dullness over the years. If you know that this is a possibility, then you can guard yourself against it. It all depends on what kind of a professional teacher you want to be—poor teachers are most often *made*. They were not born that way.

A data-based approach to self-accountability is much more satisfying and effective than attempting to convince yourself or anybody else of your teaching effectiveness through anecdotal records that were developed mostly from eyeballing. It is easy to say, "My students learn a lot, are well behaved, and like me." It is more difficult when someone says, "How do you know all this?" If you have relied on eyeballing, you then bring out the reminiscences and anecdotes and try to convince the listener through testimonials. It is much easier and better to be able to say, "I know it because I have taken the time to assess it and here are the data that prove it." The parent, department head, or principal who hears and sees that will be convinced.

Another very important tool for self-accountability is the development of a monitoring system for student performance (see Chapter 11) and the establishment of a record-keeping system so that student progress can be charted across time. Ultimately, the best test of your teaching effectiveness is the degree to which the students in your classes learn and grow. It is certainly in your best interests to have good data to show exactly what you are accomplishing in your program. These kinds of data can also be very useful in making changes in your program. For example, if physical fitness tests show that the majority of your students lack upper body strength, then perhaps activities stressing the upper body need to be incorporated in the program. Or, if data show that students provide only average ratings for their attitudes toward physical education, then perhaps the emotional climate of the setting needs to be examined and improved. These data can also be used to show administrators and parents exactly what is being accomplished in the program. This serves as a good public relations device and also is a straightforward measure of self-accountability.

Role Conflict

Physical education teachers are often also employed as coaches. Far too often, indeed, men and women are hired first of all for what they can coach and only secondarily for their teaching expertise. It is probably true that many undergraduate physical education majors have coaching as their first interest and teaching as a secondary interest (Locke, Siedentop, and Mand 1980). For these students, teaching on a daily basis is a secondary career choice.

A case has been made in this text for the fact that teaching, when well done, is a complex set of actions that requires the full attention and devotion of the person doing the teaching. When this difficult role is placed against a person's role as a coach, the result is often a serious case of role conflict.

A **role** is defined as a pattern of expected behaviors for a specific position in some segment of society (Locke and Massengale 1978). Each of us has been in a student role and a son or daughter role. Some of us have been in roles as parents, teachers, and coaches.

Three kinds of role conflict are particularly bothersome in physical education. **Interrole conflict** exists when one person occupies different roles that require incompatible patterns of behaving. A physical educator experiences interrole conflict when practice interferes with a teacher's meeting, when scouting interferes with family obligations, when planning for practice interferes with planning for daily teaching, and so on.

Intrarole conflict occurs when one person must respond to incompatible expectations from different people or groups. Thus, a coach must deal with some parents who want only to win and with others who see school athletic participation as a developmental experience. The teacher must deal with those who expect a "fitness first" approach and those who are most interested in group sport skill development.

How Real and Prevalent Is Role Conflict?

Chu (1981) studied teacher coaches and reported that 87 percent felt that their school administrations compelled them to coach in order to maintain their positions as teachers. One teacher coach put it this way:

> I think it is assumed that if you're in physical education, you are responsible for coaching teams. If I gave up the varsity baseball job, I would probably lose the physical education position. There was one guy who refused to coach because of the low extra pay and they took him out of physical education and made him a permanent driver's education teacher—the administration, the principal did that. [p. 40]

A majority of subjects in this study also indicated that they would have to "put up with" teaching physical education classes in order to coach.

Segrave (1981) studied 267 teacher coaches and reported that 62 percent of the total sample indicated coaching as the preferred role rather than teaching. For those who had been varsity athletes while in college, 71 percent indicated coaching as the preferred role. For those who had not been varsity athletes, 53 percent indicated coaching as the preferred role.

Massengale (1981) suggests that teacher coaches are seldom fired for teaching inadequacy, yet demonstrated skill and competence in teaching seldom compensates for coaching a losing team. Noncoaching teachers do not work under the unequal reward system that so strongly affects the lives of teacher coaches. Thus, they seldom can appreciate the conflict experienced by the teacher coaches.

The answer to the question is that role conflict is very real and is prevalent in American schools.

Finally, **load conflict** refers to the incompatible expectations that arise from the combined loads of teaching and coaching. This conflict often interacts with interrole conflict, especially when the person is away from home often, is under psychological stress, and becomes physically exhausted from the sheer length of the work day. Teacher coaches often arrive at school between 7:30 and 8:30 A.M., teach a full complement of classes, and begin coaching at 4:00 P.M. The practice session might end at 5:30 or 6:00, but by the time that equipment is put away and students have showered and left the premises, the coach usually cannot leave until 7:00. During a competitive season, this hectic schedule may be made even worse by scouting trips and away game travel dates.

The roles of teaching physical education to regular students during the day and coaching athletes in interscholastic sport teams differ in a number of important ways (Locke and Massengale 1978). The two roles most often differ in terms of the relevance of each to the professional's career advancement. The two roles tend to differ in the level of technical preparation and competence perceived necessary for successful entry. There certainly seems to be a difference in the way in which people view the need for continuous upgrading of expertise in the two roles. Conventional wisdom supports the notion that the requirements of daily preparation differ in the two roles. Certainly, in one of the roles, the person's performance is regularly evaluated, often by people who become very much involved themselves in the performance (other students, parents of students, administrators, and so on). Regular evaluation of performance entails general agreement as to what constitutes good performance in at least one of the roles.

The students served in the two roles also tend to differ. They tend to be homogeneous in one and heterogeneous in the other. They are always volunteers in one and seldom in the other. They have different levels of skill, the one group being an elite group in the school. The kind of contact the person has with students in the two roles differs markedly. In the one, the contact is often with large numbers for short periods of time, in a fairly relaxed and not very intimate setting. In the other, the contact is frequent, with large amounts of time devoted to it, and the teacher coach shares important kinds of experiences with the students that are intense and often intimate.

As you might have guessed, the roles seem to be very different, with a much more powerful set of contingencies applying to the coaching role than to the teaching role. Although this does not always hold true (one must always be careful not to stereotype individuals), the general picture of these differences seems to be strongly in favor of the coaching role as the dominant role. The differences can be characterized as shown in Table 13-1.

It needs to be stated again that this characterization does not hold true for all physical education teachers. But it does fit the traditional stereotype of the "coach" who "rolls out the ball" during his or her instructional responsibilities and generally loafs through the day, only to turn into a human dynamo at athletic practice. It has often been said that the interscholastic coach

Table 13-1 / *Differences Between the Roles of Teacher and Coach*

Role Characteristic	Teacher	Coach
1. Relevance of role to career advancement	Low	High
2. Technical preparation required for successful entry	Low	High
3. Need for continuous upgrading (clinics, etc.)	Low	High
4. Requirements for daily preparation	Small	Large
5. Frequency of public evaluation of performance	Seldom	Often
6. Emotional involvement of evaluators	Low	High
7. Consensus about desired outcomes of performance	Low	High
8. Extent and intensity of contact with students	Low	High
9. Homogeneity of students worked with	Low	High
10. Degree of voluntarism among students	Usually low	Always high
11. Motivation of students worked with	Differs greatly	Mostly high
12. Skill level of students worked with	Differs greatly	Highest in school
13. Intensity and intimacy of contacts with students	Mostly low	Often very high

does the best job of teaching in the school and the physical educator the worst job—*and they are the same person*! Table 13-1 explains why that stereotype is sometimes accurate.

Locke and Massengale (1978) found this caricature to be more accurate than inaccurate:

> It is clear, however, that load conflicts and teacher/coach conflicts constitute widespread and intensively experienced role problems for the teacher/coach. In the case of load conflict more than one half and in the case of teacher/coach conflict nearly a third of all respondents judged those problems to have "great" or "very great" significance.

Furthermore, their data indicated that role conflict for the physical educator coach was higher than for the classroom teacher coach. The literature on role conflict indicates clearly that when conflict exists, people tend to select one role as the major role. They then use the demands and expectations of this role to provide the basic framework within which they make decisions about the other role(s). If a teacher coach chooses coaching as the dominant role, then he or she makes decisions about teaching within the framework of expectations and needs of the coaching role. The teaching role becomes secondary and the time and effort devoted to it become more and more commensurate with its lowered status in the person's life. The literature also suggests that making decisions about the relative priorities of the two roles tends to reduce the tension and anxiety that was created by the role conflict.

Although the official policies of the school suggest that teaching is the top priority, the facts seem to indicate that the realities differ considerably from the official rhetoric. Massengale (1981, p. 51) has made the following observation based on a review of the available evidence: "For all practical purposes, it appears that most teacher coaches fail to resolve their occupational

Coaching Interscholastic Sport Teams: The Pay Is Low and the Hours are Long

The most common method for reimbursing teacher coaches for the extra work they do as coaches is to provide them with supplementary pay through a supplementary contract. Chu (1981) reports that teacher coaches in his study received between $1.74 per hour and $0.32 per hour for the time they devoted to their coaching. It appears that the average pay for a coach is somewhere near $1.00 per hour for the time he or she puts into the coaching assignment—not exactly a get-rich-quick strategy!

How much time do they spend? The following data from the Chu (1981) study indicate the imbalance of time devoted to teaching and coaching:

	Males			Females	
Class Contact	Class Preparation	Coaching	Class Contact	Class Preparation	Coaching
Hours During the Coaching Season					
18.4	2.7	44.2	18.8	4.1	27.2
Hours During the Noncoaching Season					
18.4	2.7	2.5	18.8	5.4	3.7

One interesting point in these data is the fact that teachers and coaches do not seem to devote more time to preparation for their teaching in their noncoaching seasons.

role conflict, attempt withdrawal, and then make a large commitment to the coaching portion of the role and a small commitment to the teaching portion." This commitment to coaching is often tacitly encouraged by departmental or school administrators through the adjustment of assignments (Templin 1981). For example, coaches are often assigned a "planning" period during the final period of the official school day. Although planning periods are supposed to be used for the preparation of teaching, everybody clearly understands that the teacher coach will use it to prepare for the day's practice session. Teacher coaches are also often given study hall or hall duty assignments in lieu of classes with the understanding that the lightened responsibility will give them time to plan for practices, review films, and attend to other aspects of their coaching assignments.

That is not a pretty picture. It is believed to be an accurate picture. And it is most probably related to the current phenomenon in teaching known as **burnout**—the point at which the total demands of being a professional educator exceed the abilities and resources of the person to continue productively in his or her many roles.

There is no answer to role conflict in physical education. The most desirable solution would be a different pattern of staffing in schools, one that would allow those who are primarily interested in coaching to do that more exclusively and those who are primarily interested in teaching to do that, without having to worry about "saving themselves" for an afternoon practice. However, to expect such a dramatic shift in staffing patterns in the near future is unrealistic. Perhaps the best that can be done now is to sensitize future teacher coaches to the problems of role conflict and to impress on them the need to sustain a responsible teaching effort. To provide only this knowledge and some "cheerleading" about a continued effort in teaching will not do the job. If dual roles are to continue to be the status quo, then strong accountability mechanisms for good teaching need to be developed in American schools.

Continuing to Develop as a Professional

There is no one best way to continue to develop and improve your teaching skills—there are *many* different ways to do so. No doubt you are aware of some of the ways as a result of being in your physical education major program. Each person must try to find that way of continuing to develop that best suits his or her needs. Several avenues for professional development will be suggested here, but no order of importance should be assumed. Some teachers like to subscribe to professional journals and belong to associations, often attending their conventions. Others prefer to visit outstanding local programs, to see firsthand what their colleagues are doing. There is no evidence to suggest that one way is necessarily better than another. What is important, however, is that each person continues to try!

The books you have encountered as a physical education major are one source of professional development. However, it would be less than honest to say that many of them are relevant to the needs and interests of schoolteachers New books do get published each year. It is important that you try to stay abreast of what is being published. One of the new books might just become an important part of your professional development.

Professional journals can be an excellent source of new ideas for the practicing teacher. *The Journal of Physical Education, Recreation, and Dance*, published by the American Alliance for Health, Physical Education, Recreation, and Dance, is an example. Your state association may publish a state journal, and numerous general education journals are available. The key here is to find one that consistently has practical ideas that can be put to use in your teaching and that has articles that prompt you to think seriously about what you are doing. Both functions are important. Both can help you grow and develop in your teaching.

Professional organizations often sponsor conventions and workshops that might provide useful practical information and also insights into the problems of teaching. However, do not expect that every session is going to be valuable to you. Organizations must respond to a set of diverse interests. If a few of your interests and needs are attended to seriously and well, then you can count yourself lucky. Conventions also provide another important service: they create an atmosphere within which professionals with common interests can come together. Often, the informal conversations held at conventions prove to be of more value than the formal program. And conventions can be fun, too!

Local school agencies often sponsor inservice training programs. It is quite common now for teachers to have several working days a year freed for inservice education. Physical educators within a school system would do well to band together to make sure that their particular needs and interests are being served in the inservice program. To remain silent is to simply accept what school administrators think would be a useful inservice program.

School visitations can be an excellent source of professional growth. Many teachers can now get leave from their duties for a day or a half-day to visit another school to view the physical education program and talk to the physical educators there. This kind of firsthand knowledge of how other physical educators do their jobs can be a rich source of ideas about activities, management, instruction, and evaluation.

Finally, colleges and universities offer a large range of courses designed for teachers who seek to further their education and, at the same time, to improve their teaching. Often, the accumulation of credit hours beyond the bachelor's degree leads to pay increases in the school system's salary schedule. Practicing teachers should look for university courses that offer practical help in the critical areas of schooling. They should also seek out courses that help them to think more creatively and seriously about the many problems that confront American education today. Occasionally, it is possible to find a graduate course that serves both of these goals—and that kind of course should be taken. Unfortunately, few colleges and universities offer graduate credit for advanced skill techniques. This is one of the most serious shortcomings of graduate physical education, especially the part of it that is supposed to respond to teachers' needs. What could be more useful than a graduate course in activity areas in which you need upgrading, or new activity areas that were not yet popular when you were in your major program? You would do well to seek out colleges and universities that are sensible enough to provide graduate courses in activity areas. Upgrading your own activity competencies is an important way to grow in your professional role.

Improving Schools

Education has been under attack, for one reason or another, for many years. Will schools get better? Most of us will respond to that question with a quick yes simply because we have been raised to believe that things do get better and because we no doubt believe that we can help them to become better. But improvement does not *necessarily* occur with the passage of time. Schools may get worse, public support may continue to wane, programs and facilities may continue to deteriorate, dissatisfaction may become more widespread, and critics may become even more vocal and strident. It is only when this latter view is taken seriously by each of us that we can begin to think seriously about improvement.

The new teacher has always been a major source of improvement in schools. The new teacher brings new ideas, a fresh enthusiasm, and infectious optimism. But there are fewer new teachers each year than has been typical for most of this century. Teachers tend to stay longer in their positions simply because economic conditions have decreased their mobility. Lack of funds in local districts has caused administrators to cut back on teaching staffs, often leaving vacated positions unfilled. Still, there is much the new teacher can do to improve schools *if* he or she decides that effecting change is part of being a professional teacher. As Ryan (1970) has argued forcefully, the chances for change are small if new teachers do not seize the opportunity:

> The first year of teaching is the beginner's initiation into the profession. Like other initiation rites, whether into the role of infantryman or fraternity man, it is a period of intense learning and also a trial. . . . In particular, initiations make defenders and believers. This is true of the first year teacher, too. Having passed the test . . . the survivor is no longer as critical of the system. This allegiance to the status quo is particularly unhealthy at this time. Presently there is a growing awareness within the larger community that the schools need fundamental changes if they are to be a vital force in the lives of our children. If the beginning teachers are not the agents of reform, the chances for real change are small. [p. 190]

The major problem with this scenario is that most first-year teachers have not *prepared* to be change agents! Without the skills necessary to effect change, the first-year teacher tends to be less effective than would be possible if he or she had some developed change skills and some experience as a change agent.

Can our schools get better? Of course they can! Goodlad (1979) has described the characteristics of schools that have achieved great success—with the implication that attempting to develop these characteristics in all schools would lead to marked improvement. The first characteristic is that the school must run with a certain amount of autonomy and that the chief executive (principal, superintendent, headmaster, or headmistress) must exert a considerable amount of leadership.

A second characteristic is that the school must have a sense of mission that gives it an identity. The identity causes the faculty and students to feel a sense of participation and ownership for what goes on in their school and how it is perceived by the public. This situation leads to school pride, which, in turn, motivates dedication among the staff and students.

A third characteristic of successful schools is the central role of the principal as a leader in creating the sense of mission just described. A principal who makes his or her position on issues clear and is perceived as a strong, independent leader is almost always associated with successful schools.

A final characteristic is that the support structure that provides aid to the school must be strong and committed to helping the individual schools achieve their missions. This support structure begins with the superintendent and central administration and ends with the building maintenance staff. The support structure is seen as *aiding* the individual school to achieve its mission and therefore functions in a positive, helping relationship.

The individual teacher cannot create these factors. But the individual teacher can provide support for the kinds of administrators and administrative structure described. The individual teacher is often in a position to help to define the kind of administrator and administrative structures that are developed and maintained within a school system.

Things can get better, but they won't get that way through sloganeering. Daily work is needed, starting at the level of the individual teacher and reaching up to the top tier of administration. Then schools get better.

CHAPTER 14

Instruments for Measuring Teaching and Its Outcomes

To recapitulate, recording is the terminal event of a complex series that begins with defining the response class of interest, proceeds through observing, and culminates in creating a permanent record of the behavior. . . . The permanent record that remains after defining, observing, and recording have taken place is the only evidence that measurement actually occurred, and the quality of the entire process cannot exceed the characteristics of that record.

> James M. Johnston and H. S. Pennypacker, *Strategies and Tactics of Human Behavioral Research* (1980)

CHAPTER OBJECTIVES

To define reliability and explain its importance in systematic observation

To differentiate among traditional methods for assessing teaching

To explain and provide examples of systematic observation methods

To combine observation methods into a system to accomplish a specific purpose

To explain the steps necessary to build an observation system

To explain how observers are trained

To calculate the reliability of observational data accurately

To differentiate among the purposes and methods of the examples of observation systems

To observe teacher and student behavior reliably

Teaching skills will improve to the extent that trainee teachers have a chance to practice specific skills and get reliable feedback about progress toward goals. To expect such improvement without feedback is wishful thinking. The research literature in teacher education is not very helpful when it comes to the outcomes of intern experiences such as student teaching. There is no evidence to defend the proposition that merely putting trainee teachers into a real setting will *automatically* improve their teaching. Quite to the contrary, there is evidence to support the notion that the teaching skills of student teachers actually (in terms of the skills emphasized by the training program) deteriorate.

For teaching skill to improve, there should be goals, feedback on a regular basis, and a chance to improve. This implies that practice teaching experiences need to be supervised, at least in the sense that the experiences must be observed and data collected in order to provide feedback for the trainee teacher. But supervision must also include the *systematic* collection of data if it is to be useful. Supervision that is done intuitively, with little more than note taking to collect data, is unlikely to be powerful enough to account for improvement. That is not just an opinion. It is a statement of fact backed by a substantial body of research. The research on traditional forms of supervision is so dismal that Mosher and Purpel (1972, p. 50) concluded their review of it with the statement that "the inescapable conclusion to be drawn from any review of the literature is that there is virtually no research suggesting that supervision of teaching, however defined or undertaken, makes any difference."

Throughout this text I have pointed out that there are many potential sources for the improvement of teaching—fellow students, instructors, supervisors, cooperating teachers. For these people to provide useful supervisory information, they must observe your teaching efforts *systematically*; that is, they must look at what you do through the lenses of an observation system. In order to do this well, they must acquire some basic observational skills and practice them enough that they can provide reliable information to you.

Reliability in observational data collection is of great importance. The term **reliability** has many meanings in scientific literature; in this text it is defined as the degree to which two people, using the same definitions, looking at the same person, at the same time, record the same behavior. Why is reliability important? Suppose that a peer or instructor observes your teaching during the first week of a teaching experience and records the behavioral interactions and feedback statements you make to your students. This becomes your baseline performance. Suppose another observation is taken the next week, and your interaction and feedback rates are considerably lower. Now the question is "Who changed—you or the observer?" If the observer changed (perhaps interpreting the definitions differently or perhaps just not being as accurate), then you will get misinformation and maybe even a poor evaluation. That is why it is important for the data collected on teaching to be reliable—so that it can reasonably be assumed that the data reflect faithfully what actually happened during the teaching episode. This chapter discusses techniques for collecting reliable information on teaching.

Most data gathering in science is accomplished by automatic recording systems. Exercise physiologists automatically record the heart rate of subjects prior to, during, and after exercise. The behavior in this case is the heartbeat, and it is made observable by placing electrodes on the skin and transmitting the impulse to a machine that continuously and automatically prints out the fluctuations in heart rate. Kinesiologists collect data on action of the muscles in much the same way. These data are accurate and reliable and provide a convenient permanent record of some crucial aspects of human behavior. But the behaviors of importance in teaching cannot be recorded by transmitting impulses via electrodes. Most often the behaviors in question must be observed by another human being. It is probably true that most socially significant behavior is seldom convenient, in that it is not easily observable, and this lack of convenience creates measurement problems that often demand the use of human observers.

When one human is used to observe the behavior of another human it is important that steps be taken to ensure the reliability of the observations. If psychology has told us anything in the past 50 years, it has told us clearly that the facts and our perceptions of the facts may differ considerably. If I observe your teaching skills, I may be viewing them from my history of experience and interpret things differently from the way someone else would. If during subsequent observation sessions I detect some change in your teaching performance, it is important that steps be taken to assure that the change occurred in your teaching performance and not in my observations. As you well know, we all have a tendency to see what we want to see, and we are particularly susceptible to the influence of suggestion. If your cooperating teacher tells your supervisor that you have "really improved" in some aspect of your teaching, all evidence indicates that your supervisor will tend to see you as improved whether or not any change has occurred. Therefore, it is important to collect data that give reliable evidence of your progress and are not susceptible to the whims of suggestion or the distortions of perception that so commonly plague inadequate observation systems. Methods for assessing the reliability of observations are presented later in this chapter.

Traditional Methods for Assessing Teaching

For many years teacher educators and teaching researchers attempted to assess teaching and its outcomes through a variety of methods such as intuitive judgment, eyeballing, anecdotal records, checklists, and rating scales. In teaching research, these methods have long been abandoned because they were shown to be unreliable and not valid as measures of teaching. But for some reason they are still widely used as methods for gathering data on teaching for supervisory purposes. Even though experts and texts consistently caution against using such methods, they are still used more often than is systematic observation. The main features of these traditional methods and their shortcomings are described as follows.

Intuitive Judgment

The method of **intuitive judgment** implies that an experienced supervisor, knowledgeable about teaching, watches a teacher teach and then makes a careful, overall judgment about what was seen. The intuitive method implies a wealth of knowledge about teaching research and about the realities of daily teaching in schools, all brought to bear on the events of a teaching session in such a way as to be able to evaluate it sensitively and usefully. This global approach to supervision is simply inadequate if it is the main method used. Trainee teachers do not need overall estimates as much as they need specific information. Also, intuitive methods tend to focus far too much on the teacher and not enough on the students. Intuitive judgment becomes useful only when it is used as an addition to a systematic observation methodology.

Eyeballing

The most common form of feedback used in preparing teachers is what I refer to as **eyeballing**. The supervisor or cooperating teacher simply watches you teach for a period of time. No notes are taken, no checklist is used, no data are recorded. After the session, the supervisor discusses the teaching performance with you. Some very specific incidents may be brought up. Some very valuable information may be brought to your attention, but it is unlikely that any information will be passed along that will help you improve your teaching skills systematically. As an observation method, eyeballing is very susceptible to errors in perception due to misconceptions, previous history, or suggestion. Far too often feedback generated from eyeballing is insignificant and is useless for improving teaching skills.

Eyeballing can be a valuable technique if it is used in addition to a systematic method of observing and recording behavior. Eyeballing has potential value because the observer is usually a trained professional, a master teacher, who can see complexities of interaction during teaching that are too subtle to be picked up by a systematic observation program. But if eyeballing is the primary observation source from which feedback is generated, then it is unlikely that a sufficient amount of reliable information will be made available to you.

Anecdotal Records

If an observer keeps notes on what goes on during an observation session and uses these notes to discuss the session with you, the system is referred to as the use of **anecdotal records**. Anecdotal records are a more extensive and reliable method of eyeballing. The observer relies exclusively on general perceptions of what is going on, but these perceptions are written down. This assures that valuable information will not be lost during the observation session. It provides a much sounder base for conducting an interactive feedback session. Depending on the thoroughness and complexity of the note taking, this can be a valuable source of information for precisely the same reasons that eyeballing can be valuable; that is, the person taking the notes is usually an experienced professional who can see the sometimes subtle and complex elements that contribute to a successful teaching performance.

Anecdotal records suffer from the same problems that plague eyeballing. The fact that a piece of information is written down does not ensure that it is an accurate perception of what is going on. Furthermore, it is highly unlikely that information generated through anecdotal records is sufficiently precise to allow you to gauge your progress toward highly specific goals. Anecdotal records appear to have their greatest potential when used in addition to the systematic observation format that generates precise information on well-defined performance categories.

Checklists and Rating Scales

In the past the most common method of systematic observation was the use of checklists. A **checklist** is a list of statements or characteristics about which an observer makes a judgment. The judgment is often a yes or no decision. Sometimes it involves use of a scale so that the space between the yes-no points is graded to allow for a range of possible responses such as *often, sometimes, infrequently, never*.

The checklist method has one dubious advantage and a number of very serious drawbacks. The advantage is that it provides the appearance of a true data-based approach to the improvement of teaching skills. By using a checklist as a terminal evaluation instrument, the supervisor is giving a pseudo-scientific wrapping to a very casual approach to evaluation. If the checklist is used in successive observation sessions as a learning tool rather than strictly as a terminal assessment tool, the same advantage is gained. The benefit gained from the use of checklists is derived primarily by the supervisor; it provides a false sense of security, the illusion that the feedback given the intern is based on some hard evidence rather than mere eyeballing.

Checklists are notoriously unreliable. The statements or characteristics on the checklist are not defined sufficiently to ensure reliable observations. To make a rating on the initiative shown by an intern is virtually impossible unless the characteristic labeled *initiative* is defined so that the intern, the supervisor, and other interested parties have some common understanding of its meaning and some examples of initiative and lack of it.

Rating scales are often thought to be more precise and sophisticated if they involve a large number of choice points. The rating scale shown here has nine choice points ranging from always to never.

Always   1   2   3   4   5   6   7   8   9   Never

This kind of rating device is highly unreliable. The illusion of greater precision and sophistication is gained at the cost of reliability. The fact is that the fewer the choice points, the more reliable the ratings. However, this is balanced by the fact that fewer choice points provide less precise information. One is left with a dilemma: a choice between reliable, imprecise information and more precise yet less reliable information. Neither is acceptable as a primary data collection format for a program that is serious about helping interns improve their teaching skills.

Rating scales are useful when information generated from simple choice points is of sufficient value to help improve teaching skills. In this case, rating scales are quick, efficient, and reliable. Checklists are useful for recording tasks completed. They serve as good reminders of the number of tasks to be completed, the nature of those tasks, and the time at which they are completed. But this use of checklists is little more than record keeping and should not be seen as a substitute for actual data collection.

Systematic Observation Methods

The systematic observation of teachers teaching has revolutionized teaching research and has led to important discoveries about the nature of effective teaching (see particularly Chapters 3 and 4). Systematic observation is the foundation on which teaching research has been built. It should also be the foundation on which teaching skills are developed. Systematic observation is simple to do—it requires only some basic understandings and a little practice. The data produced through systematic observation become the information used to help teachers to improve. In most cases, a simple summary of the raw data is all that is needed. No sophisticated statistical analysis is necessary. Adding, subtracting, and dividing are all that is required to develop very meaningful and useful information about teaching. The primary techniques of systematic observation are event recording, duration recording, interval recording, group time sampling, and self-recording.

These methods for observing and recording behavior have been used extensively in many areas of research dealing with human behavior. Having been used extensively, their reliability is well demonstrated. These methods are included also because they are easy to learn and easy to use. They require no apparatus more sophisticated than a tape recorder or a stopwatch. They have been used reliably by researchers, teachers, and students (Siedentop 1981).

Reliable use of these methods depends a great deal on how well the various performance categories are defined. Given adequate definitions, the methods are easy and reliable. They can usually be learned in one or two practice sessions. Most difficulties in using the methods arise more from problems in definition of performance categories than from technical errors associated with the observation systems.

Event Recording

Once a performance category has been defined adequately, it can be observed most simply by making a cumulative record of the number of discrete instances that it occurs within a specified time period. This results in a frequency count of the events as they occur (Hall 1971). Your supervisor may record the number of your positive interactions with students. Your cooperating teacher may count the number of times students break specified class rules. You may count the number of trials that two students have at a skill during a class session. Event recording produces a numerical output that can easily be converted to a rate per minute. The value of converting to rate per minute is that performances from different occasions can be compared because they are classified in common units—that is, rate per minute.

Event recording is one of the most useful methods of collecting meaningful data; any action or reaction of a student or teacher and any aspect of interaction between student and teacher that can be defined can be measured by counting the number of times it occurs. Concepts such as cooperation, competition, competitive effort, sportsmanship, and aggressiveness can be given new meaning by defining them in terms that can be observed and then by counting them as they occur.

Event recording can be done continuously; that is, several categories of teacher behavior can be observed via event recording for an entire teaching session. The length of a session is easily determined, and the data can be converted to a measure of rate per minute. Often it is too time consuming and fatiguing to do event recording for an entire session. Also, other observations may need to be made. A valid measure of teacher behavior can be obtained by doing event recording for a short time period and repeating it at intervals throughout a teaching session. For example, it is usually quite satisfactory to do 3-minute periods of event recording and to do five such intervals in a teaching period. If the five recording intervals are spaced throughout the period, a valid sample of the teacher's behavior is gained even though only 15 minutes of the session are devoted to the data collection. This concept of sampling behavior rather than recording it continuously is important to any data-based approach to the improvement of teaching.

Duration Recording

Event recording is useful if the most meaningful understanding of a behavior can be gained by having some idea about the frequency with which it occurs. For example, one way to better understand the efficiency of a learning environment is to have some idea about the number of trials that students need to practice a skill. Event-recording intervals placed periodically throughout a session give valid and reliable information that can be seen as number of trials per minute.

Sometimes, however, the frequency of a behavior does not yield the most useful information. Suppose that you want to get some measure of the degree to which a student is participating in your class. The first task would be to define participation and nonparticipation. It would not be appropriate to use event recording to study participation. One single participation (an event) might last for a long time, and another single participation (another event) might last for a short time. To know that two events occurred would not help you understand a student's rate of participation. It would be far better to record the amount of time a student spends in activity that you have defined as participation. A stopwatch could be turned on and off according to a student's participation; the resulting cumulative time would be the most accurate measure of participation.

Duration recording uses time as a measure of behavior. The raw data derived from duration recording is expressed in minutes and seconds. A student might participate for a total of 21:30 in a 30-minute class (21 minutes and 30 seconds). These raw data can be converted to a percentage figure that permits comparisons among students and among various sessions. The data are converted by dividing the total time of a recording session into the time derived from duration recording. The resulting measure is expressed as a percentage of total time spent in participation.

As with event recording, it is often inefficient to do duration recording continuously for an entire teaching session; samples can be done with duration recording. Three 5-minute samples of duration recording spaced periodically throughout a teaching session provide valid information about the percentage of time spent in any defined behavior. In this case the percentage figure is derived by using the total time of the recording intervals rather than the total time of the class. The output is still in percentage of time spent in a defined behavior category.

Duration recording is useful for any behavior category in which the length of time spent engaged in the behavior provides the best estimate of the importance of the behavior. This is true for both teacher behavior, such as the amount of time spent giving instructions to the class, and student behavior, such as the amount of time spent in managerial activity or participation.

Interval Recording

Another technique for providing meaningful data on teaching is interval recording. The term **interval recording** refers to observing behavior for short time periods (intervals) and deciding what behavior best characterizes that time period. For example, the total time period might be divided into 10-second intervals. In the first interval, the teacher is observed. In the second 10-second interval, the observer records the behavior category that best represents what he or she just observed. In interval recording, consecutive intervals are used to first observe and then record. Intervals should be small, usually no longer than 20 seconds and sometimes as small as 6 seconds. The observation interval does not have to be of the same length as the recording interval. Usually, the recording interval can be shorter, especially as observers grow more skilled or when a small category system is used in which fewer decisions are necessary.

The data generated from interval recording are expressed as a percentage of intervals in which each behavior occurs. However, because the intervals represent a precise measure of time, the interval technique can also be used to estimate time involvements. Interval recording has the advantage of being highly reliable. The instructions as when to observe and when to record can be preprogrammed on a cassette and the observer cued through an ear jack on the tape recorder.

Interval recording has been used successfully to observe teacher behavior, student behavior, and measures such as academic learning time. Observers should strive to use as short an interval as can be and still have reliable data. The only problems usually encountered using interval techniques are when the intervals are so long that several behaviors can occur and the observer has a difficult time deciding which behavior to record. A short interval (6–12 seconds) normally avoids that problem. If a 10-second observe and 10-second record interval system is used, there will be one data point gathered every 20 seconds, three per minute, and 90 per 30-minute teaching episode. The total of 90 data points is usually sufficient to ensure the **validity** of the behavior being observed; that is, what is recorded faithfully represents what actually happened in the setting.

Group Time Sampling

One technique used to gather periodic data on all members of a group (typically a class or specific subset of a class) is **group time sampling**. Group time sampling has also been referred to as **Placheck recording** (Planned Activity Check). At regular intervals throughout the observation session, the observer quickly scans the group and counts the number of students engaging in the behavior category of interest. This scan typically takes no more than 10 seconds, even for a fairly large class. A smaller group could be scanned in 5 seconds. Once a student is counted, the observer does not return to that student even if her or his behavior changes. The goal is to observe each individual at a moment in time and to record the number of the total group engaged in a particular behavior category. Behavioral observations for categories such as effort, participation, productivity, and appropriate behavior lend themselves well to the group time-sampling technique. Periodic measures of criterion variables such as academic learning time could also be taken in this way.

The group time-sampling method is used as follows. The observer always scans in a specified direction, usually from left to right. A specified amount of time is taken for the scan (usually 10 seconds). However, this is dependent on the total number in the group, because with larger groups progressively more time is required to complete the scan. The number of people engaged in the behavior category is counted. It is always easiest to rate the behavior category in which the fewest are engaged. For example, if you are rating productive and unproductive behavior, and most students are engaged in productive behavior, it is easiest to count those engaged in unproductive behavior. The number engaged in productive behavior can be calculated simply by subtracting the number engaged in unproductive behavior from the total. Again, it is best to convert these raw data into a percentage figure. This is done by noting the size of the total group and dividing the total into the appropriate figure. Thus, a percentage of students engaged in productive behavior can easily be calculated by dividing the total number of students into the number engaged in productive behavior.

Group time samples should be spaced periodically throughout a class session. Because they take only 10 seconds to complete, they need not prevent the observer from doing other observations during the time between intervals. Eight group time samples spaced evenly through a 40-minute session will take only 1:20 of observation time (1 minute, 20 seconds) yet they will yield valid information concerning the behavior of the group.

Self-Recording

Often a behavior of interest can be self-recorded. A student might sign in the time at which he or she arrives for class or practice. Students might record the number of tasks they complete in a gymnastics or volleyball unit. A teacher might keep record of the number of times he or she interacts with a particular student who is considered to be in need of a greater number of teacher-student interactions.

Self-recording is important for two reasons: (1) behaviors of interest can be recorded without the presence of an observer, and (2) the teacher can initiate a measure of self-control over his or her teaching performance. Often behaviors can be recorded as tallies on a notebook or clipboard. Many have used golf wrist counters to keep event recording tallies on their own performance.

Sometimes an intermediary mechanism is useful. For example, a teacher can use a tape recorder to record a half-hour teaching session. The tape can later be coded for categories of teacher verbal behavior by the teacher him- or herself.

Combining Observation Techniques in One System

The choice of an observation technique should make sense in terms of the behavior being observed. Feedback from a teacher to a student is best observed with event recording—the most meaningful measure of feedback is either as a rate (number of feedbacks per minute or per a 30-minute teaching lesson) or as a ratio (percentage of total feedbacks that were delivered accurately or percentage of total feedbacks that had specific information content). Useful information about feedback can also be developed through an interval format. But duration recording doesn't give useful information about feedback. Knowing the length of a feedback interaction doesn't tell us much about it.

Student learning opportunities can be gauged as a measure of time using duration recording or interval recording. Thus, total amount of time spent in active learning is a very meaningful piece of information. So too is the percentage of intervals in which a student was engaged in academic learning time. Student learning opportunities can also be observed through event recording, accrued by counting the number of trials per 30 minutes that occur among members of a class.

Variables such as student on-task behavior can be observed in a number of ways, through event recording (number of instances of off-task behavior), duration recording (percentage of total time spent on task), interval recording (percentage of total intervals spent on task), or group time sampling (percentage of students off task). The choice of which one to use will most often be dictated by considerations such as reliability and economic use of the observer's time. The goal should be to get the most reliable data possible with the most efficient use of the observer's time (using less time to get reliable data on on-task behavior leaves more time to observe something else).

Many observation systems incorporate more than one kind of observation technique. This can be done quite easily through sampling the various behaviors in question. The goal should be to sample them regularly and to have the samples spread out across the entire time period. If all the teacher behavior data were collected in the first 15 minutes of a teaching episode and all the student behavior data in the second 15 minutes, the data would not yield a true picture of what went on throughout the entire period. It is much better to sample a small amount of teacher behavior, then move to student behavior, then back to teacher behavior, and so on throughout the entire observation period. For example, the following 4-minute cycle of observations uses event recording for teacher behavior and group time sampling for student on-task behavior and student learning time:

10 seconds	Group time sample number of students off task
10 seconds	Record
10 seconds	Group time sample number of students in ALT-PE
10 seconds	Record
20 seconds	Rest
60 seconds	Event record teacher behavior
10 seconds	Group time sample number of students off task
10 seconds	Record
10 seconds	Group time sample number of students in ALT-PE
10 seconds	Record
20 seconds	Rest
60 seconds	Event record teacher behavior
4 minutes	Total time

With this format, the 4-minute cycle could be repeated seven times in a 30-minute observation period, leaving 2 extra minutes for rest. The seven cycles would produce fourteen group time samples for off-task behavior, fourteen group time samples for academic learning time-physical education, and fourteen minutes of event-recorded teacher behavior data. Because each cycle was distributed well across the total time, together they represent a very faithful picture of what actually happened.

This is all accomplished with just one observer. That observer is aided tremendously (and the data made more reliable) if the particular patterns of observe and record are preprogrammed on a cassette tape with simple cues such as "Observe student off-task behavior," "Record student off-task behavior," "Begin one minute of teacher behavior event recording," "End teacher behavior event recording" and "Begin one-minute rest." An ear jack should be used so that the cues are heard only by the observer and therefore are not intrusive in the setting where the observations are taking place. Ideally, a very small tape recorder could be placed in a pocket, so that the entire apparatus would be as unobtrusive as possible. The tape recorder should be battery powered so that the observer is free to move about. Batteries should be checked often so that the time intervals on the tape are as accurate as possible.

By sampling behavior rather than observing it continuously and with the development of multitechnique observation systems, the amount of information collected by one observer can be substantial. This observer can be an instructor, a peer intern, a helping student, a cooperating teacher—or the teacher him- or herself, if the session is videotaped.

Developing an Observation System

The best observation systems are always those created for specific purposes within a local program, systems that reflect clearly the major emphases within a teacher preparation program and are specific to the goals of any particular teaching episode. Literally hundreds of systems are now in use. Even in physical education, the number of available systems is large (see Cheffers 1977). Sometimes a system developed in one place for a particular purpose is useful *as is* in another place. But those situations are few and far between. Often, a system is *adapted* for local purposes, changed slightly so that it better reflects the goals of a specific teaching episode.

Once the observational techniques described in the previous section are mastered, the adaptation of existing observational systems or the creation of entirely new ones is quite simple. If proper attention is paid to appropriate sampling of behavior and the categories are very well defined, observational systems from the very simple to the quite complex can be developed and refined with little trouble. The purpose of this section is to describe the steps necessary to develop observational systems.

What to Observe

The complexity of an observation system is determined by the number of specific goals to be achieved in a teaching episode or a series of teaching experiences. Microteaching episodes usually have a very limited set of goals requiring only a simple observation system. Student teaching usually requires a much more complex observation system that reflects the major overall goals of the experience and whatever immediate specific goals are being worked on in a given teaching episode.

Complexity is also related to the number of decisions an observer must make. If a 5-category teacher feedback system is being used, the level of decision making is quite simple. If a 24-category teacher behavior system is being used, the decisions are usually more complex. If several different observational techniques are being used at the same time by one observer, this too adds to the complexity of the system.

Chapter 2 presented an assessment model that consisted of teacher process variables, student process variables, and student outcome variables. Methods for regularly recording student performance were reviewed in Chapter 11. The variables considered in the present chapter are teacher and student process variables.

I have categorized the on-site assessment of teacher and student behavior as follows. Category 1 focuses on the observation of discrete teaching variables such as questioning, giving feedback, reinforcing appropriate student behavior, and desisting misbehaviors. Category 2 focuses on analytic units, combinations of teacher and/or student variables that define an important aspect of the teaching and learning process. Examples of analytic units are managerial episodes and the cycle of teacher prompt, student response, and teacher feedback. Category 3 focuses on criterion process variables, those student process variables that provide direct, ongoing evidence of student learning. Examples of criterion process variables are academic learning time-physical education (ALT-PE) and number of learning trials per unit of time.

In order to develop a successful observational system, the developer must decide which assessment level meets the specific needs of the teaching experience. An observation system for a major field experience of student teaching might very well include measures in all three categories. For example, it might be very useful to develop an observation system that revealed managerial episode length (an analytic unit), sampled important teacher behaviors (discrete teacher process variables), and periodically sampled student ALT-PE (criterion process variable). An example of this kind of system can be found on page 280.

The decision concerning what to observe, therefore, is quite important simply because the feedback generated from observations will help to change future teaching efforts in a positive direction. Very complex systems should be used only when (1) the goals of a teaching experience are several and (2) the observers have sufficient training to use a complex system reliably. Systems should always be developed from the simple to the complex. Observational skills are like any other skills—they improve with practice for which there is adequate feedback. The following list gives some examples of the kinds of teaching skills described in this text that are amenable to systematic observation. The list is meant to be suggestive rather than exhaustive.

Teacher Process Skills

Number of managerial prompts per managerial episode
Number of positive and/or negative behavior reactions per managerial episode
Rate of reinforcement for appropriate student behavior
Rate of nags for inappropriate student behavior
Ratio of properly timed desists to total desists
Ratio of properly targeted desists to total desists
Duration of instructional episodes
Number of major points per instructional episode

Rate of positive feedback
Rate of corrective feedback
Ratio of feedbacks with specific information to total feedbacks
Ratio of properly asked questions to total questions
Rate of prompts, hustles, and other instructional cues
Rate of smiling
Percentage of interactions with value content
Frequency of modeling
Ratio of individual to group direct feedback
Instances of appropriate punishment

Analytic Units

Length of managerial episodes
Accuracy of prompt-response-feedback cycle
Frequency of successive prompt-response-feedback cycles
Ratio of properly timed desists to total desists
Ratio of properly targeted desists to total desists
Length of instructional episodes
Appropriateness of teacher response to student-initiated contacts
Amount of time in active supervision
Percentage of intrusions dealt with successfully (overlapping)
Frequency of smoothness errors
Frequency of momentum errors

Criterion Process Variables

Percentage of total time in ALT-PE
Rate of student responding per unit of time
Percentages of total time in activity, management, and instruction
Percentages of student behavior on task and off task
Number of skill objectives reached per student

Obviously, there is no lack of things to look for! A small, short, peer-teaching episode might focus only on active supervision and feedback skills. Thus, a system would be built that would categorize feedback in a manner consistent with what the program teaches about feedback and also monitors and rates the teacher's strategies for active supervision. A general supervision instrument for student teaching would be more complex and would take into account several variables, including at least one good measure of a criterion process variable.

How to Build the Observation System

The first step in building a system is to choose the variables to be observed. This process was explained in the preceding section. The second step is to choose the observation technique; that is, to decide whether the variables chosen would best be observed through event recording, duration recording, interval recording, or group time sampling. This decision is made on the basis of two factors: (1) the *match* between the technique and the variable and (2) the integrating of the various techniques into a total system. If the observation system is small, limited to only one or a few variables, then the match between the technique and the variables should guide the decision. This means that, first, most teacher behaviors are best observed through event recording. Second, certain analytic units such as managerial episodes are most meaningfully observed through duration recording (merely counting the frequency of managerial episodes doesn't reveal much of interest—it is their length that counts!). And, third, an overall criterion process variable such as ALT-PE is best observed through interval techniques in which the intervals are quite short.

But if there are several variables to observe, then the system must be built in such a way that allows one observer to do several things. In this case, measures of ALT-PE might best be gathered with group time sampling because it requires less observer time than does interval recording. The time saved can be used observing other variables through other techniques.

Once variables have been chosen, carefully defined, and observational techniques chosen, the next step is to develop the actual coding instrument. A **coding instrument** is a record sheet that enables an observer to record observations most efficiently. Several examples of coding instruments appear in this chapter. They should be developed for observer efficiency, which means that they make the process of transferring the observation to the coding sheet as easy as possible. For example, after several years of using duration recording and transferring durations to coding sheets in columns, one research group discovered a much easier process, that of building a *time line*. The use of a time line enables an observer to make a simple mark across the line to show when one kind of activity stops and another starts. This was not only simpler for the observer but provided a much more useful *picture* of what had happened and was more easily interpretable to the person for whom it would become feedback.

A portion of a time line is shown in Figure 14-1. This time line is six minutes long and is divided into 10-second units. The observer merely draws a line through the time line when one activity, such as a management episode

Figure 14-1. *Time Line*

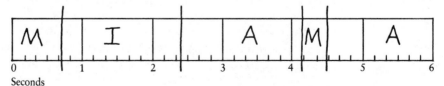

0   1   2   3   4   5   6
Seconds

M = Management Time
I = Instructional Time
A = Activity Time

(M), ends and an instruction (I) activity begins, or when a transition (T) activity ends and a practice (P) activity begins. Later the time line can be examined to calculate total time spent in the various activities. This method is simple and efficient. It also is a useful format for providing feedback because the teacher can then actually *see* the flow of activities as they occurred in the lesson.

Like observation instruments, coding sheets should be developed for specific, local purposes. It is unlikely that a coding sheet developed in one place will be exactly what is needed in another place. The point is to develop an instrument that reflects as precisely as possible the decisions made concerning the goals of the teaching episode and the techniques through which the variables will be observed.

Coding sheets such as the general supervision instrument shown on page 280 provide a large amount of information on one sheet. Several techniques are used, and a place is provided in which to summarize the information. This provides useful feedback for the teacher and a convenient way of storing collected data on teaching for future reference. There should always be an area on the coding sheet itself (either at the top or on the back) to provide relevant information concerning the teacher, the setting, students, duration of the total observation period, and other pertinent information. If this information is included, the completed coding sheet becomes a valuable record that can be used for feedback, for research, and for eventually establishing realistic goals and expectations for future experiences.

How to Do the Observations

Choosing relevant variables, matching observation techniques to the variables, and developing the coding sheet for transferring the observations to a permanent record represent the actual building of an observation instrument. What remains is to put it into use, to ensure that it can be used reliably.

Preprogramming an audiotape to cue the observer is an important contribution to systematic observation, especially for systems that use different techniques, sample behavior, or are interval systems. Of course, if you are simply using a five-category event-recording instrument to monitor teacher feedback, the audiotape feature is unnecessary. But, if observers need to sample behavior, switching from the observation of one variable to another, or switching from teacher to students, the cues on a preprogrammed tape can greatly simplify the task for the observer and thus increase the chances of obtaining reliable data.

The observer should be as unobtrusive as possible and still be in position to get the necessary data. If teacher verbal behavior is being observed, then the observer should plan to move around, keeping in close proximity to the teacher, yet staying as inconspicuous as possible. Students will react to the presence of an observer, but will react less and less the longer the observer is in the setting. Teachers too will react—and tend at the beginning to be on their "best behavior." Across time, however, the demands of teaching are such that teachers will tend to behave more normally, attending to the needs of their students and the immediate situation rather than thinking constantly about being observed. Still, unobtrusive observation should be sought.

The observer should have all that is needed to complete the observations, including (1) extra coding sheets, (2) extra pencils, and (3) a clipboard or some other firm surface on which to place the coding sheet, (4) strong batteries if a portable tape recorder is being used to provide preprogrammed cues, and (5) copies of all definitions for categories under observation. The observer should be at the setting in plenty of time to be prepared for the beginning of the teaching session. The data can be summarized while the teacher is ending the class and taking care of after-class supervision. The data can then be used as feedback when the teacher has the time available to study them and react to them. Supervisory conferences should be based on the data and should use the data as a foundation from which to examine and interpret what went on.

Training Observers

This text has emphasized that observational skills are easily acquirable and that reliable observations can be made by peers, instructors, cooperating teachers, supervisors, or by teachers themselves if the teaching sessions are videotaped. In each instance, the observer, no matter who it might be, needs to have sufficient training to ensure the collection of data that meet minimal reliability standards. Most of the observation techniques described in this chapter and the observation systems shown as examples can be learned to an adequate degree of reliability in a short period of time, often as little as two to four hours. More complex systems will take a little longer. The steps in training observers are clear-cut and have received widespread agreement in the literature concerning systematic observation:

1. Observers learn definitions from printed materials. Definitions should contain sufficient examples so that distinctions among categories are clear. Good definitions are the single most important ingredient in collecting reliable data. When observers are having problems, the difficulty is almost always traceable to definitional problems.
2. Observers study a written transcript of a teaching lesson and categorize the behaviors from the transcript. This process can be done as "homework" and tends to eliminate many errors and remedy major misconceptions.
3. If useful, observers discuss the categories, the examples, the transcript, and other issues.
4. Observers practice observations on a videotape. The tape should have been coded by an experienced observer so that the trainee can compare his or her data with that of an experienced observer. This process helps to establish observer accuracy. The term **observer accuracy** refers to the degree to which an observer agrees with a precoded standard.

5. Observers practice in the field. Observers should always practice in pairs so that interobserver reliability can be calculated. The term **interobserver reliability** refers to the degree to which two independent observers working with the same definitions viewing the same subjects at the same time record similar data. The two (or more) observers can then discuss discrepancies and resolve issues.

6. Throughout the training process, a decision log should be kept. A **decision log** is a record of observer disagreements and how they were resolved. Periodically, the definitions should be reviewed in light of the information developed through the decision log and changes made to fit the decisions concerning how to handle various situations.

7. Observers practice until they have met a minimal reliability standard. In behavioral observation research, using interobserver agreement calculation techniques (see next section), a criterion of 80 percent is typically required before observers can begin to collect data that are used for research. A slightly less stringent requirement is no doubt acceptable if the purpose of the observation is to generate feedback for teachers in training.

8. Reliability should be checked often to ensure that observers are applying the code accurately. This is analogous to calibrating a weight scale regularly. The observer needs to be "calibrated" too.

Calculating the Reliability of Observation Data

There are several reasons why it is important to ensure that observations are reliable. First, reliable observations indicate whether or not the definition of a teacher or student performance category is sufficiently clear and adequate. A poorly defined teacher or student performance category almost guarantees unreliable observations. When a reliability check indicates a low reliability, the situation is most often remedied by clarifying the definition of the performance categories.

A second reason for estimating reliability is to make sure that changes noted in teacher or student performance are due to the teacher or student and not to the observer. Observers often tend to see what they want to see, either consciously or unconsciously biasing the observations by their feelings about how they want the experience to turn out. This does not mean that an observer is unprofessional or incompetent. It does mean that all of us are subject to this tendency.

A third reason for checking reliability is to ensure that the changes noted in the observations do indeed reflect what is going on in the class. If observations indicate that a teaching intern decreases management time from one week to the next, he or she can take pride in the improvement to the degree that the observations are known to be reliable. If they are not reliable, then the results hardly differ from those generated by eyeballing.

This text emphasizes a data-based approach to improving teaching skills. If this model is used and certain improvements occur in your teaching skills, it is crucial that you, the school in which you teach, and the college or university at which you study have confidence that these improvements are real. Such confidence is directly related to the reliability of the recordings made during the intern experience.

The term **reliability** refers to the degree to which independent observers agree on what they see and record. In this sense the term **independent observers** can be taken to mean that one observer could not detect recordings being made by another observer. This criterion is usually satisfied by having observers placed far enough apart so that no visual or auditory cues could be used to detect the observations being made. If a tape recorder is used for a coding format, reliability checks can be made by splicing an extra ear jack into the ear jack line and allowing for sufficient cord to have the observers sit approximately 10 feet apart.

The general formula for computing reliability is

$$\frac{\text{Agreements}}{\text{Agreements + Disagreements}} \times 100 = \text{\% of agreement}$$

For event recording, duration recording, and permanent product measurement, reliability can be calculated by dividing the data of the observer who has the lower number of instances or time by that of the observer who has the higher number of instances or time.

If event recording is being used to judge the number of social interactions that a student has during a period, and one observer records 14 while a second observer records 12, the reliability would be computed as follows:

$$\frac{12}{14} \times 100 = 86\% \text{ reliability}$$

If duration recording is being used to measure the amount of time a teacher spends verbalizing to the class, and one observer records 12:30 while a second observer records 13:10, the reliability would be computed as follows:

$$12:30 = 750 \text{ seconds}$$
$$13:10 = 790 \text{ seconds}$$

$$\frac{750}{790} \times 100 = 95\% \text{ reliability}$$

If attendance is being self-recorded by students as they enter class, the teacher, student helper, or observer can unobtrusively check the students as they record their attendance. If such an observer agreed with each student as he or she checked in, the reliability would be 100 percent. If, in a class of 30 students, the monitor disagreed with the check-in of 2 students, the reliability would be computed as follows:

$$\frac{28}{30} \times 100 = 93\%$$

Table 14-1 / *Sample Data from Independent Observers for Two Students*

	Observer A		Observer B	
Interval	Student 1	Student 2	Student 1	Student 2
1	U	P	U	P
2	U	U	U	P
3	P	P	P	P
4	U	P	P	P
5	P	P	U	U
6	P	P	U	P
7	P	U	P	U
8	P	P	U	P
9	U	U	P	U
10	P	P	P	P
11	P	P	P	P
12	U	P	P	P

Note: P = Productive.
U = Unproductive.

For interval and group time-sampling recordings reliability is determined by estimating the degree to which the independent observers agree or disagree for each interval or sample recorded. Suppose that interval recording was used to rate the degree to which two students were engaged in productive learning behavior during a physical education class. The raw data of the time sampling might appear as in Table 14-1.

To compute reliability, the observations by interval for each student must be compared. Any interval for which the observers have recorded the same rating indicates agreement. Any interval for which they have recorded different ratings indicates disagreement. If the raw data are rearranged so that the observations of the two observers for each student can be compared, the agreements and disagreements become immediately apparent.

Table 14-2 shows observations that are clearly in disagreement. For Student 1, the seven circled intervals indicate seven disagreements. For Student 2, the two circled intervals indicate two disagreements. There are 12 intervals, so the reliability would be computed as follows:

Reliability for Student 1   *Reliability for Student 2*

$$\frac{5}{5+7} \times 100 = 42\% \qquad \frac{10}{10+2} \times 100 = 83\%$$

Obviously there is some problem with these data. A reliability of 80 percent is usually considered necessary for research purposes. With a low number of intervals (12), a reliability of 75 percent would probably suffice. But these data indicate a substantial discrepancy and must be considered unreliable. The observers should attempt to clarify the definitions of productive and un-

Table 14-2 / *Sample Data Scored for Disagreements Between Observers*

	Student 1		Student 2	
Interval	Observer A	Observer B	Observer A	Observer B
1	U	U	P	P
2	U	U	U	P
3	P	P	P	P
4	U	P	P	P
5	P	U	P	U
6	P	U	P	P
7	P	U	U	U
8	P	U	P	P
9	U	P	U	U
10	P	P	P	P
11	P	P	P	P
12	U	P	P	P

productive learning behavior, using examples of each to come to a greater agreement about the performance category they are observing.

Reliability for group time sampling (GTS) is determined by computing how much the independent observers agree for each group time sample recorded. Suppose that you want to check the degree to which your students are engaged in active learning. After defining what you consider to be active learning, you could conveniently sample this category using GTS. Suppose that you do one group time sample every 3 minutes during a 30-minute period. This would provide ten samples per period and would give you a good idea of the degree to which your students were involved in active learning. Let's assume that you have 24 students in your class and that your cooperating teacher is doing a reliability check. The raw data for the group time sample recordings might appear as in Table 14-3.

Table 14-3 / *Group Time Sample (GTS) Data*

	Your Observation	Cooperating Teacher
GTS 1	12/24	14/24
GTS 2	18/24	19/24
GTS 3	17/24	17/24
GTS 4	14/24	14/24
GTS 5	10/24	12/24
GTS 6	12/24	10/24
GTS 7	14/24	14/24
GTS 8	20/24	21/24
GTS 9	22/24	22/24
GTS 10	20/24	20/24

Reliability is computed most easily by counting the disagreements for each GTS. Because you recorded 12 active learners in the first GTS and the cooperating teacher recorded 14, there were two disagreements; because there are 24 students in the class, there were 22 agreements. In the 10 GTS shown there is a total of 8 disagreements, which subtracted from the total possible of 240 (10 × 24 class members) shows 232 agreements. The reliability is computed as usual:

$$\frac{232}{232 + 8} \times 100 = 97\%$$

This shows a very high reliability, which should give you confidence that your observations of the degree to which your students are engaged in active learning are accurate. Incidentally, the hypothetical data show that during the middle portion of the class session the percentage of students engaged in ac-

---

Progress Check

Compute reliabilities from the following data.

1. Using a time-sampling format, you and an independent observer record 48 agreements and 11 disagreements.
2. Using duration recording, two independent observers record 8:34 and 9:01. (Don't forget to convert the data to seconds for computation.)
3. Doing GTS's on your class, one observer records 21 students on task while a second observer records 17 students on task.
4. Your supervisory team is checking the positive and negative feedback statements you make to your students. The cooperating teacher records 14 positive feedbacks and 8 negative feedbacks. The supervisor records 15 positive feedbacks and 7 negative feedbacks. (After you compute the reliabilities, convert the data to rate per minute, assuming that the observations were made during a 20-minute observation period and that the data collected by the cooperating teacher are used.)

Answers
1. 81% reliability
2. 95% reliability (Did you convert the minutes to seconds before starting?)
3. 81% reliability (Notice that you can compute reliability without having to know the number of students in the class.)
4. Positive feedback = 95% reliability Rate = .7 per minute
  Negative feedback = 88% reliability Rate = .4 per minute

tive learning was barely 50 percent, a fact that might encourage you to examine what in the organization of the class caused half the students to be inactive for such a substantial portion of the instructional time.

Examples of Observation Systems

Systematic observation is not a mysterious process. Once goals are determined and very precise and specific behavioral definitions agreed to, the process of observation is quite easy, no more difficult than (1) paying attention to the right cues at the proper time, (2) sticking carefully to the definitions agreed to, and (3) either counting or timing the frequency or duration of a teacher behavior, student behavior, or some combination thereof (an analytic unit such as a managerial episode). This chapter has provided a step-by-step outline of how to build a useful observation system, how to train observers, and how to determine the degree to which reliable data are being collected. The remainder of the chapter is devoted to examples of observation systems. But a reminder needs to be stated. Although some of these systems might be useful in settings other than those for which they were created, it is more likely that they will serve best as *examples* from which ideas may be generated for developing observational systems that serve specific goals in local settings. The examples included were chosen to illustrate the major observational techniques described earlier in this chapter; that is, event recording, duration recording, interval recording, and group time sampling. Self-recording examples can be found in Chapter 11.

Student Time Analysis

Information concerning how students spend their time can be extremely useful for making judgments about instructional strategies. Two examples are presented. One divides time into three categories and lists the results in columns (see Figure 14-2). The other uses five categories and a time line approach (see Figure 14-3). Each, of course, requires duration recording.

In Figure 14-2, duration recording was used to classify physical education class time into three categories. A clock or stopwatch was used to record the duration of each instance of the three categories. The time was jotted down as the next sequence began. These data could be expressed as a percentage of the total class time, which in this case was 40 minutes. You will notice that an undue amount of time was spent in management and "teacher talk," and that not quite half of the class time was spent in active learning. These data show a situation that badly needs to be changed, especially in the large amount of time devoted to management.

In Figure 14-3, the time line is crossed with a mark whenever events change from one category to another. The abbreviations are used to indicate which amount of time was devoted to each category. The percentage of total

Record of Time Allotment in Class

Class: *9TH GRADE / MR. ALLEN*   Date: *1/9*   Time: *2:00-2:40*

Teacher Talk (Demonstration and Instruction)	Management	Active Learning
3:06	1:17	6:18
1:08	1:24	5:20
4:30	0:46	3:50
2:06	0:40	4:25
1:10	2:50	___
___	1:50	19:13
12:00	1:00	
	0:20	
	___	
	8:47	

Figure 14-2. *Sample Duration-Recording Format*

time is shown in the summary on the bottom. (The figure was developed by Kenneth Alexander, Ohio State University, for a secondary methods field experience.)

Teacher Reaction Analysis

Teachers react to students—to their skill attempts, to their strategy choices, to their effort, to their social behavior, and to their organizational behavior. A substantial effort has been made in this text to redirect teacher reactions into positive categories. As Figure 14-4 shows, feedback can be broken down into many different categories. The choice of what level of complexity to use is determined by the goals of the teaching episode.

Two simple formats for coding feedback are shown in Figures 14-5 and 14-6. In Figure 14-5, general, informational (that is, specific), and value feedback are categorized as positive or negative. The tally marks refer to feedback directed to an individual student. The letter *g* refers to feedback directed to a group. In this example, each of the four event recording intervals was 5 minutes in length.

Figure 14-6 can be used to record skill and behavior feedback that is positive or corrective and specific or general. Total frequencies (using event recording) are tabulated, and a rate per minute is calculated on the basis of the length of the observation period. This instrument would be appropriate for a beginning teaching episode in which teachers in training were first attempting to improve their interaction styles.

Figure 14-3. *Sample Time Line Format*

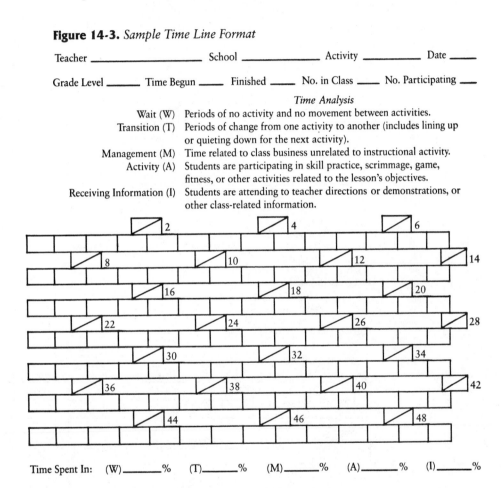

Teacher _____ School _____ Activity _____ Date _____

Grade Level _____ Time Begun _____ Finished _____ No. in Class _____ No. Participating ___

Time Analysis

Wait (W) — Periods of no activity and no movement between activities.

Transition (T) — Periods of change from one activity to another (includes lining up or quieting down for the next activity).

Management (M) — Time related to class business unrelated to instructional activity.

Activity (A) — Students are participating in skill practice, scrimmage, game, fitness, or other activities related to the lesson's objectives.

Receiving Information (I) — Students are attending to teacher directions or demonstrations, or other class-related information.

Time Spent In: (W)_____% (T)_____% (M)_____% (A)_____% (I)_____%

Figure 14-4. *Levels of Complexity in Coding Feedback*

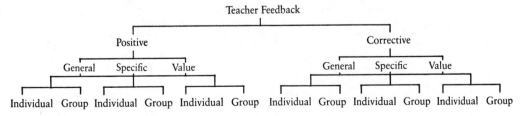

Type of Feedback	Five-Minute Intervals				
	1	2	3	4	Total
+ Gen	‖‖‖ ‖ q	‖‖ q	‖‖‖	‖‖ qq	20
+ Info	‖‖	qq‖	qqq‖q	‖‖‖	19
+ Value	‖ qq	‖‖	‖	q‖	9
– Gen	‖	‖ q	‖	‖‖	9
– Info	‖ q	‖‖‖	‖ qq	‖ q	13
– Value		‖ q	q	‖‖	6

Summary of Data

Totals	Rates per Minute	Ratios or Percent
Positive feedback = 48	Positive feedback = 2.4	Positive/Negative = 48/28
Negative feedback = 28	Negative feedback = 1.4	= 1.7
All feedback = 76	All feedback = 3.8	Info/Total = 32/76 = 42%
Feedback directed to		Value/Total = 15/76
individuals = 56		= 20%
Feedback directed to		Individual/Group = 56/20
group = 20		= 2.8

Figure 14-5. *Format for Coding Feedback*

Feedback Statements	Skill Feedback		Behavior Feedback	
	Positive	Corrective	Positive	Negative
Specific				
General				
Total				
Rate per Minute				

Figure 14-6. *Format for Recording Skill and Behavior Feedback*

Observing a Specific Teacher Behavior

Sometimes it is necessary to focus on one teaching skill in order to emphasize its importance and provide feedback for improvement. In that case, an instrument can be developed that focuses solely on that skill and is sufficiently specific to provide good information on which improvement can be based. The example shown in Figure 14-7 is for the skill of questioning. Examples of other teaching skills for which separate instruments might be developed are desisting, enthusiasm, demonstrations, and active supervision.

Figure 14-7 focuses on each question as it is asked. The question is categorized, and specific aspects of the questioning technique are observed and recorded (such as whether the teacher used the name of the person to answer first and whether the student was given adequate time to respond). A space for summary data and comments is provided on the bottom of the coding sheet.

Figure 14-7. *Completed Observation Form for Questioning Skills*

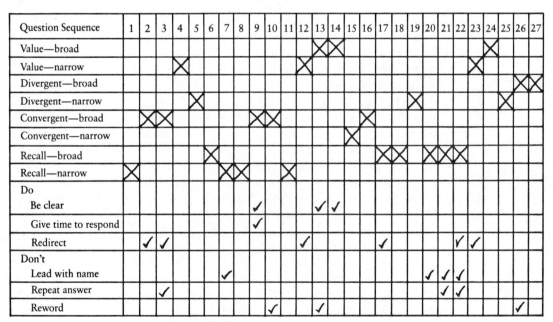

Summary: Percent of Questions

Value = 22%

Divergent = 18%

Convergent = 22%

Recall = 37%

Total broad = 59%

Total narrow = 41%

Ratio of Do/Don't = 10/10 = 1/1

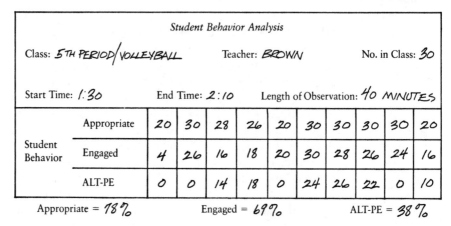

Student Behavior Analysis

Class: *5TH PERIOD/VOLLEYBALL*   Teacher: *BROWN*   No. in Class: *30*

Start Time: *1:30*   End Time: *2:10*   Length of Observation: *40 MINUTES*

Student Behavior	Appropriate	20	30	28	26	20	30	30	30	30	20
	Engaged	4	26	16	18	20	30	28	26	24	16
	ALT-PE	0	0	14	18	0	24	26	22	0	10

Appropriate = *78%*   Engaged = *69%*   ALT-PE = *38%*

Figure 14-8. *Observation Form for Analyzing Student Behavior*

Student Behavior Analysis

The time analysis shown earlier provides useful information about students. So too will a student behavior analysis. What follows is an example of a simple, time-efficient coding system for developing information concerning the behavior of students. The student behavior is sampled frequently rather than observed continuously. A group time-sampling technique would clearly be the appropriate method for this observation format. The system shown in Figure 14-8 has 10 group time samples. For a thirty-minute lesson, one would be taken each three minutes. Each time sample would take approximately 10 seconds, so that all three categories would take 30 seconds. This means that only five minutes of total observation time is necessary to generate this information. The categories in this system are not mutually exclusive. A student can be behaving appropriately but not be engaged. A student can be engaged but not be in ALT-PE. The total number of students in the class is needed in order to calculate the percentages for the summary data.

Any specific aspect of student behavior could be observed itself or included as a part of a more complex observational system. An important aspect of student behavior, number of successful learning attempts, can also be self-recorded by students or checked by monitors as indicated in Chapter 11. Systematic observation of student behavior is one of the best ways for teachers to develop information that is useful in making decisions about instructional strategies and management techniques.

Management Skill Analysis

Effective teachers are first of all effective managers. This text has devoted much attention to managerial skills, and these skills are so important that it is quite likely that separate observation instruments might be developed through which data can be generated to provide feedback to teachers in training concerning their managerial performance. Two examples of managerial coding formats are shown. Figure 14-9 is a beginning management skills observation instrument; the categories are less complex and fewer skills are observed. The skills observed are the basic management skills of positive teacher interaction, maintaining appropriate student behavior, reducing the number of managerial prompts needed to manage successfully, and reducing the length of time spent in management. Figure 14-10 includes those basic skills, subdividing the interaction skill categories into more specific categories and adding more advanced skills such as modeling, extinction, targeting, and timing, as well as providing minimal information on variety of interactions and use of voice.

The data from Figure 14-9 show that much work is needed—these data were taken from a baseline observation session, which means that no specific attempt has yet been made to improve any of these skills. The rate of appropriate behavior is too low. The teacher has a negative interaction style. The teacher needed to use too many managerial prompts, and the managerial episodes were too long, particularly the beginning and ending episodes. Event recording was used to monitor the behavioral interactions. Duration recording was used to monitor the length of managerial episodes. Group time sampling was used to generate eight separate estimates of the level of appropriate behavior in the class. The data are summarized for the teacher at the bottom of the coding sheet.

Figure 14-9. *Filled-In Coding Format for Beginning Management Skills*

Behavioral Interactions											
Three- or Five-Minute Event-Recording Periods	+	−	+	−	+	−	+	−	+	−
	//	⧫⧫ /	/	///		////		⧫⧫ ///	/	////
Managerial Episodes — Length	2:47	0:58	3:16	1:42	1:36	2:30				
Managerial Episodes — Number of Managerial Behaviors	⧫⧫	///	⧫⧫ //	///	⧫⧫	////				
GTS for Appropriate Behavior	22/28	25/28	24/28	21/28	26/28	22/28	24/28	20/28		

Class: JONES 8TH GRADE   Date: 11/7   Starting time: 9:30   Ending time: 10:10

Data Summary
Rate of + reactions per minute = 0.27   Total time in management = 12:49
Rate of − reactions per minute = 1.67   Average time per episode = 6/769 = 128 SECONDS = 2:08
Ratio +/− reactions = 4/15 = 1/4   Average number of managerial behaviors per episode = 4.5
                                               Percentage of appropriate behavior = 184/224 = 82%
Comments: BASELINE - 2ND OBSERVATION
BEGINNING AND ENDING MANAGEMENT MUCH TOO LONG
FOCUS ALMOST TOTALLY ON NEGATIVE INTERACTION
IT APPEARS THAT LONG MANAGEMENT EPISODES CONTRIBUTE TO
INAPPROPRIATE BEHAVIOR

The coding sheet for advanced management skills (Figure 14-10) is taken from a third observation after baseline assessment was completed and the improvement in performance is readily seen. The negative interaction rate is down, and the positive rate is up with a greater number of positives than negatives. The managerial episodes length is greatly reduced, as well as the number of managerial prompts needed to achieve that more efficient managerial strategy. The interaction analysis is more useful here because of the greater specificity of the category system, indicating that too many general positive feedbacks were given. Moving from general feedback to specific positive feedback would probably be the next step for this teacher. Information on other managerial skills is written in by the observer. The students are better behaved, a 93 percent rate having been achieved. All in all, this teacher has less management time with less managerial teaching behavior, a more positive climate, and better student behavior. That is the essence of improved managerial skills.

Figure 14-10. *Filled-In Coding Format for Advanced Management Skills*

		Behavioral Interactions											
Length of Event-Recording Time = FOUR 5-MINUTE INTERVALS' 20 MINUTES		Positive (+)					Negative (−)						
		Direction		Nonverbal		Initiated by + Behavior	Direction			Nonverbal			Comments
		I	S	G	F	G	C		I	S	G	F	G	C	
	General	///		††† ///	//	/	///	††† /	/			////	///⌐+		STARING DOWN
	Specific	††† ††† /				///	/// NOT ENOUGH HERE	////			††† /			
	General—value	/	/	///										
	Specific—value	///	///	††† /			//		//			///		//	
Voice and Variety		GOOD JOB — ††† // TOO MANY VOICE GOOD ON GROUP DIRECTED												
Managerial Episodes	Length	0:32	0:47	0:16	1:02	0:18							
	Number of management behaviors	//	///	//	///	//							
GTS for Appropriate Behavior		22/24	24/24	21/24	22/24	20/24	23/24	24/24					
Use of modeling:	MUCH BETTER-USE OF JOHN TO MODEL FOLLOWING INSTRUCTIONS WELL-DONE-MOST GROUP FEEDBACK HAS INFO AND VALUE CONTENT †††						Rating of targeting:	MORE POSITIVE SPECIFIC FOR GETTING ORGANIZED QUICKLY-MORE POSITIVE FOR BILLY AND WALTER					
Use of extinction:	STILL HAVE TROUBLE IGNORING NANCY ///						Rating of timing:	MUCH BETTER-WATCH "STARING DOWN" REACTION-GOOD DESIST ON CLASS DURING DRILL CHANGE					

Class: CHAPMAN 4TH   Date: 3/16 3RD OBSERVATION AFTER BASELINE   Starting time: 1:10   Ending time: 1:52

Data Summary

+ interaction/minute = 2.4
− interaction/minute = 1.3
Ratio of +/− = 48/26 = 2/1
% of interactions initiated by + = 23%

% of interactions nonverbal = 15/74 = 20%
Contact nonverbal/noncontact = 8/15 = 50%
% of interactions—specific = 43/74 = 58%
% of interactions—value = 26/74 = 35%

Total time in management = 2:55
Average time per episode = 0:35
Management behavior per episode = 2.4
% of appropriate behavior = 156/168 = 93%

**Descriptive
Teacher-
Student
Behavior
Systems**

277

Descriptive Teacher-Student Behavior Systems

One of the main functions of systematic observation is to provide thorough descriptive information about what is going on in an educational setting so that changes can be discussed and implemented. Although there are many ways to provide such a descriptive analysis, I have found that an interval-recording system is well suited to providing complete, reliable data on teacher and student behavior.

Figure 14-11 shows an interval system developed to describe teacher and student behavior in an elementary camp setting, a situation in which elementary students went to a resident school camp for a period of a few days. Many

Figure 14-11. *Interval Coding Sheet (Camp)*

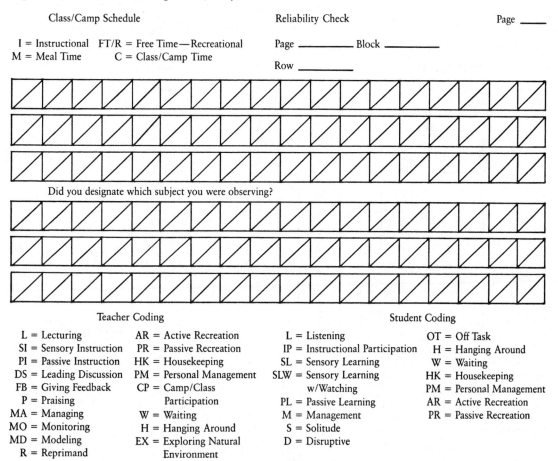

Class/Camp Schedule   Reliability Check   Page _____

I = Instructional   FT/R = Free Time—Recreational   Page _____ Block _____
M = Meal Time   C = Class/Camp Time
                                              Row _____

Did you designate which subject you were observing?

	Teacher Coding		Student Coding
L = Lecturing	AR = Active Recreation	L = Listening	OT = Off Task
SI = Sensory Instruction	PR = Passive Recreation	IP = Instructional Participation	H = Hanging Around
PI = Passive Instruction	HK = Housekeeping	SL = Sensory Learning	W = Waiting
DS = Leading Discussion	PM = Personal Management	SLW = Sensory Learning	HK = Housekeeping
FB = Giving Feedback	CP = Camp/Class	w/Watching	PM = Personal Management
P = Praising	Participation	PL = Passive Learning	AR = Active Recreation
MA = Managing	W = Waiting	M = Management	PR = Passive Recreation
MO = Monitoring	H = Hanging Around	S = Solitude	
MD = Modeling	EX = Exploring Natural	D = Disruptive	
R = Reprimand	Environment		

Interaction: Attachable to all previous codes
S = Student Interaction
T = Teacher Interaction

of the categories described are useful for any educational setting; that is, giving feedback, praising, off task, and instructional participation. Other categories were developed specifically for the camp setting; that is, sensory instruction, housekeeping, and personal management (Moore 1977).

The interval coding sheet allows the observer to (1) observe the teacher for one interval (typically no more than 10 seconds), (2) record what the teacher was doing, (3) observe one student for 10 seconds, (4) record what

Figure 14-12. *Interval Coding Sheet (School)*

Observational Recording Record

Recorder _____ Teacher _____ School _____ Page _____

Grade _____ Environment _____ Activity _____ Date_____

Time Started _____ Time Finished _____ Reliability Check: Yes _____ No _____

	1	2	3	4	5	6	7	8	9	10	11	12	13	14	15	16	17	18	19	20
C																				
B																				
I																				

	21	22	23	24	25	26	27	28	29	30	31	32	33	34	35	36	37	38	39	40
C																				
B																				
I																				

	41	42	43	44	45	46	47	48	49	50	51	52	53	54	55	56	57	58	59	60
C																				
B																				
I																				

	61	62	63	64	65	66	67	68	69	70	71	72	73	74	75	76	77	78	79	80
C																				
B																				
I																				

Climate		*Behavior*					
Management	M	Lectures or Orients	LO	Teacher Modeling +	TM +	Skill Feedback General +	FG +
Instruction	I	Asks Questions	AQ	Teacher Modeling −	TM −	Skill Feedback Specific +	FS +
Activity	A	Answers Questions	WQ	Student Modeling +	SM +	Skill Feedback General −	FG −
Waiting	W	Listening	L	Student Modeling −	SM −	Skill Feedback Specific −	FS −
Interaction		Monitoring	MO	Praise General	PG	Skill Feedback Corrective	CF
Individual	I	Nonfunctional	NF	Praise Specific	PS	Teacher Officiating	TO
Group	G	Managing	MG	Nags	N	Teacher Participation	TP
Class	C	Physical Contact	PC	Nasties	N −		
Male	M	Hustles	H	Punishment	P		
Female	F						

that student was doing, (5) observe a second student for an interval, (6) record what that student was doing, and (7) return to the teacher for the next interval, starting the cycle all over again. A second option to this format is to consider the student observation interval as a group time sample and record what the majority of students in the class are doing within that short interval.

Each interval space is divided in half by a line running from the lower left of the space to the upper right of the space. The space on top of this line is used to indicate what kind of "time" is being observed: instructional time, meal time, recreation time, or class or camp time. The bottom half of the space is used to record the letter abbreviation for the category that best represents what went on in that interval. An "S" or a "T" can be attached to any of the codes to indicate an interaction, teacher to student (T), or student to student (S). These data when summarized would be expressed in percentage of intervals in which each of the categories occurred. A rough estimate of time could also be developed.

Figure 14-12 shows an interval system used to describe teaching behavior in physical education or sport settings. The interval system has three "tiers" and requires three decisions for each interval. The top tier is used to describe the "climate" or the prevailing focus of the class during an interval. Four climate categories are listed at the bottom of the coding sheet. The second tier is used to describe what the teacher was doing during the interval. There are 25 categories from which to choose for this decision, a rather complete set of categories describing most of the important functions fulfilled by teachers and coaches. The third tier is used if the behavior involved an interaction. The choices here are whether the interaction was directed toward a group, an individual, or the entire class and whether, if an individual, it was a male or female student. This coding format provides 80 intervals. With a 10-second observe and a 10-second record format, almost 27 minutes of teacher behavior can be coded on one sheet. Again, as with most interval systems, what is actually recorded is the letter abbreviation for the category chosen.

A General Supervision Instrument

During culminating field experiences in a methods class or during student teaching, it is often useful for a program to adopt a general supervision instrument that will be used for all student teachers. This provides needed emphasis in these important experiences for the major goals of the program, a means for evaluating the degree to which the program is meeting those goals, a means for evaluating the individual student, and a means for comparing the relative performances of several students.

The instrument shown in Figure 14-13 (developed by Dr. James Currens, at Baldwin-Wallace University) uses event recording for teacher feedback and behavioral interactions. It uses a time line for duration recording of the important aspects of how time is used in the teaching session. It uses group time

Record of Student Time Allotment in Class, Behavioral Interactions, and Skill Feedback Statements

Observer _____ Date _____ School _____ Grade _____ Environment:
Time Started _____ Time Finished _____ Total Minutes Observed _____   Experimental _____
Number of Students in Class _____ Activity _____ Student Teacher _____   Generalization _____

(Time Analysis Codes: I = Instruction; A = Activity; M = Management)

	Skill Feedback Statement					
Time Analysis	Positive		Corrective		Negative	
	General	Specific	General	Specific	General	Specific
Total Management Time _____						
% Management Time _____						
Total Instructional Time _____						
% Instructional Time _____						
Total Activity Time _____						
% Activity Time _____						
Total						
Rate P/M						

	Behavioral Interactions			
Group Time Sample Analysis	Positive		Negative	
	General	Specific	General	Specific
% Appropriate Behavior _____				
% ALT-PE _____				
Total				
Rate P/M				

Figure 14-13. *General Supervision Instrument*

sampling to monitor levels of appropriate student behavior and academic learning time. The entire data set is summarized at the bottom of the sheet. It needs to be emphasized that these data are collected by one observer. Peer teaching interns, college supervisors, or public school cooperating teachers can all learn to do this kind of coding with minimal training.

The data are not so complex that they cannot be summarized quickly, often during the brief period when the teacher is ending the class. The data can then become immediately useful for an on-the-spot supervision conference. The data also are tremendously useful in many other ways, especially to the program and those who make decisions about it.

References

Anderson, W. Introduction. In W. Anderson and G. Barrette, eds., *What's Going On in the Gym. Motor Skills: Theory into Practice*, 1978, Monograph 1.

Armstrong, R., Cornell, R., Kraner, R., and Roberson, E. W. *The Development and Evaluation of Behavioral Objectives*. Worthington, Ohio: Jones, 1970.

Baird, H., Belt, W. D., Holder, L., and Webb, C. *A Behavioral Approach to Teaching*. Dubuque, Iowa: Brown, 1972.

Baley, J. *Gymnastics in the Schools*. Boston: Allyn & Bacon, 1965.

Banathy, B. *Instructional Systems*. Belmont, Calif.: Fearon, 1968.

Bane, M. J., and Jencks, C. The schools and equal opportunity. *Saturday Review of Education*, September 16, 1972, *55*, 37–42.

Barnes, W. How to improve teacher behavior in multiethnic classrooms. *Educational Leadership*, April 1977, *35*, 511–515.

Beale, H. *Are American Teachers Free?* New York: Scribner's, 1936.

Becker, E. *Beyond Alienation*. New York: Braziller, 1967.

Berliner, D. *Tempus educare*. In P. Peterson and H. Walberg, eds., *Research on Teaching: Concepts, Findings and Implications*. Berkeley, Calif.: McCutchan, 1979.

Birdwell, D. The effects of modification of teacher behavior on the academic learning time of selected students in physical education. Unpublished doctoral dissertation, Department of Physical Education, Ohio State University, 1980.

Bloom, B., ed. *Taxonomy of Educational Objectives. Handbook 1: Cognitive Domain*. New York: McKay, 1956.

Bloom, B. Learning for mastery. *Evaluation Comment*, May 1978, *1*.

Boehm, J. The effects of competency-based teaching programs on junior high school physical education student teachers and their pupils. Unpublished doctoral dissertation, Department of Physical Education, Ohio State University, 1974.

Boyer, E. Education issues. *New York Education Quarterly*, Summer 1981, *12*, 2–4.

Brophy, J., and Good, T. *Teacher-Student Relationships: Causes and Consequences.* New York: Holt, Rinehart & Winston, 1974.

Burlingame, M. Socialization constructs and the teaching of teachers. *Quest*, 1972, *18*, 40–56.

Cassidy, R., and Caldwell, S. *Humanizing Physical Education.* 5th ed. Dubuque, Iowa: Brown, 1974.

Charters, W. W., and Waples, D. *The Commonwealth Teacher-Training Study.* Chicago: University of Chicago Press, 1929.

Cheffers, J. Observing teaching systematically. *Quest*, 1977, *28*, 17–28.

Cheffers, J., and Mancini, V. Teacher-student interaction. In W. Anderson and G. Barrette, eds., *What's Going On in the Gym. Motor Skills: Theory into Practice*, 1978, Monograph 1.

Chu, D. Functional myths of educational organizations: College as career training and the relationship of formal title to actual duties upon secondary school employment. In V. Crafts, e., *1980 National Association of Physical Education in Higher Education Proceedings.* Champaign, Ill.: Human Kinetics Publishers, 1981.

Cohen, A. Technology: Thee or me. *Educational Technology*, 1970, *10*, 57–60.

Costello, J., and Laubach, S. Student behavior. In W. Anderson and G. Barrette, eds., *What's Going On in the Gym. Motor Skills: Theory into Practice*, 1978, Monograph 1.

Crockenberg, V. Poor teachers are made, not born. *Educational Forum*, 1975, *39*, 189–198.

Cruickshank, D. R., and Applegate, J. H. Reflective teaching as a strategy for teacher growth. *Educational Leadership*, 1981, *38*, 553–554.

Darst, P. The effects of a competency-based intervention on student-teacher and pupil behavior. Unpublished doctoral dissertation, Department of Physical Education, The Ohio State University, 1974.

Denemark, G. Goals for teacher education: A time for decision. In *Time for Decision in Teacher Education* (1973 Yearbook of the American Association of Colleges for Teacher Education). Washington, D.C.: American Association of Colleges for Teacher Education. 1973.

Denemark, G., and Espinoza, A. Educating teacher educators. *Theory into Practice*, 1974, *13*, 187–197.

Dubey, R., Endly, V., Roe, B., and Tollet, D. *A Performance-Based Guide to Student Teaching.* Danville, Ill.: Interstate, 1972.

Duke, D. Looking at the school as a rule-governed organization. *Journal of Research and Development in Education*, 1978, *2*, 116–126.

Dunkin, M., and Biddle, B. *The Study of Teaching.* New York: Holt, Rinehart & Winston, 1974.

Emmer, E., and Evertson, C. Synthesis of research on classroom management. *Educational Leadership*, January 1981, *39*.

Evertson, C., and Brophy, J. Process-outcome relationships in the Texas Junior High school study. Paper presented at the meeting of the American Educational Research Association, Toronto, Canada, April 1978.

Evertson, C., Anderson, C., Anderson, L., and Brophy, J. Relationships between classroom behaviors and student outcomes in junior high mathematics and English classes. *American Educational Research Journal*, 1980, *17*, 43–60.

Ferritor, D. E., Buckholdt, D., Hamblin, R. R., and Smith, L. The noneffects of contingent reinforcement of attending behavior on work accomplished. *Journal of Applied Behavior Analysis*, 1972, *5*, 7–17.

Gage, N. L. *Teacher Effectiveness and Teacher Education*. Palo Alto, Calif.: Pacific Books, 1972.

Gage, N. *The Scientific Basis of the Art of Teaching*. New York: Teachers College Press, 1978.

Galloway, C. Teaching is more than words. *Quest*, 1971, *15*, 67–71.

Glasser, W. *Reality Therapy*. New York: Harper & Row, 1965.

Glasser, W. *Schools Without Failure*. New York: Harper & Row, 1969.

Goodlad, J. Can our schools get better? *Phi Delta Kappan*, January 1979.

Griffin, P. Observations and suggestions for sex equity in coeducational physical education classes. *Journal of Teaching in Physical Education*, Spring 1981, *1*, 12–17.

Hall, R. V. *Managing Behavior*. Part 1. Meriam, Kans.: H & H Enterprises, 1970.

Hamilton, K. The effects of a competency-based format on the behavior of student-teachers and high school pupils. Unpublished doctoral dissertation, Department of Physical Education, The Ohio State University, 1974.

Hayman, J., and Moskowitz, G. Behavior patterns and training needs of first-year teachers in inner-city schools. *Journal of Classroom Interaction*, 1975, *10*.

Hellison, D. Humanism in physical education. Paper presented at the Northwest Regional Conference on Secondary Physical Education, Portland, Ore., November 1973a.

Hellison, D. *Humanistic Physical Education*. Englewood Cliffs, N.J.: Prentice-Hall, 1973b.

Holt, J. *How Children Fail*. New York: Pitman, 1964.

Huber, J. The effects of a token economy program on appropriate behavior and motor task performance of educable mentally retarded children in adapted physical education. Unpublished doctoral dissertation, Department of Physical Education, The Ohio State University, 1973.

Hughley, C. Modification of teacher behaviors in physical education. Unpublished doctoral dissertation, Department of Physical Education, The Ohio State University, 1973.

Jackson, P. *Life in Classrooms*. New York: Holt, Rinehart & Winston, 1968.

Jackson, P. The way teaching is. In K. Ryan and J. Cooper, eds., *Kaleidoscope: Readings in Education*. Boston: Houghton Mifflin, 1980.

Johnson, D. *Reaching Out: Interpersonal Effectiveness and Self-Actualization*. 2nd ed. Englewood Cliffs, N.J.: Prentice-Hall, 1981.

Johnston, J. M., and Pennypacker, H. S. *Strategies and Tactics of Human Behavioral Research*. Hillsdale, N.J.: L. Erlbaum Assocs., 1980.

Kalectaca, M. Competencies for teachers of culturally different children. In W. Hunter, ed., *Multicultural Education*. Washington, D.C.: American Association for Colleges for Teacher Education, 1974.

Kent, I., and Nicholls, W. *I Amness: The Discovery of Self Beyond Ego*. Indianapolis: Bobbs-Merrill, 1972.

Kleibard, H. The question in teacher education. In D. McCarty, ed., *New Perspectives in Teacher Education*. San Francisco: Jossey-Bass, 1973.

Kounin, J. *Discipline and Group Management in Classrooms*. New York: Holt, Rinehart & Winston, 1970.

Kozol, J. Free schools fail because they don't teach. *Psychology Today*, 1972, *5*, 30.

Leonard, G. *Education and Ecstasy.* New York: Delacorte Press, 1968.

Locke, L. Teacher education: One minute to midnight. In *Preparing the Elementary Specialist.* Washington, D.C.: American Association for Health, Physical Education and Recreation, 1973.

Locke, L. The ecology of the gymnasium: What the tourists never see. *Proceedings of SAPECW* (Spring 1975). (ERIC Document Reproduction Service No. ED 104 823)

Locke, L. Research on teaching physical education: New hope for a dismal science. *Quest*, 1977, *28*, 2–16.

Locke, L. Learning from teaching. In J. Jackson, ed., *Theory into Practice.* University of Victoria Physical Education Series. Victoria: British Columbia: University of Victoria, 1979.

Locke, L., and Massengale, J. Role conflict in teacher/coaches. *Research Quarterly*, 1978, *49*, 162–174.

Locke, L., Siedentop, D., and Mand, C. The preparation of physical education teachers: A subject-matter-centered model. In *Undergraduate Physical Education Programs: Issues and Approaches.* Washington, D.C.: American Association for Health, Physical Education, Recreation and Dance, 1981.

Lortie, D. *Schoolteacher: A Sociological Study.* Chicago: University of Chicago Press, 1975.

McDaniel, T. The teacher's ten commandments: School law in the classroom. *Phi Delta Kappan*, June 1979, *60*, 703–708.

McKenzie, T. Development and evaluation of a behaviorally-based teacher center for physical education. Unpublished doctoral dissertation, Department of Physical Education, The Ohio State University, 1976.

McKenzie, T., and Rushall, B. Effects of various reinforcing contingencies on improving performance in a competitive swimming environment. Unpublished paper, Department of Physical Education, Dalhousie University, 1973.

McLeish, J. Effective teaching in physical education. Victoria, British Columbia: Department of Education, University of Victoria, 1981. Mimeo.

Madsen, C., and Madsen, C. *Parents, Children, Discipline: A Positive Approach.* Boston: Allyn & Bacon, 1972.

Madsen, C. H., and others. An analysis of the reinforcing function of "Sit down" commands. In R. K. Parker, ed., *Readings in Educational Psychology.* Boston: Allyn & Bacon, 1968.

Mager, R. *Preparing Instructional Objectives.* Belmont, Calif.: Fearon, 1962.

Mager, R. A universal objective. *Improving Human Performance: A Research Quarterly*, 1973, *3*, 181–190.

Massengale, J. Role conflict and the occupational milieu of the teacher/coach: Some real working world perspectives. In V. Crafts, ed., *1980 National Association of Physical Education in Higher Education Proceedings.* Champaign, Ill.: Human Kinetics Publishers, 1981.

Medley, D. *Teacher Competence and Teacher Effectiveness.* Washington, D.C.: American Association for Colleges of Teacher Education, 1977.

Medley, D. The effectiveness of teachers. In P. Peterson and H. Walberg, eds., *Research on Teaching: Concepts, Findings, and Implications.* Berkeley, Calif.: McCutchan, 1979.

Metzler, M The measurement of academic learning time in physical education. Unpublished doctoral dissertation, Department of Physical Education, The Ohio State University, 1979.

Moore, G., Descriptive behavior analysis in a resident school camp. Unpublished doctoral dissertation, Department of Physical Education, The Ohio State University, 1977.

Morgenegg, B. Pedagogical moves. In W. Anderson and G Barrette, eds., *What's Going On in the Gym. Motor Skills: Theory into Practice*, 1978, Monograph 1.

Morris, J. Diary of a beginning teacher. *National Association of Secondary School Principals Bulletin*, October 1968, 6–22.

Mosher, R., and Purpel, D. *Supervision: The Reluctant Profession.* Boston: Houghton Mifflin, 1972.

Mosston, M. *Teaching Physical Education.* Columbus, Ohio: Merrill, 1966.

Myrick, R. Growth groups: Implications for teachers and counselors. *Elementary School Guidance and Counseling*, 1969, 4, 35–42.

NEA Reporter, January 1980.

Novak, M. *The Joy of Sports.* New York: Basic Books, 1976.

Oliver, B. The relationship of teacher and student presage and process criteria to student achievement in physical education. Unpublished doctoral dissertation, Department of Physical Education, Stanford University, 1978.

Olsen, P. Graduate education and new jobs in education. *Theory into Practice*, 1974, 13, 151–158.

Osgood, E., and others. *The Measurement of Meaning.* Urbana: University of Illinois Press, 1957.

Patterson, A. Professional malpractice: Small cloud, but growing bigger. *Phi Delta Kappan*, November 1980, 62, 193–196.

Pieron, M. From interaction analysis to research on teaching effectiveness: An overview of studies from the University of Liège. Unpublished paper, Department of Physical Education, The Ohio State University, November 1980. Mimeo.

Pieron, M. Research on teacher change: Effectiveness of teaching a psychomotor task in a microteaching setting. Paper delivered at the American Association of Health, Physical Education, Recreation and Dance Convention, Boston, April 1981. Mimeo.

Popham, W. J., and Baker, E. *Systematic Instruction.* Englewood Cliffs, N.J.: Prentice-Hall, 1970.

Postman, N., and Weingartner, C. *Teaching as Subversive Activity.* New York: Delacorte Press, 1969.

Powell, L. *Communication and Learning.* New York: American Elsevier, 1969.

Premack, D. Rate differential in monkey manipulation. *Journal of the Experimental Analysis of Behavior*, 1963, 6, 81–89.

Premack, D., and others. Reinforcement of drinking by running: Effect of fixed ratio and reinforcement time. *Journal of the Experimental Analysis of Behavior*, 1964, 5, 91–96.

Quarterman, J. A descriptive analysis of physical education teaching in the elementary school. Unpublished doctoral dissertation, Department of Physical Education, The Ohio State University, 1977.

Rate, R. A descriptive analysis of academic learning time and coaching behavior in interscholastic athletic practices. Unpublished doctoral dissertation, Department of Physical Education, The Ohio State University, 1980.

Raths, L., Harmin, M., and Simon, S. *Values and Teaching*. Columbus, Ohio: Merrill, 1966.

Rife, F. Modification of student teacher behavior and its effect upon pupil behavior. Unpublished doctoral dissertation, Department of Physical Education, The Ohio State University, 1980.

Rink, J. Development of an instrument for the observation of content development in physical education. Unpublished doctoral dissertation, Department of Physical Education, The Ohio State University, 1979.

Rogers, C. *Freedom to Learn*. Columbus, Ohio: Merrill, 1969.

Rogers, J. On introducing contingency management. *National Society for Programmed Instruction Newsletter*, April 1974, *13*.

Rolider, A. The effects of enthusiasm training on the subsequent behavior of physical education teachers. Unpublished doctoral dissertation, Department of Physical Education, The Ohio State University, 1979.

Rosenshine, B. Evaluation of classroom instruction. *Review of Educational Research*, 1970, *40*, 279–300.

Rosenshine, B. Content, time and direct instruction. In P. Peterson and H. Walberg, eds., *Research on Teaching: Concepts, Findings, and Implications*. Berkeley, Calif.: McCutchan, 1979.

Rosenshine, B., and Furst, N. Research in teacher performance criteria. In B. Smith, ed., *Research in Teacher Education*. Englewood Cliffs, N.J.: Prentice-Hall, 1971.

Rushall, B., and Siedentop, D. *The Development and Control of Behavior in Sport and Physical Education*. Philadelphia: Lea and Febiger, 1972.

Ryan, K. *Don't Smile Until Christmas*. Chicago: University of Chicago Press, 1970.

Ryan, K., and Cooper, J. *Those Who Can, Teach*. Boston: Houghton Mifflin, 1972.

Segrave, J. Role preferences among prospective physical education teacher/coaches. In V. Crafts, ed., *National Association of Physical Education in Higher Education Proceedings*. Champaign, Ill.: Human Kinetics Publishers, 1981.

Siedentop, D. Behavior analysis and teacher training. *Quest*, 1972, *19*, 26–32.

Siedentop, D. *Physical Education: Introductory Analysis*. 3rd ed. Dubuque, Iowa: Brown, 1980.

Siedentop, D. The Ohio State supervision research program: Summary report. *Journal of Teaching in Physical Education*, Spring 1981, 30–38.

Siedentop, D., Herkowitz, J., and Rink, J. *The Physical Education of Children*. Englewood Cliffs, N.J.: Prentice-Hall, in press.

Siedentop, D., and Olson, J. The validity of teacher behavior observation systems in physical education. In L. Gedvilas, ed., *Proceedings of National College Physical Education Association for Men, 1978*.

Siedentop, D., and Rife, F. Developing a learning environment for badminton. *Ohio High School Athlete*, 1974, *33*, 17–19.

Siedentop, D., Rife, F., and Boehm, J. Modifying the managerial effectiveness of student teachers in physical education. Unpublished paper, Department of Physical Education, The Ohio State University, 1974.

Silberman, C. E. *Crisis in the Classroom*. New York: Random House, 1970.

Simon, S., Howe, L., and Kirchenbaum, H. *Values Clarification*. New York: Hart, 1972.

Singer, R., and Dick, W. *Teaching Physical Education: A Systems Approach*. Boston: Houghton Mifflin, 1974.

Smith, L., and Geoffrey, W. *The Complexities of an Urban Classroom.* New York: Holt, Rinehart & Winston, 1969.

Soar, R., and Soar, R. M. Emotional climate and management. In P. Peterson and H. Walberg, eds., *Research on Teaching: Concepts, Findings and Implications.* Berkeley, Calif.: McCutchan, 1979.

Stallings, J. How instructional processes relate to child outcomes in a national study of Follow Through. *Journal of Teacher Education,* Spring 1976, 27, 43–47.

Stallings, J. Allocated academic learning time revisited, or beyond time and task. *Educational Researcher,* 1980, 9, 11–16.

Stephens, T. *Social Skills in the Classroom.* Columbus, Ohio: Cedars Press, 1978.

Stewart, M. Teaching behavior of physical education teachers in the natural environment. *College Student Journal,* 1980, 14, 76–82.

Sulzer, B., and Mayer, G. Behavior Modification Procedures for School Personnel. Hinsdale, Ill.: Dryden Press, 1972.

Templin, T. Teacher/coach role conflict and the high school principal. In V. Crafts, ed., *National Association for Physical Education in Higher Education Proceedings.* Champaign, Ill.: Human Kinetics Publishers, 1981.

Tumin, M. Schools as a social organization. In R. Corwin and R. Edelfelt, eds., *Perspectives on Organizations: The School as a Social Organization.* Washington, D.C.: American Association of Colleges of Teacher Education, 1977.

Tyler, R. *Basic Principles of Curriculum and Instruction.* Chicago: University of Chicago Press, 1950.

Weinstein, G., and Fantini, M. *Toward Humanistic Education: A Curriculum of Affect.* New York: Praeger, 1971.

Westcott, W. Effects of teacher modeling on the subsequent behavior of students. Unpublished doctoral dissertation, Department of Physical Education, The Ohio State University, 1977.

Whitehurst, G. Academic responses and attitudes engendered by a programmed course in child development. *Journal of Applied Behavior Analysis,* 1972, 5, 283–292.

Williams, R., and Anandam, K. *Cooperative Classroom Management.* Columbus, Ohio: Merrill, 1973.

Wynn, C. Teacher competencies for cultural diversity. In W. Hunter, ed., *Multicultural Education.* Washington, D.C.: American Association of Colleges for Teacher Education, 1974.

Young, R. The effects of various reinforcement contingencies on a second-grade physical education class. Unpublished doctoral dissertation, Department of Physical Education, The Ohio State University, 1973.

Index

DATE DUE

7/27/88	OCLC		
8/23			
12-8-88	UC		
AUG 2 6 1991			
7/26/84 (16) MAY 1 6 2005			